CUSTOM, COURTS AND COUNSEL

Custom, Courts and Counsel

Selected Papers of the 6th British Legal History Conference Norwich 1983

Edited by
Albert Kiralfy, Michele Slatter
and Roger Virgoe

Routledge
Taylor & Francis Group
LONDON AND NEW YORK

First published in 1985 by
FRANK CASS AND COMPANY LIMITED

This edition published 2013 by Routledge
2 Park Square, Milton Park, Abingdon, Oxon OX14 4RN
711 Third Avenue, New York, NY 10017

Routledge is an imprint of the Taylor & Francis Group, an informa business

First issued in paperback 2016

British Library Cataloguing in Publication Data

British Legal History Conference
(6th : 1983 : Norwich)
Custom, courts and counsel : selected papers of the 6th British Legal History Conference, Norwich 1983.—(The Journal of legal history, ISSN 0144-0365; vol. 5, no. 3)
1. Law—Great Britain—History and criticism
I. Title II. Kiralfy, A.K.R. III. Slatter, Michele IV. Virgoe, Roger V. Series
344.1'009 KD532

ISBN 0-7146-3265-1

These Conference papers first appeared in a Special Issue on 'Custom, Courts and Counsel' of *The Journal of Legal History*, Vol.5, No.3, published by Frank Cass & Co. Ltd.

ISBN: 978-0-714-63265-0 (hbk)
ISBN: 978-1-138-99058-6 (pbk)

Contents

Ecclesiastical Sanctuary in Thirteenth-Century Welsh Law

HUW PRYCE

The granting of sanctuary by churches was never solely a matter for ecclesiastics in medieval Europe. By providing partial immunity from legal processes it created problems of law enforcement that concerned secular rulers and lawyers too.[1] The aim of this paper is to show how Welsh jurists of the thirteenth century conceived and treated of sanctuary and its secular legal consequences. Three aspects will be discussed in particular: (1) the inviolability of churches; (2) the exceptions to and restrictions on seeking asylum; and (3) the secular legitimation of churches' sanctuary rights.[2] Before opening the main discussion, however, it may be helpful to outline the historical and conceptual background of ecclesiastical sanctuary in medieval Wales.

We do not know when Welsh churches first claimed and exercised the power to protect persons seeking refuge from their enemies or their legal obligations. No collections of secular and ecclesiastical law such as illuminate sanctuary elsewhere in early medieval Europe survive from Wales, and our earliest evidence is contained in the Llandaf charters, some of whose references to violation of sanctuary appear to belong to original records dating from the eighth century and later.[3] In the late eleventh and early twelfth centuries Welsh hagiographers claimed substantial sanctuary rights for their churches, as did the final editors of the Book of Llandaf.[4] The territorial protection of saints and their churches was praised by twelfth-century poets[5] and by Gerald of Wales. Gerald, however, complained that this protection was abused by men who, having fled from the animosity of their princes, then used the churches as based from which to launch attacks of their own.[6] Other twelfth-century sources confirm Gerald's view that, in a society of rapidly changing political alliances, sanctuary could promote violence as well as protect people from it.[7]

The origins and development of ecclesiastical sanctuary in Wales are further illuminated by the terms used for it in the lawbooks and other sources. Indeed, to speak of 'sanctuary' is misleading if by that is meant the institution recognised by the canon law of Gratian's *Decretum* (*c.* 1140) and later texts. The key Welsh word is *nawdd*, cognate with Old Irish *snádud* and argued to derive from a Celtic root, **snád–*, meaning 'protect'.[8] The earliest instances of *nawdd* in Welsh occur in the purely secular context of battle, where it clearly stands for physical protection or quarter, and this sense continued into the period of the lawbooks.[9] The legal texts, principally in the opening tractate on the court, also attest to a secular concept of *nawdd*. There each member of the court possesses powers of *nawdd* 'protection' whose duration or geographical extent varies according to the protector's status.[10] The purpose of this *nawdd* is not stated and we therefore do not know whether, like the *snádud* of Early Irish law, it meant 'the power to accord to another person immunity from all legal processes',[11] or simply protection of life and limb for whatever reason. Sparing a person from death certainly appears to be the principal secular meaning of *nawdd* in the non-legal sources.

The archaic concept of *nawdd* as a protection bestowed by individuals was attributed by poets to secular rulers as well as to God and His saints.[12] By the end of the eleventh century, and probably much earlier, churches seem however to have transformed *nawdd* into a territorial concept. The protection of a saint was held to extend permanently over land and churches consecrated to him. Thus *Braint Teilo*, a document setting forth the privileges of the church of Llandaf, claimed jurisdiction for the church over breakers of its *nawdd*, both within and outside the *llan* or church-enclosure. Saints' Lives resemble the Llandaf material in asserting the privilege of *refugium*, the normal Latin translation of *nawdd*, in generous territorial terms.[13] Twelfth-century vernacular poetry presents a similar picture, and in addition to the word *nawdd* used a compound of it, *noddfa*, 'field of protection', which also occurs in prose texts of the following century, including the lawbooks. *Noddfa* is almost always used with regard to churches and underlines their success in establishing a territorial concept of *nawdd*.[14]

When the earliest extant Welsh lawbooks were being written down in the thirteenth century it is very likely that the secular institution of *nawdd* had been exclusively appropriated by the church, and adapted to an ecclesiastical concept of sanctuary. This concept was embodied in the term *refugium*, the standard Latin equivalent of *nawdd* in Welsh law. *Refugium* was an unusual term for sanctuary in medieval Europe and is attested predominantly in Irish and Welsh sources.[15] These would appear to have derived it from Old Testament accounts of the Levitical *civitates refugii*, 'cities of refuge', to which those who had killed by accident or in ignorance might flee.[16] *Refugium* was used to translate the *nawdd* pertaining to the church of Llandaf in the early twelfth century and, by the middle of the thirteenth, in the Latin texts of Welsh law, rendered secular and ecclesiastical *nawdd* alike.[17] This may indicate that *nawdd* in its legal sense had by then become primarily an ecclesiastical attribute. The secular *nawdd* granted by members of the royal court is barely witnessed outside the lawbooks' archaic tractate on the court, and was almost certainly obsolete by the thirteenth century.[18]

Welsh jurists thus had to come to terms with churches which had established territorial rights of sanctuary in which were fused secular and biblical concepts of protection. In what follows I will concentrate on legal rules contained in lawbooks from Gwynedd in North Wales, principally the Book of Iorwerth, originally compiled during the first half of the thirteenth century and whose oldest manuscripts date from *c.* 1250. This is one of three main groups of vernacular lawbooks, the other two being the Book of Cyfnerth (deriving in its present form from mid-Wales) and the Book of Blegywryd (from south-west Wales). In addition to these we have five redactions in Latin.[19] Although these other lawbooks include statements on churches' rights of sanctuary and some of them are extant in thirteenth-century manuscripts, it is those from Gwynedd – particularly the Book of Iorwerth (containing a unique short tractate on sanctuary)[20] and the collection of case law, *Llyfry Damweiniau* – which provide the most detailed evidence for ecclesiastical *nawdd* or sanctuary in thirteenth-century Welsh law. Further, comparison of this evidence with the rules in the other lawbooks, as well as with records from the 1260s and 1270s relating to the dioceses of Bangor and St Asaph, strongly suggests that it reflected contemporary concern in Gwynedd with the secular legal consequences of ecclesiastical sanctuary, and was not merely the conservative copying of obsolete law.[21]

I

The recognition of the inviolability of churches was clearly a prerequisite for their effective provision of sanctuary. Twelfth- and thirteenth-century canon law prescribed spiritual penalties in order to secure restitution for sacrilege, and was reinforced in Wales by the provincial legislation of Canterbury.[22] Native law and ecclesiastical practice in North Wales differed somewhat from these canonical norms, however, although the desire to preserve the immunity of churches was no less. The Book of Iorwerth rules that whoever does wrong to a mother-church shall pay fourteen pounds, or seven pounds if the offence takes place in the cemetery. In both instances half of the amount goes to the abbot, provided that he is ordained and educated, and half to the priest and community (*clas*). Seven pounds was also due for a wrong done in another church, or chapel, to be divided equally between the priest and the parson.[23]

Versions of this rule occur also in the Book of Cyfnerth, three of the Latin Redactions, and the Book of Blegywryd.[24] Their textual relationship is complicated, but here we need only note two points in particular.

The first is that all versions seem to descend from a common archetype which laid down tariffs compensating churches for injuries. In some versions such a payment is termed a *dirwy*, the normal word for a fine to the king in Welsh law. In this instance, however, *dirwy* seems to bear the usual meaning of its Old Irish cognate, *díre*, namely 'honour-price'.[25] Sacrilege was thus conceived as an injury to the honour of the saint and his church, and indeed *iniuria* is the word used by one Latin redaction to describe payments to a mother-church and its daughter.[26] This conception would appear to be of pre-thirteenth century, and even of pre-Norman, origin. It occurs in the demonstrably archaic passage of Welsh law on the seven bishop-houses of Dyfed, in which properly ordained abbots are entitled to seven pounds for injury done to them, and invites comparison with provisions in early medieval laws from other parts of Europe, including Ireland.[27] Seven pounds represented considerable compensation in Welsh law: the *dirwy* or fine to the king amounted to only three pounds, and the rule on sacrilege thus reflects at least the aspiration to, if not the attainment of, high status by churches in Wales.

The second important point to emerge from a comparison of the versions of this rule is that in all texts except that in the Book of Iorwerth the payments are said to come from those taking sanctuary in the church. Rather than upholding the inviolability of churches in general these texts therefore proclaim ecclesiastical jurisdiction over refugees, in clauses which would seem to have been added to the rule as it originally stood. Offences by sanctuary-takers are, however, considered by the Book of Iorwerth in its short tractate on sanctuary. This states that if a person commits an offence to the value of one legal penny in the *noddfa* or sanctuary-place, and on account of this faces a claim, he is not entitled to protection from the *nawdd* or sanctuary that he has wronged unless he can renew it in another sanctuary. Similarly, if a person commits an offence while under the protection of relics he may no longer be protected by them.[28] The latter rule is found also in the thirteenth-century compilation of case law, *Llyfr y Damweiniau*, and is followed by a further statement that someone striking a blow with a weapon while protected by relics loses their protection.[29] The jurists of Gwynedd, then, denied sanctuary to men who committed offences and acts of violence in it, and in this they resembled their canonist contemporaries.[30] The rule in the other lawbooks, however, simply asserts the church's entitlement to heavy fines from persons who committed offences or, according to some versions, fought while in sanctuary.[31] This rule retains the idea of sacrilege as a wrong to be amended by rendering the appropriate honour-price, as opposed to an abuse of ecclesiastical immunity that *ipso facto* denied the offender any further protection.

As we have seen, the jurists of thirteenth-century Gwynedd appear to have distinguished between sacrilege in general and offences in a sanctuary by those taking refuge there. In the former case they reproduced an archaic rule stipulating payments; in the latter they denied further protection to the offenders, although presumably still requiring restitution to the church. We have good evidence that churches in North Wales claimed and received fines or amends for sacrilege in the thirteenth century, although the amounts differ from those of the lawbooks. Thus in the arbitration between Richard, bishop of Bangor, and Llywelyn ap Gruffudd, prince of Gwynedd, in 1261, it was declared that the *emenda* for sacrilege and fighting in three churches pertained exclusively to the bishop.[32] Witnesses at bishop Anian's inquest into the episcopal rights of St Asaph in 1274 testified that wrongs committed in churches and cemeteries had been punished by confiscation to the bishop of all the offender's movables, and two years later the same church complained to the archbishop of Canterbury that Llywelyn claimed the right to punish sacrilege and that the prince kept all the ensuing fines.[33] It was possibly after this letter was written in December 1276 that Goronwy ap Heilyn and his accomplices bound themselves to pay the bishop for the *iniuria* done by them to the church of Llanarmon. Goronwy himself promised to pay thirty pounds and the others sums of four pounds and one pound.[34] It should be noted that none of these examples refer specifically to sacrilege by persons taking sanctuary. It is possible therefore that the Book of Iorwerth reflected contemporary practice in distinguishing offences by persons in sanctuary from sacrilege by those making no claim to protection from the church.

All the lawbooks agree that the inviolability of churches extended to an area beyond the cemetery. The rule on payments to churches in the Books of Cyfnerth and Blegywryd, and in the Latin redactions, refers to this area as the *noddfa*, literally 'field of protection' but significantly translated in one Latin redaction as *villa* or 'township'.[35] The Book of Iorwerth, in its brief tractate on ecclesiastical *nawdd*, states that the refugee may move about without relics not only in the cemetery but also beyond it, in the *corflan*, while his beasts may stay with those of the church for as far as they could go and return to their byre again.[36] This provision is strikingly confirmed by Gerald's observations on sanctuary in major Welsh churches at the end of the twelfth century.[37] The dimensions of the *corflan* are specified in a subsequent rule as a radius the length of a legal acre (i.e. 120 yards) around the cemetery.[38] The *corflan* thus extended further than the sixty paces laid down as the maximum immunity of churches in canon law,[39] as must have the *noddfa* of the other legal texts, and this would suggest that ecclesiastical sanctuary in Wales was comparable, for example, with that set forth by the legislation of the early Irish church or with the chartered sanctuaries of medieval England.[40]

Having defined the territorial extent of sanctuary the tractate then rules on its temporal duration: if a church claims that it may protect a man without his making amends for seven years or longer, and the secular lord opposes this, the church must have lawful witnesses who will uphold that privilege.[41]

II

So far we have seen how the jurists sought to defend and to define the inviolability of churches. Next I wish to examine how, in the interests of safeguarding legal obligations and processes, Welsh law tried to limit the taking of sanctuary. The most important material is contained in the short tractate on ecclesiastical sanctuary in the Book of Iorwerth. It opens by denying *nawdd* from three legal obligations, two of which have just been explained in the preceding tractate on suretyship.[42] The first of these, *gorfodogaeth*, is a kind of criminal suretyship, whereby the *gorfodog* guarantees the good behaviour of his charge and bears responsibility for any misdeeds that the latter may commit. Earlier, in the section on *gorfodogaeth*, it is stated that if the *gorfodog* takes sureties from his charge, in order to ensure compensation for any loss incurred as the result of his duties, then the latter is not entitled to *nawdd* from the sureties.[43] This may be the meaning of the rule in the sanctuary tractate, but more probably it prohibits the *gorfodog* himself from seeking sanctuary and thereby encouraging lawlessness.

Mechniaeth 'suretyship' is the second obligation from which *nawdd* is denied. This certainly included a debtor trying to avoid paying a debt guaranteed by a surety, for such evasion is explicitly prohibited earlier in the lawbook.[44] It may also include a surety who sought *nawdd* from his obligations. This eventuality is forbidden in a tetrad found in Latin Redaction B, a mid-thirteenth-century lawbook with north Welsh connections.[45] The tetrad lists four men for whom there is no *refugium* anywhere, the last being a non-performing surety. The sentence in fact reads awkwardly, beginning with the words 'Captivus de fideiussione' – 'a captive or slave on account of suretyship' – followed by the explanation that this is a surety who, not denying his suretyship after the death of his debtor, had not secured the repayment of the debt. While it is evident from other rules of Welsh law that a surety's obligations did not cease with the debtor's death, nowhere is it suggested that a surety who failed to fulfil his obligations in such circumstances became a captive or slave.[46]

The reference to *captivus* probably derives from a desire by the author of the text in Redaction B to preserve the last of the four men denied *nawdd* in the Welsh version of this tetrad, namely the king's *caeth* or slave, while proposing a new rule concerning sureties.[47] Latin Redaction

E in fact omits the *captivus* at this point and makes better sense.[48] The Welsh version of the tetrad upholds the rights and prerogatives of the king, denying *nawdd* not only to his slave, but also to a breaker of the royal peace, a hostage given voluntarily to the king and a *cwynossog*, 'supper-giver', who fails in his duty to feed the king. The reference to *cwynossog* was clearly obsolete by the thirteenth century, and is replaced by an excommunicate in the Latin version.[49]

Returning to the exceptions to sanctuary in the Book of Iorwerth the most difficult to interpret is the third, *goresgyn*. Sanctuary from *goresgyn* was prohibited because, like *gorfodogaeth* and suretyship, it was acknowledged. What, then, did it mean? The thirteenth-century law-books of Gwynedd have no other examples of the word. In the southern Welsh lawbooks *goresgyn*, or its variant *gweresgyn*, are used to denote the acquisition of the possession of land, which could be challenged in an action of *camweresgyn*, 'false acquisition of possession'.[50] Possibly once a person had accomplished *goresgyn*, and it had thus become acknowledged, he could not seek sanctuary if such an action was brought against him. This would match the maintenance of legal obligations and processes sought by the rest of the triad.

Thus far we have considered outright prohibitions on taking sanctuary. What restrictions were placed, however, on a person who had successfully reached a sanctuary? Firstly, as we have seen, protection could be terminated if the person committed sacrilege. Secondly, according to the Book of Iorwerth, if an offender had taken sanctuary and a claim was lodged against him on account of his unlawful act, the abbots and priests were not to protect the offender until he had made amends.[51] If no claim was made this condition did not apply, but another rule implies that amends should be made within seven years, unless the church had witnesses who would verify its right to grant sanctuary for longer.[52] Thus, as elsewhere in medieval Europe, the principal purpose of ecclesiastical sanctuary in Welsh law was to provide physical protection rather than total immunity from legal claims. This is well illustrated also by a rule in the collection of case law, *Llyfr y Damweiniau*, which states that a traitor who took sanctuary was spared execution although he still lost his patrimony as required by law.[53]

III

Lastly, the most fundamental limitation proposed by the jurists of thirteenth-century Gwynedd on ecclesiastical sanctuary was its legitimation by the secular ruler. Almost half of the short tractate on ecclesiastical *nawdd* in the Book of Iorwerth affirms that churches' title to sanctuary rights derived from the king or lord. After prohibiting *nawdd* from *gorfodogaeth*, suretyship and *goresgyn*, the passage says that if the clergy claim that they are entitled to give protection in any of these cases, it is the king, who granted the *noddfa* originally, who must decide whether he gave it to his own detriment. The tractate proceeds to assert the need for royal confirmation of a church's privileges, stating that each owner of ecclesiastical land must recite its privilege and entitlement to each new king, and if the king consents to the privilege he is to invest the church with its *noddfa*, 'sanctuary-place', and *braint*, 'privilege'. It is not clear whether the recitation of charters or other written records is implied here. The tractate's final rule states that if a church claims the right to protect an offender for seven years or more, and the territorial lord denies that he has granted it this privilege, the church must have lawful witnesses who keep its *braint*.[54] This rule lays down, then, that a church's privilege, including sanctuary, derived originally from the secular lord and was preserved by witnesses. Possibly it was their testimony which was 'recited' in the earlier clauses, in place of or in addition to a written record of the church's rights.

In the 1260s and 1270s Llywelyn ap Gruffudd clashed with the bishops of Bangor and St Asaph over ecclesiastical liberties.[55] Apart from appropriating fines for sacrilege the prince on at least one occasion disputed a church's right to grant sanctuary. In the text of the arbitration between the prince and the bishop of Bangor in 1261 it is stated that Llywelyn had seized a person in a place alleged by the church to be a *refugium*. It was agreed that, in order to decide whether this was a *locus refugii*, trustworthy persons representing both parties should be sent to the disputed place. If it could be proved before them that this was a sanctuary, Llywelyn should make satisfaction; if not, he could rejoice in his prisoner.[56] It seems that the trustworthy persons were to hold an inquest, a procedure certainly favoured by the prince and one of his bishops as a means of establishing the rights of one against the other in the 1270s. In 1274 the bishop of St Asaph held an inquest to vindicate his privileges, and in the following year Llywelyn conceded that, if the bishop lacked princely charters confirming those privileges, they should be determined according to the outcome of inquiries by trustworthy persons.[57] It is likely, then, that the legal rules prescribing the recitation of a church's privileges, and their preservation by lawful witnesses, presupposed that this confirmation by the prince would depend on the findings of an inquest.

In conclusion, the treatment of ecclesiastical sanctuary in the legal texts of thirteenth-century Gwynedd differs significantly from that of the other Welsh lawbooks. The latter, in laying down fines to churches from sanctuary-takers, are concerned essentially to proclaim ecclesiastical privilege rather than to confront legal problems resulting from it. The

Welsh version of the tetrad denying *nawdd* to four men does admittedly set a boundary between the right to grant sanctuary and the rights of the king, but goes no further than that, and in any case includes at least one element that was patently obsolete by the thirteenth century. By contrast, the Book of Iorwerth, in its unique tractate on ecclesiastical *nawdd*, seeks above all to clarify how the privilege of sanctuary impinges on secular rights and legal obligations. Its definitions of the exceptions to and restrictions on taking sanctuary, as well of the spatial and temporal limits of churches' inviolability, have a precision and attention to legal procedure lacking in the other Welsh lawbooks, and illustrate once more the greater sophistication of what Professor Dafydd Jenkins has termed the 'classical law' by comparison with that of the other legal texts.[58] Comparison with the record evidence demonstrates, moreover, that the legal problems treated by the classical law on sanctuary were of contemporary relevance in thirteenth-century Gwynedd. In short, it was an interest in the secular implications of ecclesiastical sanctuary which resulted in the most extensive and sophisticated treatment of it in thirteenth-century Welsh law.

APPENDIX

A translation of the short tractate on ecclesiastical sanctuary in the Book of Iorwerth (§71).

From *Llyfr Iorwerth*, ed. A.R. Wiliam, Cardiff, 1960, 43–4. This edition is based on BL Cotton ms. Titus Dii – ms. B in *Ancient Laws and Institutes of Wales*, ed. A. Owen, Record Commission, London, 1841. No significant variations of substance occur between the text of the tractate on sanctuary in ms. B and the texts in the other mss. of the Book of Iorwerth, although this is not so with regard to other tractates and sections of the lawbook.

1. Three things from which sanctuary (*nawdd*) is not allowed since they are acknowledged: *gorfodogaeth* and suretyship and *goresgyn*.
2. If it happens that the parsons of the church say that they can give *nawdd* against any one of those three, let it be the responsibility of the king – the man who gave them that sanctuary-place (*noddfa*) – to proclaim in what form he gave them that *noddfa*; and if he gave it against himself, let them keep what he gives to them.
3. Every owner of ecclesiastical land is obliged to come to every new king that comes, to declare to him their privilege (*braint*) and their entitlement (*dylyed*).
4. And the reason namely that they declare to him is lest the king be deceived.
5. And after they have declared their privilege to him if the king deems that their privilege is in order, let the king invest them with their privilege (*braint*) and their sanctuary-place (*noddfa*).
6. If it happens that a man does an unlawful act and from that unlawful act seeks sanctuary (*nawdd*) and [while he is] in that sanctuary a claim is made against him, the abbots and the priests are not entitled to escort [i.e. protect] him unless he makes amends for the original unlawful act.

7. If it happens that a claim is not made against him, let them escort him for as far as they are entitled to escort him.

8. If it happens that a man commits an offence to the value of a penny [while] in the sanctuary-place (*noddfa*), and a claim is made against him for the unlawful act that he has committed in the sanctuary-place (*noddfa*), he is not entitled to the sanctuary (*nawdd*) against which he committed an offence unless he renews it from another sanctuary [anew in another church.][a]

9. Whoever takes sanctuary (*nawdd*) is entitled to proceed in the cemetery and the *corflan* without relics upon him, and his beasts together with the beasts of the community (*clas*) and the abbots for as far as they may go and then reach their byre again.

10. If it happens that a man has relics upon him and he commits an offence while under [the protection of] the relics, he is not entitled to have protection (*nawdd*) or defence from the relics since he has not deserved it.

11. The dimensions of a *corflan*: the length of a legal acre [i.e. 120 yards] and its head on the cemetery, and that in a circle around the cemetery.

12. If it happens that there is a church which says that it is entitled to maintain a man in its sanctuary-place (*noddfa*) for seven years without making amends, or a period that is longer, and the lord who is over the territory opposes it on account of this and says that it does not have that privilege from him, the church must have lawful witnesses who will keep that privilege.

13. And if it has them, let it have its privilege without objection; and if it does not have them, let the church escort him as it is best entitled, or let him make amends for the unlawful act which he has committed.

NOTES

Abbreviations

BBCS	*Bulletin of the Board of Celtic Studies.*
Bleg	*Cyfreithiau Hywel Dda yn ôl Llyfr Blegywryd*, ed. S.J. Williams and J.E. Powell, 2nd edn, Cardiff, 1961.
Dw Col	*Damweiniau Colan*, ed. D. Jenkins, Aberystwyth, 1973. References to numbered sentences.
Ior	*Llyfr Iorwerth*, ed. A.R. Wiliam, Cardiff, 1960. References to numbered sections and unnumbered sentences.
LTWL	*The Latin Texts of the Welsh Laws*, ed. H.D. Emanuel, Cardiff, 1967.
WML	*Welsh Medieval Law*, ed. A.W. Wade-Evans, Oxford, 1909.

Unless otherwise stated references are to page (and line).

1. For a general account of sanctuary in western Europe, see L.-R. Misserey, 'Asile en Occident', *Dictionnaire de Droit Canonique*, ed. R. Naz, Paris, 1935–65, vol. 1, 1089–1104. On sanctuary in medieval England: J.C. Cox, *The Sanctuaries and Sanctuary-Seekers of Medieval England*, London, 1911; C.H. Riggs, Jr., *Criminal Asylum in Anglo-Saxon Law*, University of Florida Monographs, Social Sciences, No. 18, Spring 1963; R.F. Hunnisett, *The Medieval Coroner*, Cambridge 1961, Chap. III. English law on sanctuary was incorporated in Edward I's Statute of Wales (1284) c. 5: *Statutes of the Realm*, Record Commission, London, 1810–28, vol. 1, 59.

[a] From ms. C (also in mss. A, D, E, G)

2. These and other aspects of protection and sanctuary in Welsh law will receive detailed discussion in my thesis, 'Native Law and the Church in Medieval Wales', to be submitted for the D.Phil. degree at Oxford University.
3. *The Text of the Book of Llan Dâv*, ed. J.G. Evans and J. Rhys, Oxford, 1893, 211, 216, 217–18, 219, 222, 239, 259, 261, 271. For the dates of these charters, ranging from *c.* 765 to *c.* 1075, see W. Davies, *The Llandaff Charters*, Aberystwyth, 1979, 118, 119, 120–1, 124, 127–9. Although a high proportion of the references to *refugium* in *Liber Landavensis* occur in liberty formulae attributable to the early twelfth century (*ibid.*, 138, 143), this is not the case with the references cited above; more generally, the paucity of surviving written evidence from pre-Norman Wales relating to any subject makes it hazardous to dismiss an early medieval origin for sanctuary simply because the sources are largely silent about it. Further, the use of *refugium* as a term for sanctuary in Welsh sources also suggests that Welsh ecclesiastics may have conceptualised sanctuary in this biblical sense by the eighth century, as Irish ecclesiastics had certainly done by that period: see n. 14 below. I am grateful to Wendy Davies for her helpful comments on the date and significance of the references to *refugium* in the Llandaf charters.
4. *Vitae Sanctorum Britanniae*, ed. A.W. Wade-Evans, Cardiff, 1944, 68–80, 136–80 (St. Cadog's *refugium* in the *cantref* of Gwynllŵg); *Rhigyfarch's Life of St. David*, ed. J.W. James, Cardiff, 1967, 24–5 (ch. 57, in the Vespasian recension only); *The Text of the Book of Llan Dâv*, 69, 132, 154, 120.
5. *Hen Gerddi Crefyddol*, ed. H. Lewis, Cardiff, 1931, xvi. 53–6; xviii, 76–8, 140–7; xxxv. 14, 53–4.
6. *Giraldi Cambrensis Opera*, ed. J.S. Brewer *et al.*, Rolls Series, London, 1861–91, vol. 6, 203–4 (*Descriptio Kambriae*, I. 18); cf. vol. 1, 315.
7. *Brut y Tywysogyon, Red Book of Hergest Version*, ed. T. Jones, 2nd edn, Cardiff, 1973, 60, 84, 126.
8. E.P. Hamp, '*nawdd* "protection" and *nes*', *BBCS* 26 (1974–6), 158–60.
9. *Canu Aneirin*, ed. I. Williams, Cardiff, 1938, lines 24, 36, 633; *Llyfr Du Caerfyrddin*, ed. A.O.H. Jarman, Cardiff, 1982, Poem 34, lines 3, 6, 7; *Owein or Chwedyl Iarlles y Ffynnawn*, ed. R.L. Thomson, Dublin, 1968, 29; *Historia Peredur vab Efrawc*, ed. G.W. Goetinck, Cardiff, 1976, 16, 22, 26 *et passim*.
10. *WML*, 4.21ff.; *LTWL*, 111.14–112.38 (Redaction A). Cf. J.G. Edwards, 'The Royal Household and the Welsh Lawbooks', *Trans.Roy.Hist.Soc.*, 5th ser., 13 (1963), 163–76.
11. *Críth Gablach*, ed. D.A. Binchy, Dublin, 1941, 106.
12. Secular rulers: *Llyfr Du Caerfyrddin*, Poem 3, line 34, Poem 23, lines 13, 17, 21; *Llawysgrif Hendregadredd*, ed. J. Morris-Jones and T.H. Parry-Williams, Cardiff, 1933, 26.13, 89.30. God: *Hen Gerddi Crefyddol*, xv. 21, xvi.2, xxviii.42, xxix. 37, xxxi.41. Saints: see n.4 above.
13. *The Text of the Book of Llan Dâv*, 120. Cf. W. Davies, '*Braint Teilo*', *BBCS* 26 (1974–6), 123–37; *eadem*, *Wales in the Early Middle Ages*, Leicester, 1982, 137, 167–8; and n.3 above.
14. *Hen Gerddi Crefyddol*, xviii. 140–7 (*nạwdd*); xxxv. 54 (*noddfa*). *Noddfa* in prose texts: *Brut y Tywysogyon, Red Book of Hergest Version*, 60.17, 126.7; *Historia Gruffud Vab Kenan*, ed. D.S. Evans, Cardiff, 1977, 8.4, 14.3. See also the mid-fifteenth century references to sanctuaries at St Dogmael's ('Nothvadegwell alias refugium') and Nevern ('Nothvabernach'): *Calendar of Papal Letters, Vol. IX, 1431–1447*, ed. J.A. Twemlow, London, 1912, 455, 501. *Noddfa* is used in relation to the protection of pagan temples in the Welsh version of Geoffrey of Monmouth's *Historia Regum Britanniae*: *Brut Dingestow*, ed. H. Lewis, Cardiff, 1942, 32.28.
15. *Glossarium Mediae et Infimae Latinitatis*, ed. Du Cange, vol. 7, Niort, 1886, 82; R.E. Latham, *Revised Medieval Latin Word-List*, London, 1965, 398. I am indebted to Richard Sharpe, of the Dictionary of Medieval Latin from British Sources, for confirming that *refugium* in the technical sense of sanctuary is virtually unattested in English sources. For one Scottish example, however, see *The Acts of Malcolm IV King of Scots 1153–1165*, ed. G.W.S. Barrow, Edinburgh, 1960, 246.
16. See esp. the early eighth century *Collectio Canonum Hibernensis*, *Lib.* XXVIII: *Die*

irische Kanonensammlung, ed. H. Wasserschleben, 2nd edn, Leipzig, 1885, 94–8; P. Fournier, 'Le *Liber ex Lege Moysi* et les tendances bibliques du droit canonique irlandais', *Revue Celtique* 30 (1909), 221–34, esp. 227.

17. *The Text of the Book of Llan Dâv*, 118 (Latin version of *Braint Teilo*); *LTWL*, 195.3–196.15, 217.28 (Redaction B).
18. Cf. D. Jenkins, 'Introduction', *Celtic Law Papers*, ed. *idem*, Brussels, 1973, 15.
19. For general introductions to the Welsh lawbooks see D. Jenkins, *ibid.*, 8–13, and 'The Medieval Welsh Idea of Law', *Tijdschrift voor Rechtsgeschiedenis* 49 (1981), 323–4; M.E. Owen, 'Functional Prose: Religion, Science, Grammar, Law', *A Guide to Welsh Literature*, ed. A.O.H. Jarman and G.R. Hughes, Swansea, 1976–9, vol. 1, 268–9. The Book of Cyfnerth may well also have derived from Gwynedd originally, but by the mid-13th century it had been superseded there by the Book of Iorwerth: D. Jenkins, 'A Family of medieval Welsh lawyers', *Celtic Law Papers*, 121–33.
20. *Ior* §71: translated in the Appendix.
21. This north Welsh evidence cannot of course be assumed to represent native law on sanctuary elsewhere in thirteenth-century Wales.
22. *Corpus Iuris Canonici*, ed. E. Friedberg, Leipzig, 1879–81, vol. 1, 815–16, 818, 820; vol. 2, 654–7 (*Decretum*, C.17 q.4, cc.6,7,12,14,21; Decretals of Gregory IX, *Lib.* 3, t.49); *Councils and Synods ... relating to the English Church. II. A.D. 1205–1313*, ed. F.M. Powicke and C.R. Cheney, Oxford, 1964, 581 (Council of Merton and Westminster 1258, c.15), 762–4 (Ottobuono's Legatine Council of London 1268, c.12). The former canon was cited in the statutes of Richard de Carew, bishop of St David's, 1259: *Episcopal Acts and Cognate Documents relating to Welsh Dioceses, 1066–1272*, ed. J. Conway Davies, Cardiff, 1946–8, vol. 1, 400 (c.24; cf. c.23).
23. *Ior* §43/9–12; *Ancient Laws and Institutes of Wales*, ed. A. Owen, Record Commission, London, 1841, vol. 1, 78–80 (V.C.I. xliii.20–1).
24. *WML*, 113.19–114.7 (this text is incomplete: cf. University College of North Wales ms. 21108, p.96); *LTWL*, 217.20–30 (Redaction B), 337.27–38 (Redaction D), 461.23–32 (Redaction E); *Bleg*, 42.29–43.13.
25. *The Welsh Law of Women*, ed. D. Jenkins and M.E. Owen, Cardiff, 1980, 68, 200; *Críth Gablach*, 84.
26. *LTWL*, 290.3–4 (Redaction C).
27. T.M. Charles-Edwards, 'The Seven Bishop-Houses of Dyfed', *BBCS* 24 (1970–2), 247–50; K. Hughes, *The Church in Early Irish Society*, London, 1966, 134–6.
28. *Ior* §71/8, 10.
29. *Dw Col* §§200, 201.
30. *Corpus Iuris Canonici*, vol. 2, 657 (Decretals of Gregory IX, *Lib.* 3, t.49, c.10).
31. For fighting, see *LTWL*, 217.27–8 (Redaction B), 337.34–6, 338.1–2 (Redaction D), 461.29–30 (Redaction E); Bleg., 43. 8–11, 21–3.
32. *Councils and Ecclesiastical Documents relating to Great Britain and Ireland*, ed. A.W. Haddan and W. Stubbs, Oxford, 1869–71, vol. 1, 490–1.
33. National Library of Wales, Peniarth ms. 231B, p. 125; *Councils and Ecclesiastical Documents*, vol. 1, 514.
34. Peniarth ms. 231B, p.82.
35. *LTWL*, 217.24 (Redaction B). Cf. n.13 above.
36. *Ior* §71/9. Although most mss. read *corfflan* 'burial ground' (<*corff* 'body'), I accept Professor Dafydd Jenkins' suggestion that the original form was *corflan* (<*corf* 'boundary, defence'), and that the idea of it as a burial-ground developed later through its being adjacent to the *mynwent* 'cemetery': *Llyfr Colan*, ed. D. Jenkins, Cardiff, 1963, 156.
37. *Giraldi Cambrensis Opera*, vol. 6, 203 (*Descriptio Kambriae* I. 18).
38. *Ior* §71/11; another version occurs in *Dw Col* §198. Legal acre: *Ior* 82/4–5; cf. T. Jones Pierce, 'A note on ancient Welsh measurements of land', *Archaeologia Cambrensis* 97 (1943), 195, 202.
39. *Corpus Iuris Canonici*, vol. 1, 815 (*Decretum* C.17 q.4 c.6).
40. *Die irische Kanonensammlung*, 174–9 (*Collectio Canonum Hibernensis*, *Lib.* XLIV); K. Hughes, *The Church in Early Irish Society*, 148–9; J.C. Cox, *Sanctuaries and*

Sanctuary-Seekers of Medieval England, Chs. V–IX.
41. *Ior* §71/12–13.
42. *Ior* §71/1.
43. *Ior* §70/3.
44. *Ior* §62/14.
45. *LTWL*, 258.3–8. North Welsh connections: *ibid.*, 40–4.
46. *WML*, 87.13–17; *LTWL*, 125.37–40 (Redaction A), 254.6–8 (Redaction B), 369.24–31 (Redaction D); *Bleg*, 42.7–12; *Ior* §64/10.
47. *WML*, 124.25–125.7; *LTWL*, 371.4–8 (Redaction D); *Bleg*, 109.22–9.
48. *LTWL*, 502.28–30.
49. For the archaic nature of the *cwynossog*, see T.M. Charles-Edwards, 'A Comparison of Old Irish with Medieval Welsh Land Law', Oxford University D.Phil. thesis, 1971, 78–81.
50. *WML*, 53.20, 22, 24; *LTWL*, 384.3 (Redaction D); *Bleg*, 71.25, 76.11, 78. 29, 79. 1–2. Cf. D. Jenkins, 'A Lawyer Looks at Welsh Land Law', *Transactions Hon.Soc. Cymmrodorion*, 1967, 225.
51. *Ior* §71/6.
52. *Ior* §71/7, 12–13.
53. *Dw Col* §199.
54. *Ior* §71/2–5, 12–13.
55. G. Williams, *The Welsh Church from Conquest to Reformation*, 2nd edn, Cardiff, 1976, 8–14.
56. *Councils and Ecclesiastical Documents*, vol. 1, 490.
57. *Ibid.*, 502–3, 504.
58. D. Jenkins, 'The Medieval Welsh Idea of Law', 324.

Some Problems of the Evidence of Fourteenth Century Approvers

JENS RÖRKASTEN

Although the grand jury may have been conceived as a body of witnesses, it is quite clear that by the beginning of the fourteenth century, if not earlier, its members had their information from hearsay, information that might have been heard long after a crime had been committed. A large number, perhaps the majority of crimes were committed in the absence of witnesses. This leaves the historian with a great mass of material on crime and public order, material, however, the quality of which is dubious.

The information given by approvers in their confessions and subsequent appeals must seem very helpful in this situation. After all they had first-hand knowledge and could supply exact information. Still, there have to be doubts as to whether their appeals are of better quality than the jury verdicts, indeed whether they can be trusted at all.[1]

One of the Articles of the Eyre from the time of Edward I[2] inquiring as to who forced approvers to appeal innocent people, a clause in the Ordinances of the reign of Edward II,[3] quite clearly stating that prisoners were being forced to become approvers by officials, and the reiteration of these complaints in the Parliament of 1326/27,[4] all suggest that there was widespread abuse of this institution and that consequently information given by approvers has to be treated with care. The case in the *Rotuli Hundredorum*[5] of a sheriff who solved a dispute about a sale of a horse by procuring the appeal of an approver in his custody against the seller may serve as an example of innocent people being unjustly appealed. The fact that there are a number of cases in which persons are indicted of a crime together with someone who later turns approver but does not appeal those already indicted is an indication that, on the other hand, culprits could be omitted in the appeal. In the gaol delivery rolls there are several examples, even detailed descriptions, by prisoners who complain that they were forced to become approvers.[6] Among various methods of maltreatment and torture the application of the *peine forte et dure* is mentioned.[7]

As a background to this the high rate of acquittal of the appellees and the execution of almost all approvers ('natural' deaths in prison, clergy and fugitives excepted) can be understood. Even in cases where there was additional strong suspicion against the appellee the jury usually found a verdict of not guilty.

Another reason to doubt the credibility of approvers is the fact that out of approximately one thousand three hundred and ten approvers between 1307 and 1330, four hundred and eighty-two withdrew their appeals prematurely. Others stayed mute when asked to proceed during the trial.

Apart from the abuse that undoubtedly took place prisoners had good reasons to turn approver and in prison certainly had many chances to derive information from fellow prisoners and construct an appeal which in itself is of no great historical value today. Approvers were paid and thus far better off than poor prisoners who had to rely on alms. Even more important, appellees had to be brought to the prison where the approver was held and this meant a delay in the procedure.[8] Thus prisoners who turned approver certainly had an incentive to appeal people who were in distant counties and accuse them of crimes committed far away, so that their capture, as well as the arrival of the petty jury, would take some time, time that could possibly be used for an escape or maybe even to learn to read in order to claim benefit of clergy later.[9]

Do we have to conclude from all this evidence that approvers' appeals have to be dismissed as fiction of no historical value? There can be no doubt that the system was abused but the question is: did this abuse really always influence the approver's appeals? Several types of abuse in connection with approvers can be recognised: (i) during the trial the approver withdraws his appeal and describes how he was forced to accuse either innocent persons or persons unknown to him; (ii) in an inquest it is presented that a prisoner was forced to turn approver; (iii) in an inquest it is presented that an approver was hindered from accusing certain persons; (iv) a former prisoner brings an action against officials who pretended that there was an approver's accusation against him; (v) someone who was actually appealed but was to be released *ad manucaptionem* was not released until he had bribed officials; (vi) appellees who were not to be released *ad manucaptionem* were allowed to leave prison after having bribed officials.

In the first three types of abuse it has to be assumed that the appeals or at least parts of them were false. In the fourth type it is not clear whether an approver made accusations at all. The arrest in one of the examples was made by the bailiff 'saying and assuring that he had a warrant to attach because of an appeal made by some approver, where he had no warrant'.[10] An approver's appeal in this case was not even necessary: arrest could also be made under pretence of an indictment.[11] In the last two types not the approver but the appellee was maltreated; there is no reason to assume that the appeal was false.

Another important question is whether the appellees really were always innocent, as is suggested by the high acquittal rate and as is said in most of the complaints recorded in the Hundred Rolls. Looking for an answer to this question the historian has to study the behaviour of the juries and it has to be pointed out that approvers as confessed felons had hardly any credibility. That they were the King's approvers does not mean that juries were eager to believe them. In this connection the 'Mirror of Justices' can be regarded as a valuable source, as it states that one of the pleas against an approver's appeals was that an approver had 'lost his free voice and forfeited every right and every action'.[12] The lack of credibility of often poor, even vagrant, self-confessed felons was not the only reason for juries to acquit appellees. In the Statute of Winchester communities were threatened with punishment for undiscovered crimes.[13] It is only logical that this resulted in a certain hesitation to present undiscovered crimes at all. Jury members would hurt themselves and their neighbours if they – by the conviction of an appellee – would admit that a crime had been committed which they had not presented.[14] The fact that the majority of caught appellees were only accused of being receivers of stolen goods, an accusation that was very difficult to prove, and were tried by their neighbours, may serve as another explanation of the high rate of acquittal. Some cases demonstrate that for the approver's fate conviction or acquittal of appellees did not matter.[15] After one Norfolk approver's appeals had been successfully concluded he was asked whether any of his appellees were still alive, which he denied, whereupon he was hanged. Finally it must not be forgotten that a certain number of appellees were convicted, the jury confirming the allegations made by the approvers. The high rate of acquittal of appellees neither justifies doubt in the appeals nor proves that abuse was widespread. Rather it is an indication of public opinion on approvers.

A further important question is whether prisoners who later turned king's evidence had the chance to concoct false information in gaol. Apart from prisoners who were forced to do so by officials, people caught on indictment or on suspicion who had been in gaol for some time certainly could construe false appeals which nowadays seem plausible. A number of prisoners, however, either appealed by other approvers or caught at the suit of the victim of the crime, often with the mainour, asked for a coroner as soon as they had been arrested, in order to appeal confederates. Since during the procedure before the coroner no other prisoners seem to have been present in these cases the existence of deliberately falsified information can be ruled out.[16]

The financial situation of prisoners, as mentioned above, may have been another reason for prisoners to make appeals, but even though the large majority of approvers did not have any chattels, in ninety-seven cases it can be proved that the prisoners did have chattels, sometimes even revenues from land.

In many cases – cases involving Newgate prisoners have to be excepted because there prisoners who had committed crimes in various counties were held centrally – it can be observed that the appellees came from the approver's dwelling place or from neighbouring villages and that equally the crimes were committed in the same area.[17] Many approvers seem not to have used the delaying tactics available to them. Furthermore entries stating that none of the appellees had been caught are very few. The sheer number of caught appellees not only demonstrates the significance of approvers within the criminal law but also proves that many people named in appeals did exist and were not fictitious. At the appeal of 17 Oxford approvers more than 50 appellees were caught, while more than 120 appellees named by 39 Kent approvers and more than 220 appealed by 49 approvers in Gloucestershire and Herefordshire were arrested.

There remains, however, the problem of the large number of withdrawn appeals. Did withdrawal really always mean that the information given in the appeal was false? It is necessary to look at the circumstances and the description of the withdrawal because here, too, certain types can be distinguished. Apart from cases where it is explicitly said that the appeal was false,[18] withdrawal often took place when the approver was confronted with the appellees in court or before the duel. In the judicial records the events leading to the failure of the appeal are usually described as (i) *retraxit (subtraxit) se de appello suo*; (ii) *non vult prosequi appellum suum;* (iii) *dedicit appellum suum*. The first two clearly seem to describe the withdrawal of a fraudulently made appeal. In the records they can be interchanged and when approvers claim benefit of clergy the withdrawal of the appeal which sometimes precedes the claim is expressed in the same words. However, *dedicere* can also mean 'to contradict',[19] namely to make contradictions when the appeal had to be repeated meticulously in court. Accusations against twenty or even more confederates and the reporting of as many crimes were not exceptional and errors on the approver's side must have occurred. Even the *non vult prosequi* clause, although it is not clear what motives might have induced approvers not to follow suit, cannot automatically be interpreted as the revocation of a false appeal. After all, it has to be mentioned that of one hundred and eighty-six out of one thousand three hundred and ten approvers between 1307 and 1330 it can be demonstrated that they did follow suit and correctly repeated their accusations.

All this neither negates the allegations of extortion carried out by officials against prisoners nor proves the truth of the information given in the appeals, but the background and the circumstances of the appeal are not as unfavourable as on first sight.

The uncertainty of the value of the information is due partly to the different appearance of the appeals on the gaol delivery rolls and the coroners' rolls. On the gaol delivery rolls only parts of an appeal are given and in an abbreviated form: omissions of details and inconsistencies remind the reader that the proceedings were in court – after all only the caught appellees are mentioned. The appeals themselves did not matter here. The impression given by the coroners' rolls is quite different. Here the original appeals are recorded. Most of them are coherent; itineraries of prisoners can be reconstructed; apart from information on the crimes they also report what happened to the booty, and where the criminals hid. Short phrases and seemingly unimportant remarks indicate the quality of appeals: asked to give the date of a crime, a prisoner says it was in summer[20] – he might just as well have invented a date; an approver knows all the home towns of his appellees except one[21] – this could have been added as well if the appeal had been false; on the last day of his appeal another approver mentions a crime that was disturbed by the hue and cry being raised and was never actually carried out;[22] another approver says he thinks that a certain Roger was secretly planning and supporting crimes but he is not sure.[23] Passages like these together with vivid descriptions of the crimes, sometimes even the exact description of a companion,[24] do not prove but raise the probability of the truth of appeals. More convincing are instances where appellees have to be suspected of having a criminal background, when they are – apart from approvers' appeals – also appealed or indicted of other crimes. Unfortunately in many of these cases it is not possible to find out whether the approver could have acquired information about such an indictment earlier because in the records no dates are given, so that the date of the arrest is unknown. However, when an approver appeals a prisoner who is held in another gaol[25] or the indictment is made in one county and the approver imprisoned in another[26] suspicion seems to be justified. It is still more convincing when people are independently appealed by two, sometimes three approvers of crimes of a similar nature, for example the harbouring of felons.[27] Between these appeals there can be intervals of several years and it seems unlikely that one prisoner used an earlier appeal as a pattern. It is still better when the appellee is also indicted of the same crime to which the approver confessed. In one of these cases the indictment was made more than two years after the appeal so that the approver cannot have acquired the information in prison.[28]

It has been mentioned above that many appellees were caught after the appeal and that in spite of a high rate of withdrawal many approvers followed suit. The basis for this was that they recognised the appellee. That they did so is in itself no proof that their accusations were justified; still, there are cases showing not only that accuser and accused had known each other before but that they knew of their respective criminal records. In these examples a coroner proves at the allegation of either the approver or the appellee that either appeal or defence are invalid because one of the parties earlier had abjured the realm.[29] The proof of the approver's claim of his appellee's previous abjuration or the acceptance of an appellee's exception against an accusation because the approver had earlier abjured the realm must be more than coincidence.

Another striking feature, seemingly speaking against the appeals, in reality, however, confirming them, is the omissions or deviations which can be recognised as deliberate. An approver A appeals five people of murder;[30] approver B appeals at least one of them of the same crime.[31] In connection with another crime a second person is appealed by both of them. Neither approver mentions the other, probably because they were in prison together, trying to avoid each other and only revealing their connection by parts of their appeals. Even the confessions of two other prisoners who also were imprisoned together, the one almost constantly referring to the other as his companion, the other not mentioning the first except once and similarly not referring to a single crime confessed by the first except their last crime, when they were caught together, do suddenly make sense when the dates of the crimes and the localities where they were committed are compared. There are chronological gaps in the second approver's appeals into which fit all the incidents reported by the first. In this case only one approver tried to avoid the other while his former companion had chosen a different tactic. The two versions given in the appeals of two other approvers, Henry and Alexander, are another example: Henry's wife is among the appellees of Alexander. She is accused of having received a jacket to the value of 20d. Henry, who of course knows of the receipt – after all Alexander and he committed the theft together – accuses another woman, who also is involved elsewhere in both their appeals, of having received this jacket, and then adds that after his confession this woman gave the jacket to his wife. As both appeals match exactly apart from this discrepancy, Henry's attempt to exonerate his wife is obvious. So, I think, is the authenticity of their confessions.

In general, crimes were reported to and recorded by the coroner in the order in which they came to the prisoner's mind. After bringing them into chronological order, the interesting even though not surprising observation can be made that few crimes date from distant years but many from recent months. This is quite natural but in itself also a confirmation of the appeal, because the cleverness to invent an appeal so natural in its appearance can neither be presupposed, nor was it required.

It is unfortunate that so few coroners' rolls survive because sooner or later one of the inquests resulting in a verdict of homicide committed by unknown thieves would be sure to match up with an approver's confession. A jury's report of the death of an inhabitant of Harrowden (Northamptonshire) who was killed on 26 September 1321 in Harrowden when he disturbed felons breaking into a neighbour's house seems to confirm the story an approver told two months later confessing that he and others stole from a man in Harrowden cloth to the value of 25s. The omission of the killing in the appeal is not surprising because according to the jury the felons took to flight after having struck down the victim.[32] There are many other examples of homicides described as having been committed by unknown thieves on the one hand and on the other as having been committed during a street robbery or a burglary, which do not exactly match but still fit together.

The veracity of the appeals made by approvers is almost impossible to prove. The evidence against their having any value at all seems at first sight to be overwhelming. This may be due in part to the survival of a greater number of gaol delivery rolls, which cast doubt on the information, than coroners' rolls. Still, the evidence as a whole cannot be dismissed, either because of official malpractices or because of the high acquittal rate of appellees. Every confession has to be taken seriously if it does not contradict itself, cannot be proved to have been forced upon a prisoner, and contains certain attributes, details for example, which are a sign of inside information. In these cases approvers' appeals do form a valuable source for the study of crime and the upkeep of public order.

NOTES

I should like to thank Dr John Post for his helpful advice. Responsibility for errors and omissions is, of course, my own.

1. The negative connotations of 'approvers' seem to have had some influence on historical research as well as legal literature. Already in Fitzherbert's *La Graunde Abridgement* of 1514 or 1516 (here used the edition of 1577), pp. 213a, 214b, 218a, and in Sir Robert Brooke's *La Graunde Abridgement* of 1568 (here used the edition of 1573), p. 182b, cases where the approver system was abused predominate. Coke in his *Third Part of the Institutes of the Lawes of England* (here used the edition of 1648), p. 91 mentions malpractices by gaolers, and Sir Mathew Hale in *Historia Placitorum Coronae* (1736, re–pr. 1971), ii. 226, states that 'more mischief hath come to good men by these kind of approvements by false accusations of desperate villains, than benefit to the public by the discovery and convicting of real offenders, gaolers for their own profits often constraining prisoners to appeal honest men'.

   Such comments discouraged historians from studying the subject systematically, apart from the article by F.C. Hamil, 'The King's Approvers' in *Speculum*, xi (1936), pp. 236–58. Neglected in Pollock and Maitland and Holdsworth's basic works on the history of English law, the 'despised approver', when mentioned, was largely used as an example of the negative aspects of the medieval penal system and law. See, e.g., M. Bassett, 'Newgate prison in the Middle Ages', *Speculum*, xviii (1943), pp. 233–46. Approvers also figured in accounts of the coroner's office, the most detailed being R.F. Hunnisett, *The Medieval Coroner*, Cambridge (1961), p. 71 ff.

   More positively, Hamil did think that approvers had been useful in 'breaking up bands of robbers, thieves and murderers and the receivers of their goods' and R.B. Pugh stressed 'the authentic ring' of their stories – R.B. Pugh, *Some Reflections of a Medieval Criminologist*, Raleigh Lecture in History, British Academy, 1973, p. 18. J.B. Post has pointed out the chance of using the material to reconstruct underworld relationships, especially of the poorest classes on which few sources are available – J.B. Post, 'Criminals and the Law in the Reign of Richard II', Oxford Ph.D., 1976, p. 295. More recently Barbara Hanawalt has made use of appeals by approvers in her study, *Crime and Conflict in English Communities, 1300–1348*, Cambridge, Mass., 1979. The following attempt at the evaluation of such appeals is largely based upon the judicial records of the reign of Edward II.

2. *Statutes of the Realm*, Record Commission (1810) (hereafter *Statutes*), i.235.
3. *Statutes*, i. 165.
4. *Statutes*, i. 253.
5. *Rotuli Hundredorum*, Record Commission (1812), i. 457.
6. E.g. JUST 3/214/3, m.8 (Henry de Ewyas approver).
7. E.g. JUST 3/48, m.8 (John Bonde approver).
8. *Statutes*, i. 41.
9. G.O. Sayles (ed.), *Select Cases in the Court of King's Bench*, vol. vii. Selden Soc. lxxxviii (1971), p. 33.
10. JUST 1/254, m.3 'dicendo et asserendo se habere warrantum ad ipsum attachiendum ratione cuiusdam appelli facti super ipsum per quendam probatorem ubi nullum habuit warrantum ...'.
11. Attempts to curtail abuses of indictments and approvers are mentioned by H.M. Cam, *The Hundred and the Hundred Rolls*, 1930, p. 228.
12. *The Mirror of Justices*, ed. W.J. Whittaker, with an introduction by F.W. Maitland, Selden Soc., vii (1893), p. 99.
13. *Statutes*, i.96.
14. It should be pointed out that an approver was convicted only for the crime he initially confessed to in his appeal and – after the first appellee had been acquitted – for his false appeal.
15. JUST 3/49/1, mm. 22, 25d, 27 (John Macke approver).
16. During a court session a coroner describes the circumstances under which an appeal was made: JUST 3/48, m.8.
17. R.B. Pugh, *Imprisonment in Medieval England*, Cambridge (1968), p. 116. Cf. *Fleta*, ed. H.G. Richardson and G.O. Sayles, ii, Selden Soc. lxxii (1953), p. 93, where the extra authority of the Newgate gaol delivery justices is mentioned.
18. Approvers allege either maltreatment or a state of diminished responsibility: see note 6 and also JUST 3/222, m.26.
19. R.V. Latham, *Revised Medieval Latin Word List*, Oxford (1967), p. 135, s.v. dedicere.
20. JUST 1/476, m.1.
21. JUST 2/94A, m.1d.
22. JUST 2/94A, m.1d.
23. JUST 3/222, m.6d., 'nescit quod idem Rogerus est culpabilis de aliqua latrocinia ex certa sciencia set de credulitate dicit quod intendit quod culpabilis est de diversis latrociniis'.
24. JUST 2/110, m.4.
25. JUST 3/222, m.13.
26. KB 27/243, rex, rot. 6d.
27. JUST 3/51/3, mm.8, 18; JUST 2/110, m.4 (Alexandere le Cartere, approver); JUST 3/51/4, mm.6–8; JUST 2/110, m.5 (Robertus Erneys approver).
28. JUST 3/18/5, mm.23d, 27, 27d; JUST 3/19/8, mm.27d, 34, 39; C.258/6, no.18b, (John le Cartere approver). Cf. also JUST 3/222, m.27 (John Spynnesmale approver) and JUST 1/767, (Thomas de Horstede approver).
29. Plea against an appeal – JUST 3/119, m.7; pleas of approvers – JUST 3/48, m.24d, JUST 3/49/1, mm. 18, 20.
30. JUST 3/51/3, mm.8, 10d, 18; JUST 2/110, mm.3,4 (Robert de Redinges approver).
31. JUST 3/51/3, m.18d (Ralph de Auston approver).

32. JUST 2/109; m.5; JUST 3/51/3, m.15. The dating, however, poses a problem in this case. According to the jury the crime took place on 26 Sept. 1321, a Sunday. The approver said he committed the crime on 4 Oct. 1321, the following Sunday. There remains, of course, the possibility that one of the entries was misdated, that it should have said 'after' or 'before' Michaelmas. However, even if this was the case the point I am making remains unaffected.

The Admissibility of Defence Counsel in English Criminal Procedure

J.B. POST

For many centuries, English criminal procedure presented a moral paradox which was epitomised, without originality but with unaccustomed attention to the law, by that great procedural reformer, Lord Chief Justice Jeffreys. 'I think it is a hard case', he told a defendant on treason charges in 1684, 'that a man should have counsel to defend himself for a two-penny-trespass, and his witnesses examined upon oath; but if he steal, commit murder or felony, nay, high-treason, where life, estate, honour, and all are concerned, he shall neither have counsel, nor his witnesses examined upon oath'. He then spoiled this enlightened sentiment by refusing to create a contrary precedent,[1] and in this he was, for once, in the mainstream of judicial opinion. In his day it was universally accepted that defendants in capital causes were not permitted counsel. There were two recognised exceptions: first, defending counsel were admitted in cases brought by the obsolescent procedure of appeal; second, counsel might be admitted, at the instance of a defendant on indictment and with the consent of the court, to put points of law only. These two rare circumstances still left the generality of defendants in capital causes without the right of recourse to professional advice or representation. The rule was relaxed, by statute, for high treason upon indictment in 1696 (and upon impeachment in 1747), and for felony upon indictment in 1836.[2] No detailed account of the rule and observance of it has appeared, although there are critical collections of precedents in Hawkins's *Pleas of the Crown* and Howell's *State Trials*,[3] and good historical summaries are also accessible.[4] This article does not set out to analyse practices in different periods or different courts, but merely to gloss, briefly, upon the origin of the rule and its character, upon the arguments used to justify it, and upon the range of interpretation and application.

'I take it to be a settled rule at common law', wrote Hawkins in 1721,[5] and so had several generations of legal commentators and practitioners. Ironically, the early precedents customarily cited – one from 1406, one from 1469 – were both appeals, in which it was noted that counsel were admissible in the appeals before the court, but were not admissible upon indictments laid on the same alleged facts.[6] The shortage of reports probably reflected the self-fulfilling absence of counsel in such cases, but at least one earlier and more direct precedent is known, in which a motion for counsel upon presentment for rape was rejected by an unknown eyre justice in 1293.[7]

Before that date, evidence for the practice upon indictment is lacking. The compiler of the 'Laws of Henry I', however, included detailed, if sometimes obscure, provisions for the use of defence counsel in capital causes between party and party.[8] While 'counsel' here is a more general term than it later became, the procedures were evidently formal and familiar, and foreshadow the use of professional pleaders by defendants in appeal which was discussed briefly but unambiguously in *Britton* in the 1290s.[9] In the intervening period, the waters are muddied somewhat by *Placita Corone*, which has a fictional appellee in larceny begging the court to 'let me be counselled by some learned person, as to how I can best defend myself', only to be told that 'that course would be clearly against the law of the land and against right'.[10] This says more about *Placita Corone* than it does about the admissibility of counsel; the author was either depicting a bullying judge or – more likely – he was ignorantly conflating the characteristics of two distinct procedures. Certainly there is no other evidence that counsel for appellees was ever denied.

Placita Corone was looking back, somewhat astigmatically, to the period when criminal prosecution by party was gradually giving place to the initiation of suits by presentment for the crown, and it must have been during this period that the rule against counsel in such cases crystallised. In the form in which the rule emerges from darkness there is none of the uncertainty or flexibility that characterises so much in the early years of recorded criminal procedure, and the principle may thus have developed in the late twelfth and early thirteenth centuries. Alternatively, it is possible that it developed, in much the same period, as part of the procedures governing crown suits upon failed appeals.

What is suggestive is that either origin of the rule would fit the earliest and most durable of the justifications offered for it. The 1293 eyre justice explained carefully: 'the king is party in this case, and sues ex officio, for which reason it is not proper that you should have counsel against the king . . .; if a woman acts against you, you shall have counsel against her, but not against the king.' Later in the case a further motion for counsel was dismissed 'because it touches the lord king'.[11] An apparently ideological principle of this kind would be entirely credible for the period, and in keeping with the burgeoning royal presence in criminal actions. The same reasoning, perhaps more artificially conceived, can be found much later: Smith wrote in *De Republica Anglorum* that 'he that shall speak for the prisoner shall be rebuked, as speaking against the prince'.[12] This possibility was taken seriously when Sir Bartholomew Shower, a well-known sycophant, rose for the defence in the first case held under the act permitting defence counsel in treason; he was at tedious pains to dissociate himself personally from any of the sentiments imputed to the defendant.[13]

It is interesting to compare this notion of the impropriety of opposing the crown with the arguments used to explain the exemption of appeals. Obviously, by the time the rule was established, defence counsel in appeal was an immemorial custom, but later writers constructed a rationale. In *Doctor and Student* we read that 'there is no appeal brought but that, of common presumption, the appellant hath great malice against the appellee',[14] while Hawkins, who in 1730 was counsel for the defence in an appeal of murder,[15] had by then already noted that 'appeals are presumed to be generally carried on with greater heat and spleen than indictments', and 'for the most part rather grounded on a desire of private revenge than of public justice'.[16] In fact it was thought to be for closely similar reasons that defence counsel had been admitted in treason cases; since, as Foster reflected, 'state prosecutions ... are carried on by the weight of the Crown and too often in the spirit of party, ... it is extremely reasonable to allow the prisoner the assistance of counsel, to the full extent of the act'.[17]

This runs counter to the doctrine of royal impartiality, which was one of the staple defences of existing practice. *Doctor and Student* sets the reasonable premiss: 'when that a man is indicted at the king's suit, the king intendeth nothing but justice with favour, and that that is to the rest and quietness of his faithful subjects, and to pull away misdoers from among them charitably, and therefore' – and this is the important and enduring corollary – 'he will be contented that his justices shall help forth the offenders as far as reason and justice may suffer.'[18] (Note the term 'offenders' to describe persons not yet convicted.) More precisely, in Hawkins's words, 'it is the duty of the court to be indifferent between the king and the prisoner, and to see that the indictment be good in law, and the proceedings regular, and the evidence legal and such as fully proves the point in issue'.[19] Such trust in the workings of impartiality led Coke and many others to promote the misleading maxim that the court is 'counsel for the prisoner'.[20]

This handsome notion was predicated upon the assumption that the case against the prisoner should be unanswerably clear,[21] and in consequence a just court would ensure that an insufficient crown case would fail. Dogmatic faith in prosecution cases was, and is, as familiar as the schismatic doubt among defendants and the wider public, but there may have been some practical justification. Professor Langbein has observed of eighteenth-century criminal trials that 'in most cases the accused had been caught in the act or otherwise possessed no credible defense', and he has commented on the preponderance of direct evidence over circumstantial evidence in an age lacking systematic and technical forensic detection.[22] If hard evidence was the only evidence likely to result in a court appearance, it is not surprising that commentators should have regarded the typical crown case as unanswerable.

Other arguments used against the admission of defending counsel were even more overtly practical, and were arguments against a change rather than justifications in principle. It was held, for example, that a prisoner conducting his own defence might impress the court with his plain honesty, or alternatively (with a bit of luck) condemn himself by inexpert mistakes.[23] More obviously, the admission of defence counsel would lengthen criminal trials in sessions which were already oversubscribed;[24] Staunford feared that counsel would be 'so wary [*covert*] in their speech that it would be too long before the truth became apparent'.[25] In 1686 Jeffreys observed that '[if] counsel must be heard to every trivial point, the courts of law would never be at an end in any trial, but some dilatory matter would be found to retard the proceedings . . .',[26] and the attorney-general used the same argument in 1691 against the bill which eventually revised the procedure in treason.[27] In the same year, Holt as lord chief justice voiced another fear, that defence counsel would increase the number of acquittals, for which reason 'never was counsel allowed to find out faults in an indictment'.[28] Traditionally, even the defendant was not allowed a copy of the indictment, in case its drafting details proved susceptible to exceptions pleaded at the trial or to writ of error sued afterwards. The fear may have been justified; Professor Cockburn reckons that 'a moderately alert attorney could probably have made mincemeat of perhaps half of the indictments considered at assizes', and he quotes two exceptional cases (not capital) in which counsel were involved and did just that.[29]

Against the background of these theoretical and practical objections to counsel, it is interesting to see the ways in which the rule was applied. There are two clear hindrances to a full appraisal of court practice: first, the sparsity of criminal reports before the late seventeenth century, and, second, the bias of surviving reports, Old Bailey apart, towards the exceptional case. These mean that it is only really possible to see the rule in action in a period throughout which it was under criticism and in process of reform. This imperfection is exacerbated by the fact that it was abuse of criminal procedure, rather than the procedures themselves, which gave rise to the criticisms in the first place. Political trials have never been very edifying, but many of those held in the 1680s and early 1690s offended even contemporaries. The Popish Plot, the Rye House Plot, and Monmouth's Rebellion cases prompted a House of Lords committee in 1691 which took evidence from legal representatives of convicted traitors,[30] and the House of Commons, in passing a bill admitting defence counsel, reported that 'their design was, to prevent those abuses in trials for treason ... by means of which, during the violence of late reigns, they had observed divers had lost their lives'.[31] We cannot necessarily suppose that these strictures would have applied to the trials which went unreported.

What we can see, heat and spleen apart, is that the rules about defending counsel were uniformly accepted, but far from uniformly interpreted and applied. In 1590, for example, at assizes, a judge refused to tell a defendant how many jurors he might challenge, on the grounds that 'I sit to judge and not to give you counsel'.[32] A century later Lady Alice Lisle, a victim of Judge Jeffreys, wrote plaintively: 'I have been told, the court ought to be counsel for the prisoner, instead of which there was evidence given from thence; which, though it were but hearsay, might possibly affect my jury. My defence was such as might be expected from a weak woman; but such as it was, I did not hear it repeated again to the jury.'[33] A contemporary noted of Cornish's trial in the same year that 'he was so beset, that the defence he, or any for him could make, would have availed him nothing'.[34] Yet contrasting examples are not wanting. When Hickford pleaded guilty to high treason, in 1571, Lord Chief Justice Catlin was at pains to advise him that he was pleading irrebuttably to the general issue, and several minutes of discussion and exhortation followed before the court reluctantly entered the plea.[35] Even Jeffreys, on his good days, can be found to have offered helpful advice to defendants, if only because he liked the sound of his own unctuous voice.

Wide variations can also be found in the degrees of assistance, short of full legal representation, which might be sanctioned for a defendant. There was some feeling that limited lay assistance did not contravene the rule. Thus we have this exchange in Russell's case (1685):

Defendant:	May I have somebody write to help my memory?
Attorney-general:	Yes, a servant.
Lord chief justice:	Any of your servants shall assist you in writing anything you please for you.
Defendant:	My wife is here, my lord, to do it.[36]

Lady Alice Lisle, who was deaf, was allowed a friend to explain the court proceedings as they went along.[37] Bateman, in 1685, gave such a display of mental distraction that his son was allowed (without an explicit ruling) to make his defence for him.[38] On the other hand, in 1681 Fitzharris's wife was nearly turned out of court for whispering to her husband about jury challenges.[39] In 1691 a defendant was denied the presence of his solicitor 'to refresh my memory', although a few years earlier another prisoner had been allowed an amanuensis who was indeed his solicitor.[40]

It was by this date rapidly becoming acceptable for prisoners to have access to counsel while awaiting trial, although it was sometimes held to be a misdemeanour for counsel to advise thus without leave of the court.[41] Stephen refers to 'this irregular and unsystematic good nature',[42] and Foster attributed it to 'the benignity of the times' in the 1690s and after,[43] but the practice was officially creeping in earlier; the attorney-general boasted in Russell's case that 'he hath been very fairly dealt with, he hath had the liberty of counsel to advise him'.[44] Well before the 1696 act the secretaries of state were issuing warrants for counsel to visit prisoners for private consultation.[45] Of course, from time immemorial, occasional prisoners had had access to legal advice – whenever a defendant rattled off a list of exceptions to his indictment we may suppose that he had been expertly rehearsed; it was the consent of the prosecution and the recognition of the courts that seem to have been novel.

The availability of legal advice to prisoners on remand promoted yet another point of ambivalence and inconsistency. It was regarded as proper for a prisoner to make and consult notes for his defence and, as in Russell's case, for someone to make his notes for him. Nonetheless there were problems. The most famous case in point was Colledge's in 1681. The defendant was allowed counsel in gaol, and allowed the use of notes; but the notes prepared by his counsel were not only disallowed, as being tantamount to counsel in court, but they were confiscated in advance and used in preparing the prosecution case.[46] One of the criteria for distinguishing Colledge's notes from those of his counsel, according to Chief Justice North,[47] was the use of the second person singular instead of the first, and indeed in Penruddock's case in 1655 the defence brief, consisting of thirty-six paragraphs of exceptions, precedents, and statutes, was cast in the first person, despite the probable hand of counsel in the matter ('18: They cannot indict us and try us all in one day, as it is in Kelloway, fol.149, 6, which the Lord Chief Justice declared to be law in the case of the Portugal ambassador's brother').[48] Sidney's counsel, on the other hand, provided him with a minute analysis of all possible procedures and evidences against him, with tabulated instructions for dealing with each ('the king's counsel will sum up the evidence to the jury. Observe if they misrepeat any part of the evidence to the jury. And call to the court to do you right in that matter').[49] In 1777 the celebrated Dr Dodd, on trial for forgery, used a speech for the defence which was written for him by the even more celebrated Dr Johnson.[50]

There was thus, in practice, some measure of legal counsel, although not representation, available to many prisoners, and it is clear on other occasions that counsel were briefed and present in court in case the defendant made a successful motion for counsel to plead on a point of law. In the case from the 1293 eyre, when counsel was refused the court ordered 'that all pleaders who are of your counsel withdraw'.[51] Four hundred years later, Russell's counsel was given leave to remain in court, but found the public occupying all the available seats.[52]

Having counsel present was one thing, however; success in a motion to admit them was quite another, and, again, depended much upon interpretation. Jeffreys's inconsistency in such rulings was remarkable even for him. In Armstrong's case he refused counsel to plead the effect of a statutory proviso upon the record of an outlawry, on the ground that 'there is no doubt or difficulty at all in the thing',[53] although there was clearly doubt in the defendant's favour, and the ruling was widely condemned. By contrast, in Rosewell's case in the same year, the defendant raised exceptions to the indictment after conviction, at which Jeffreys was vehemently critical of the attorney-general for what was in the circumstances a reasoned objection to the admission of counsel.[54] In general it seems to have been accepted by the bench that points of law might arise genuinely and usefully in the interpretation of a new statute, or of an oddity such as sanctuary or outlawry, but that exceptions to indictments, challenges to jurors, and similar routines were potentially too fruitful of dilatory trivialities to justify defence counsel.

All these minor variations in the application of the rule eventually gave place to the general relaxation of it, and it is interesting, though hardly surprising, to find that the treatment of treasons and the treatment of felonies were sharply different. When the 1696 act was passed, Holt as lord chief justice insistently applied rather questionable punctilio; in Charnock's case and in Parkyns's case he declined to anticipate the operative date of the act (which in Parkyns's case was the following day), despite plausible arguments that the preamble to the act held its provisions to be 'just and reasonable' without reference to time.[55] In 1746, when Lovat, as a peer, was impeached of high treason, fifty years of lenity upon indictment were not allowed in argument, and counsel was refused.[56] The new rule was extended to impeachment in the following year.

In felony, however, the general relaxation proceeded not by statute but by judicial discretion. In 1762 Foster could still defend the old rule ('it is impossible in a state of imperfection to keep clear of all inconveniences') without commenting upon its incidence,[57] but he must have been aware that practice was reducing its effect. When Acton, the Marshalsea turnkey, stood trial for murder in 1729, the greater part of the defence was conducted by the defendant, but his counsel intervened on procedure and on evidential points during examination and cross-examination.[58] From about 1734 onwards, Professor Langbein has detected the presence of defence counsel at the Old Bailey, at first rarely and in roles supplementary to that of the defendant, and then, gradually, dominating the defence, if still at the discretion of the bench.[59] In 1742 counsel submitted 'that although he knew by the course of the court at the Old Bailey, he was not at liberty to observe upon the prosecutor's evidence, yet he apprehended, that for the ease of the court, he might just open the nature of the defence, without making any observations upon it'.[60] The solicitor-general, in responding to Barbot's motion for counsel on a murder indictment in 1753, commented that 'by the more modern practice, the rigour of this rule hath been something relaxed', and readily consented to counsel for cross-examination and examination of witnesses.[61] It may have been for this reason that a contemporary Commons committee on the reform of the criminal law did not mention defence counsel in its various resolutions,[62] but Blackstone in 1769 thought that 'still this is a matter of too much importance to be left to the good pleasure of any judge, and is worthy the interposition of the legislature'.[63] The prolifera-tion of non-capital statutory felonies, and the increasingly regular sentence of transportation for some formerly capital offences, mocked the old rule yet further, and, by the beginning of the nineteenth century, defendants in capital and non-capital felony alike made reasonably free and frequent use of counsel both for examination of witnesses and for making the defence to the court.[64] The old rule was moribund; and by statute in 1836 it was dead.

NOTES

1. *A Complete Collection of State Trials* . . ., ed. T.B. Howell, London, 1816, vol. 10, 267; cf. Bulstrode Whitelocke, cited in J.S. Cockburn, *A History of English Assizes 1558–1714*, Cambridge, 1972, p. 121, and Bartholomew Shower, cited in J.H. Langbein, 'The criminal trial before the lawyers', *The University of Chicago Law Review*, 45 (1978), p. 309.
2. 7 & 8 William III, c.3; 20 George II, c.30; 6 & 7 William IV, c.114.
3. W. Hawkins, *A Treatise of the Pleas of the Crown* . . ., 4th edn, 1762, vol. 2, c.39; *State Trials*, vol. 5, 466n.–480n.
4. J.H. Baker, *An Introduction to English Legal History*, 2nd edn, 1978, pp. 417–18; idem, in *Crime in England 1550–1800*, ed. J.S. Cockburn, London, 1977, pp. 36–8; Cockburn, *Assizes*, 120–2; Langbein, 'Criminal trial', pp. 282–3, 307–14, and 'Shaping the eighteenth-century criminal trial: a view from the Ryder sources', *Univ. Chicago Law Rev.*, 50 (1983), pp. 123–31.
5. *Pleas of the Crown*, vol. 2, p. 400.
6. Y.B. H.7 Hen. IV f.36 pl.4; Y.B. P.9 Edw. IV f.2 pl.4.
7. Y.B. 30 & 31 Edward I (Rolls Series), 529–30; cf. Public Record Office, JUST 1/1098, mm.1–4, and D. Crook, *Records of the General Eyre*, Public Record Office Handbooks no. 20, 1983, p. 251.
8. *Leges Henrici Primi*, ed. L.J. Downer, Oxford, 1972, cc.47–9; cf. Downer's remarks at p.356, and W. Holdsworth, *A History of English Law*, London, 1903–72, vol. 2, p. 312. See also *Borough Customs*, ed. M. Bateson, vol. 2, Selden Soc. vol. 21, p. 5.
9. *Britton*, ed. F.M. Nichols, London, 1865, vol. 1, p. 102.
10. *Placita Corone*, ed. J.M. Kaye, Selden Soc. Supplementary Series vol. 4, 1966, pp. 16–17.
11. Y.B. 30 & 31 Edward I (Rolls Series), pp. 529–32.

12. T. Smith, *De Republica Anglorum: A Discourse on the Commonwealth of England*, ed. L. Alston, Cambridge, 1906, p.67.
13. *State Trials*, vol.13, 145.
14. *St. German's Doctor and Student*, ed. T.F.T. Plucknett and J.L. Barton, Selden Society vol.91, 1974, p.286.
15. *Dictionary of National Biography*, sub. art.
16. *Pleas of the Crown*, vol.2, p.401.
17. M. Foster, *A Report of Some Proceedings on the Commission for the Trial of the Rebels in the Year 1746* ..., 3rd edn, ed. M. Dodson, London, 1792, p.231.
18. *Doctor and Student*, p.286.
19. *Pleas of the Crown*, p.400.
20. E. Coke, *The Third Part of the Institutes of the Laws of England* ..., London, 1660, p.29; Hawkins, *Pleas of the Crown*, p.400.
21. Holdsworth, *History of English Law*, vol.5, pp.192–3.
22. Langbein, 'Ryder sources', p.41, and 'Criminal trial', p.281 n.56.
23. W. Staunford, *Les Plees del Coron*, London, 1557 (reprinted with introduction, 1971), p.151v; Hawkins, *Pleas of the Crown*, p.400; Langbein, 'Ryder sources', p.123; Baker in *Crime in England*, p.37.
24. Baker, *Introduction*, p.417.
25. Staunford, *Plees del Coron*, p.151v.
26. *State Trials*, vol.11, 525.
27. *Cobbett's Parliamentary History of England* ..., vol.5 (London, 1809), p.660.
28. *State Trials*, vol.12, 665.
29. J.S. Cockburn, 'Trial by the book? Fact and theory in the criminal process 1558–1625', in *Legal Records and the Historian*, ed. J.H. Baker, Royal Historical Society Studies in History, 1978, pp.64–5, and 'Early-modern assize records as historical evidence', *Journal of the Society of Archivists*, 5 (1975), pp.228–9.
30. *State Trials*, vol.9, 938–9.
31. *Cobbett's Parliamentary History*, vol.5, p.693.
32. *State Trials*, vol.1, 1278.
33. *State Trials*, vol.11, 380.
34. *State Trials*, vol.11, 466.
35. *State Trials*, vol.1, 1043–4.
36. *State Trials*, vol.9, 584.
37. *State Trials*, vol.11, 310.
38. *State Trials*, vol.11, 476, 473.
39. *State Trials*, vol.11, 476.
40. *State Trials*, vol.12, 747; vol.9, 836 (and cf. 988).
41. Hawkins, *Pleas of the Crown*, p.401.
42. J.F. Stephen, *A History of the Criminal Law of England* (London, 1883), vol.1, p.226.
43. Foster, *Report*, p.232.
44. *State Trials*, vol.9, 581; cf. vol.11, 464.
45. *Calendar of State Papers Domestic ... 1694–5* (London, 1906), pp.323–5.
46. *State Trials*, vol.8, 725–6; cf. Holdsworth, *History of English Law*, vol.9, p.232.
47. *State Trials*, vol.8, 585.
48. *State Trials*, vol.5, 784–9. For Penruddock's possible legal training, see *Dictionary of National Biography*, sub. art.
49. *State Trials*, vol.9, 823–35.
50. L. Radzinowicz, *A History of English Criminal Law and its Administration from 1750*, vol.1, London, 1948, p.459.
51. Y.B. 30 & 31 Edward I (Rolls Series), p.530.
52. *State Trials*, vol.9, 594.
53. *State Trials*, vol.10, 111; see also vol.10, 313.
54. *State Trials*, vol.10, 260–5.
55. *State Trials*, vol.13, 72; vol.12, 1381–2.
56. Holdsworth, *History of English Law*, vol.11, pp.550–1.
57. Foster, *Report*, p.231.

58. *State Trials*, vol. 17, 462–3, 468, 503.
59. Langbein, 'Criminal trial', pp. 307–14, and 'Ryder sources', pp. 124–5.
60. *State Trials*, vol. 17, 1112.
61. *State Trials*, vol. 18, 1231–2.
62. *Journals of the House of Commons 1750–4*, pp. 159–60, 190, 289.
63. W. Blackstone, *Commentaries upon the Laws of England*, vol. 4, Oxford, 1769, p. 350.
64. Old Bailey Sessions Papers, e.g. 1804 1st session 52, and 1804–5 1st session 9. For the problems in citing these printed reports, see Langbein, 'Criminal trial', pp. 267–9.

Mesne Process in Penal Actions at the Elizabethan Exchequer

D.R. LIDINGTON

In 1568, John Mayberd, mayor of Hereford, wrote to William Cecil. He had, he explained, recently received two writs out of the Exchequer. One had been addressed to the sheriffs of the city of Hereford, and the second to the mayor and bailiffs. Unfortunately, Hereford did not have any sheriffs, nor was it a county in its own right, so Mayberd had left the first writ unexecuted and was now returning it to Cecil. The second writ he had served on the defendant even though, as his letter politely pointed out, there were no bailiffs of Hereford either.[1]

This paper seeks to direct a few beams of light onto one feature of the judicial history of the Elizabethan Exchequer. Sixteenth and early seventeenth century writers agreed that one of the chief functions of the Queen's or King's Remembrancer's Office was to administer lawsuits based upon penal statutes. This assessment is borne out by the evidence of the Queen's Remembrancer's Memoranda Rolls, which list over 13,000 such cases between Michaelmas 1558 and the end of Trinity 1570.[2] Penal statutes were those laws which provided for a fixed monetary penalty to be awarded against an unsuccessful defendant. At the Exchequer, such actions were commenced by Information. Occasionally, the Attorney General would act as informer, but it was more usual for this task to be done by private individuals. A private informer was usually entitled by statute to a share of any forfeiture awarded. To commence his action, an informer would give details of his allegations to one of the Remembrancer's clerks who would then engross a summary of the case, couched in a standard form, onto parchment. This parchment bill would afterwards be exhibited before the Barons, and the informer would swear to the veracity of his Information. This done, the Barons would then authorise process to be sued out to summon the defendant into court.[3]

As the example cited at the beginning of this paper showed, the effective execution of mesne process could not be guaranteed. Perhaps it was rare for a writ to be addressed to a non-existent official. Even a correct address, however, was no certain pledge that a writ would reach its destination unimpeded. This truth must have been recognised by the Barons of the Exchequer even before 1565 when they amerced one of the court's own sworn messengers for failing to deliver no fewer than 237 writs with which he had been entrusted. Moreover, even if a writ could be delivered swiftly, it might not be executed with comparable efficiency. During 1560, the Chief Baron had to write urgently to Henry Fanshawe of the Queen's Remembrancer's Office, to explain that the sheriff of Oxfordshire was unable, owing to pressure of business, to execute all the writs which had been sent to him within the limited time allowed by law. The Chief Baron asked for new processes to be issued for all relevant cases, to be returnable on the first day of the following term.[4]

Defendants included large numbers of merchants and middlemen–traders whose occupations committed them to frequent journeys across county boundaries (or even overseas) and whom even the most zealous sheriff might find it hard to track down. The solution would have lain in devising a form of process addressed directly to the defendant, capable of being served on him anywhere, and of being delivered and executed by men other than the sheriff and his officers. Such a form of process was the Exchequer *subpoena*. The *subpoena* was addressed to the defendant, not the sheriff. It could be delivered by any individual appointed by the court, and returned *subpoenas* and affidavits found in the *bille* files of the court show that informers and their servants frequently undertook this task themselves. A defaulting defendant was held to be in contempt of court, and his person, goods and lands became liable to attachment. Yet the Queen's Remembrancer's Memoranda Rolls, the formal record of the court, contain only a handful of cases where the defendant was summoned into court by a *subpoena*.[5]

According to the Queen's Remembrancer's Rolls, the usual summons employed by the Exchequer was the writ of *venire facias*. This writ was addressed to the sheriff of the county where the defendant was supposed to reside. It instructed the sheriff to ensure that the defendant appeared, on a specified day, to answer him in the Exchequer. If, after the return of the *venire*, the defendant failed to appear, the Barons could have writs of *capias, alias capias*, and *pluries capias* issued, to compel his attendance. As a last resort, a proclamation could be made in the defendant's shire, commanding him on his allegiance to appear. A commission of rebellion could be sued out against any party who then continued to defy the court.[6]

Every penal action enrolled in the Memoranda Roll commenced with the text of the Information. Below this were written the words *super quo* and then an account of the judicial writs issued and returned, term by term, until the defendant came to court and put in his Answer. Likewise, between the enrolled Answer and the verdict of the jury there would be recorded a description of the process employed to convene the panel and send them to Westminster.[7]

However, a closer examination of the Roll reveals some problems.

More than half of all penal actions have left no record beyond the Information and the words *super quo*. Yet in these cases the clerk recorded in the margin of the rotulet that the defendant *allocutus est ad respondendum* to the offence described in the Information. The implication of this evidence, that a writ was in fact issued in such cases although not recorded in the Roll, is given extra weight by the fact that there is almost always a definite change in the hand between the Information and the entries made after the words *super quo*, but no change between the account of the writs of summons and the enrolled Answer. Whether it took two terms or ten years for the defendant to appear in court, no entry seems to have been made of the judicial summonses sued out against him until that term when his Answer was put into court and enrolled. Furthermore, the writ files of the Exchequer provide specific evidence of cases which were continued well beyond the last stage actually recorded in the Memoranda Roll.[8]

For example, in 1567 a London merchant, Adam Huchenson, was summoned by *capias* to maintain his plea. Yet the relevant entry in the Memoranda Roll shows no progress in the case beyond the joinder of issue in Michaelmas 1564.[9] Another case began with an Information brought in Easter 1563 against one Henry Campion, for retaining alien servants, and appears from the Roll to have got nowhere.

The defendant did not even put an Answer into court. But the writ file contains a writ of *venire facias juratores*, issued in Trinity 1567, ordering a panel to be selected to determine the case.[10] The parties to the action, and the clerks of the Remembrancer's Office, apparently carried on with the action, without bothering to make entries in the record of the court. In a third case, where the Memoranda Roll shows no proceedings beyond the Information, entered in Michaelmas 1562, the *bille* file contains a certificate of appearance by the defendant in Hilary 1563, and the writ file shows a *capias* issued against that same defendant in November 1566.[11]

It is not possible to dismiss such instances as occasions when writs were issued in error, after the conclusion of a case. Such things did happen, but then the returned writ would be endorsed with a note to the effect that it had been made out by mistake.[12] Conclusions must remain tentative, at least until a systematic analysis of the writ files can be undertaken, but it is reasonable to suggest that the Memoranda Rolls alone provide an inadequate record of the judicial procedures of the court. The descriptions of mesne process preserved in the Roll appear to have been entered more for form's sake than as a literal account of how defendants and juries were induced to come to Westminster. Complaints against informers included the allegation that process was regularly issued before any bill had been put into court.[13] The Exchequer evidence suggests that mesne writs were indeed written out by the clerks and dispatched to the sheriff, regardless of whether the appropriate plea had or had not been formally entered into the record.

There is, moreover, a further question. Was the *subpoena* in fact used more frequently by the court than the Memoranda Rolls suggest? The evidence of writ files and *bille* files indicates not only that a *subpoena* was issued in some cases where no process was noted on the Memoranda Roll, but also that in certain instances a writ described in the Roll as a *venire facias* was in fact a *subpoena*. The description of mesne process recorded in the Memoranda Rolls does not ring true. Between 1558 and 1570, more than 13,000 penal actions were commenced at the Exchequer. Yet in only one solitary case was the sheriff recorded as having made a return to a writ *of venire facias*.[14] In every other case where that writ was allegedly employed, the formula enrolled was that the sheriff had not returned process, but that nevertheless the defendant now came into court. In some cases at least, the whole rigmarole of *venire facias* and the involvement of the sheriff was a fiction, concealing actions by *subpoena*. For example, John See of Sandwich put in an Information during January 1561. Three Norfolk merchants were cited as defendants. The Roll describes how writs of *venire facias* were sued out and directed to the sheriff in respect of these three. One, John Taylor, appeared in Michaelmas 1561 and made his Answer. Neither of his co-defendants appeared, and the Roll states that proceedings against them by *venire facias* continued. Yet in the *bille* file for Trinity 1561 is an affidavit, sworn to by John See, declaring that he personally had served a *subpoena* on another of the defendants, Ralph Thomson of Yarmouth.[15]

An even more interesting example concerns the action initiated by William Staples, cordwainer and professional informer, against Henry Austeyn, a linen draper of London. The Exchequer issued a *venire facias* for return at the Octave of Hilary 1563. The writ was not returned, nor did the defendant appear, so a further process was addressed to the sheriffs, this time specifying the Quindene of Easter 1563.

The day dawned, no writ was returned, but the defendant came to court and made his plea. A triumph for the coercive power of the *venire facias*, and for the efficient work of the sheriffs of London? Or was it? On the London writ file for Easter 1563 appears a returned *subpoena*, addressed to Henry Austeyn and bearing a precise reference to the term and rotulet number of Staples's Information. The *subpoena* was dated 30 January, and it directed Austeyn to appear at the Quindene of Easter. It was endorsed with the words *comparuit in propria persona sua*. In other words, it was the *subpoena* which had induced the defendant to come to court, and the *subpoena* which he had returned when he made his appearance.[16]

How many other cases where the Exchequer ostensibly relied upon the sheriff and the *venire facias* in fact involved the use of a *subpoena*, served personally on the defendant by the informer? How many cases which apparently peter out after the Information were in practice occasions when a *subpoena* had been issued, but not returned, either because of a defendant's stubbornness, or an informer's lack of effort, or because of an unrecorded out-of-court settlement between the parties?[17] It is unlikely that such questions can ever be answered precisely. Any accurate quantification of the actual use made of each type of mesne process would require a careful comparison of the contents of the writ and *bille* files with those of the Memoranda Rolls. Even then, such a study would have to remain incomplete, partly because of the damage suffered by the Exchequer files during the past four centuries, and also because unreturned writs would, by definition, have left no trace in the files.

However, enough evidence survives to indicate that clerks and informers were bending the procedures of the court to suit their own interests. The types of abuse which can be inferred from the Exchequer records are those which would-be reformers of the court set themselves to eradicate. The abortive bills of 1571, Bacon's plan for special commissions to enforce the penal statutes, and the eventual Act of 1576,[18] all either directly or by implication attacked the practices of the Queen's Remembrancer's Office and sought to bring its routines under much tighter scrutiny and control. The evidence of the Exchequer suggests that legal procedure could, in Elizabethan England, be easily adapted to changing circumstances. The same evidence indicates that such changes should be attributed less to notions of the public interest than to the material ambition of the officials of the court.

NOTES

This paper is based on research undertaken for a Cambridge doctoral thesis. I am most grateful to Professor G.R. Elton for his criticisms of earlier drafts of this work. All documents cited in these notes are, unless otherwise stated, housed at the Public Record Office, Chancery Lane.

1. State Papers Supplementary SP46/14/9.
2. The equitable jurisdiction of the Exchequer has been studied by W.H. Bryson, *The Equity Side of the Exchequer*, Cambridge, 1975. The Exchequer of Pleas, which heard cases affecting Crown debtors and royal officers, still awaits its historian. Contemporary or near-contemporary accounts of the Exchequer include *The Practice of the Exchequer Court* (1658) previously attributed to Sir Thomas Fanshawe but now to Peter Osborne, Elizabeth's Lord Treasurer's Remembrancer; R. Robinson, 'A briefe collection of the Queenes Majesties Most High and Most Honourable Courtes of Recordes', ed. R.L. Rickard, *Camden Miscellany*, 20, 3rd ser., 83 (1953), p.25; L. Squibb, 'A Book of all the several officers of the Court of the Exchequer', ed. W.H. Bryson, *Camden Miscellany* 26, 4th ser., 14 (1975), pp.98–103. Exchequer: Queen's Remembrancer's Memoranda Rolls E 159/339 to E 159/360.

3. This outline account of Exchequer procedure is derived from studying the following classes of Exchequer documents: Queen's Remembrancer's Memoranda Rolls E 159; 'Bille' files E 207; Writ files E202; Entry Books of Decrees and Orders E 123; Depositions E 133 and E 134, as well as the State Papers Domestic Supplementary SP46.
4. E 159/351 Mic. 7/8 Eliz. rot. 72; SP46/13/65.
5. E.g. E 159/346 Easter 5 Eliz. rot. 18; E 159/347 Hilary 6 Eliz. rot. 318.
6. Writs are described in John Cowell, *The Interpreter*, Cambridge, 1607; by Thomas Manley, London, 1637; augmented, 1672. Examples of *capias* exist at Exchequer: Writs E 202/340. There is a record of a Proclamation on Allegiance at E 202/354/2 Hil. 9 Eliz. Case of Humfrey Wylson.

   Other writs were available to the court. For example, if a defendant could not attend because he was being detained by another court, a *habeas corpus* would be issued. E 202/357/1 Case of George Sanders.

   Where the alleged offence had included action *vi et armis* in contempt of the Crown's authority, the first summons could be by *attachias*. E 159/340 Mic. 1/2 Eliz. rot. 45.
7. E 159/339 to E 159/360.
8. E.g. Cases of Thomas Peddyngton (E 159/359 E. 5 Eliz. rot. 238 and E 202/354/2 Hil. 9 Eliz.), Sir John Constable (E 159/352 Hil. 8 Eliz. rot. 186 and E 202/354/2 Hil. 9 Eliz.), and Alexander Mynge (E 159/352 Hil. 8 Eliz. rot. 47d. and E 202/354/2 Hil. 9 Eliz.).
9. E 159/348 Mic. 6/7 Eliz. rot. 390; E 202/354/2 Hil. 9 Eliz.
10. E 159/346 E. 5 Eliz. rot. 109; E 202/354/2 Hil. 9 Eliz.
11. E 159/345 Mic. 4/5 Eliz. rot. 145; Exchequer: *Bille* E 207/29/2 Hil. 5 Eliz.; E 202/354/1 Hil. 9 Eliz.
12. E 202/354/1 Hil. 9 Eliz. Case of Leonard Smyth.
13. Exchequer: Entry Books of Decrees and Orders E 123/2/41d., E 123/3/161d.
14. E 159/340 Mic. 1/2 Eliz. rot. 79. Even in this case, the evidence is confusing. The writ was returned endorsed *non est inventus*, but the defendant appeared in court!
15. E 159/342 Hil. 3 Eliz. rot. 23, E 207/29/1 T. 3 Eliz.
16. E 159/345 Mic. 4/5 Eliz. rot. 300, E 202/340.
17. Other cases where there is evidence of a *subpoena* being used are those of Richard Smythe (E 159/346 Hil. 5 Eliz. rot. 162, E 202/340), Francis Robynson (E 159/346 Hil. 5 Eliz. rot. 198d., E 202/340), and William Weston (E 159/345 T. 4 Eliz. rot. 133, E 202/340).
18. State Papers Domestic SP 15/20/22; British Library Harleian Manuscripts 249/17 fos. 114–18; 18 Eliz., cap. 5.

Whose Prerogative in Late Sixteenth and Early Seventeenth Century England?

VICTOR MORGAN

In a speech in the early days of the Long Parliament it was a Norfolk M.P., Sir John Holland, member for Castle Rising, who complained of 'the late & great Inundation of the Prarogative Royall wch have broke out & almost overturned all our libirtyes even those [which] were best & stronglyest fortefyed'.[1] The expedients to which Charles and his advisers had resorted during the preceding eleven years of the Personal Rule may not unreasonably be thought to have been in Holland's mind on this occasion. Yet I believe there is a danger in accepting his remarks at face value, a danger of viewing the prerogative over the whole of the preceding eighty years from the vantage of the critical comments of the 1640s. In this perspective the prerogative appears as the chosen instrument of an increasingly authoritarian government. Dr Hinton has argued that the measurable increase from the 1580s in the use of the seals is evidence of increased prerogative action.[2] Some contemporary comment seems to support this case,[3] although it has been a matter of debate amongst historians as to whether the use of the prerogative is in itself evidence of despotic intent on the part of government.[4] For my part I wish to argue for the existence of a situation that is somewhat more complicated than has sometimes been allowed.[5] There are three elements to my argument and they can only be presented and illustrated in the most summary form on this occasion.

First, there are times when the fortuitous survival of evidence makes plain that what might otherwise appear to be a central, governmental, initiative in the use of the prerogative in fact arose from particular local circumstances and was pursued to meet private ends. I will illustrate an instance of this type in a moment.[6]

Second, the changing economic and social requirements of sixteenth century England found in the prerogative a flexible instrument for their needs. For example, the benefactors of charitable endowments, the founders of colleges, and the businessmen behind the rash of joint-stock trading companies of the early seventeenth century all used the prerogative to establish the corporate status of their enterprises. Professor Thorne has spoken of the similar process in the same period through which the law evolved new procedures in order to accommodate changing social and economic needs.[7]

In both these classes of use the royal prerogative provided a flexible and an accessible mechanism to meet the needs of those who required its services. It was, for example, far more readily available than was private statute through the infrequent meetings and uncertain passage of bills in Parliament.

Third, I would wish to argue that the very success of the prerogative as a means to private ends was one of the reasons for an enhancement of the status of the prerogative during the early seventeenth century.[8] However, there was a danger inherent in this reliance upon the prerogative. In the first place it was always possible that it might be used positively by the Crown in pursuance of particular, doctrinaire policies. In the second place, and partly as a consequence of the first of these changes, availability for private ends might become more restricted than once had been the case. This is, indeed, what I believe happened from the mid-1620s, and it is this which contributed to such a hard press for the prerogative in the parliamentary criticisms of the early 1640s.

These remarks on the prerogative arise from my detailed work on Cambridge University,[9] and it is from the universities that I will now draw some illustrative examples.

Let me first cite an instance of the private manipulation of the prerogative that if formal records alone had survived might have looked like a crown initiative.

Some graphic insights into the procedures involved in eliciting the royal favour for the private use of the prerogative are contained in the tale of Robert Creighton's attempt to obtain the headship of Catharine Hall in 1635.[10] He does not seem to have been an overly enthusiastic candidate: he subsequently claimed that 'I cared not for it', but that as he intended to resign his place as Professor of Greek 'this might be occasion for me to live still in ye Universitie', while 'the faithfulnes of my ten years service might perhaps have prompted me to the hopes of as great a dignitie as the Master-shippe of Catharine Hall, had I beene verie eager on the spurre of ambition'.[11] In fact, the initiative for Creighton's assault on the mastership appears to have originated with John Lothian, the senior fellow of Catharine Hall.[12]

It was Lothian who had summoned Creighton to his chamber on a Sunday afternoon in July 1635 to inform him that Richard Sibbes, the old Master, had died, and prompted him to try for the office.[13] The deposition of Thomas Buck, the University's senior bedell, who had been present at the afternoon meeting, and had talked with Lothian privately beforehand, suggests that Lothian, while himself not wishing for the office, felt isolated in the College and wanted support; Lothian told Buck that after the death of Sibbes 'he was left alone, and had not any one of ye fellows to joyn with him' while in their exculpatory depositions the fellows were later to claim 'That he onely of all the Fellowes had spoken with Mr Crighton [for the mastership] being his Countryman and acquaintance'.[14] Lothian's sense of insecurity may have derived from the means by which he had himself entered the college, as a result of a royal mandate nominating him to a fellowship.[15] Unfortunately, a reading of the statutes of the College, and consultation with Creighton's trusted friend, Thomas Shirley,[16] another fellow of Trinity College, and with Buck, revealed that he was not qualified for election, as the statutes required that the Master of Catharine Hall should be a bachelor or doctor of divinity, and at this time Creighton was only a master of arts. As Buck subsequently reflected, the means by which Lothian had obtained his own fellowship prompted him to seek the obvious means of overcoming this statutory impediment to his plans; 'and by what I then remembered concerning the manner of Mr Lothians being made fellow of the said hall did conceive that he then intended that Mr Creiton should make suit for no other l[ett]res from his M^{atie} than those wch were to be absolutely Mandatory wth a non obstante to their statute and any other thing to the contrary whatsoever.'[17] Creighton claimed that Lothian 'spake to me thus; you see if wee would wee cannot chuse you unles his Majestie dispense with our statutes; therefore if you will trie your friends at Court to procure his Majesties Letters before the Sun rise on Wednesday morning, I promise you my voice & best assistance'.[18]

Thereupon Creighton 'took horse', galloped off to Court 'and before the next day at noone I had obtayned his Majesties grant by the intercession of my Gratious Lord and Patron the Duke of Lennox'. It was at this stage that difficulties began to occur for 'finding noe Secretarie of State to attend, I was forced in that straight and narrow compend of time to use mine owne hand in the penning of his Majesties Letters'. Having some compunction about imposing himself upon an unwilling College and being loath to invoke the full force of royal authority, the letters 'I framed whollie dispensatorie, to remove those barres of Statutes' rather than mandatory, obliging the college to elect him. Returning to Cambridge that same night, at about 10 p.m., he sent the letters by Shirley to Lothian – only to be told by the latter that 'the fellowes had importun'd him and he hadd already passed a Scrutinie, & chosen an other man for the securitie of theire College'. Presumably, Lothian had not been overly concerned about succumbing to the pressures for an immediate election, as it appears from the reported conversations of the preceding Sunday that he had expected Creighton to obtain letters requiring his election rather than those which simply removed inhibitions on his candidature.[19] Lothian expressed some regret 'Wishing the Letters had been Mandatorie, or at least more powerfull, & efficacious' and told Creighton that 'yf I brought a mandate what they had done they wuld nullifie yf I brought none what they had done should stand for good'.[20] Thus, Lothian had assumed that they had made a 'hypotheticall condicionall election', that could be annulled on the expression of sufficiently strong royal wishes to the contrary. Lothian apparently advised Creighton to take horse once more and 'to returne againe to the Court for letters Mandatory' while he procrastinated over the actual admission of Ralph Brownrigg, the newly elected competitor for the office.[21] On being told this, after all his energetic exertions, Creighton appears to have had enough, 'for my part I was content to sitt downe rather than to entangle mye selfe in a twisted & interfearing business'.[22] He agreed with Lothian that his unexpected rival should be admitted and 'that his Maties l[ett]res should not be mentioned'.[23]

He should, perhaps, have been more cautious at the outset of becoming embroiled in Lothian's machinations for the irony is that this pocket academic Machiavell had at first managed to bungle his own election as a fellow of Catharine Hall for precisely the same reason that had defeated his plans for Creighton! Buck recalled that '(in regard the first le[tte]rs which it pleased his Matie to send in his behalf for the said place, were not effectually drawn up) he was enforced to procure his Maties second l[ette]rs in a more effectual manner for the obtaining of the said fellowship'.[24]

Unfortunately for all the parties involved – Lothian, Creighton and their confidants Shirley and Buck, the fellows of the College and their newly elected Master, Ralph Brownrigg – the train of events that Creighton's solicitation of Court favour had set in motion could not so readily be terminated by his opting out at this late stage. The dignity of the Crown had become engaged and what had started as a local academic plot gone awry, now called down upon its participants the wrath of the King himself. By royal order Brownrigg was suspended from his newly appointed duties as Master, the fellows pleaded their innocence, and the University's Chancellor, the Earl of Holland, demanded of the heads of the colleges a full enquiry to determine the truth of the matter, it being alleged that the election was 'not managed wth the respect that was due unto his Maties l[ett]res of dispensation'.[25] For his part Creighton attempted to exculpate himself by asserting that he had called a halt to his efforts on condition; 'always provided they gave his Majestie satisfaction, and my Lord Duke which I thought all parties were bound to doe as well of Loyaltie towards theire Soveraigne as of good manners towardes soe great a peere as my Lord Duke'.[26] The ultimate outcome was that the royal sensibilities were mollified and Brownrigg was reinstated in office.

This tale of bungling and irresolution on the part of the Scottish mafia illuminates a number of otherwise obscure aspects of University elections. First, while we know that the election of masters of the larger colleges was a matter for Crown initiative,[27] the situation at Catharine Hall suggests that even under the spartan discipline and more closely supervised regimen characteristic of the 1630s the stimulus for royal interference could still originate from *within* the University. It is only the fortuitous preservation of the records created by the bungling of matters on this occasion that provides us with this insight; there is nothing about the royal letter itself to suggest that it was prepared in the *ad hoc* way that in his deposition Creighton reveals was the case.[28] What is ostensibly a royal initiative was in fact instigated from outside the Court, and in effect provided an invitation for Court interference in order to satisfy personal and local ambitions. It is a case of private exploitation of the royal prerogative; it is also a story of a dog and its tail. Nor was it an isolated instance associated with the University.

Sir Edward Coke described how the grant of burgesses to the universities had been obtained in 1604; Cecil had moved the King for it, who 'graciously graunted and signed yt the booke being ready drawne and provided'.[29] There was little harm in this particular grant, but sometimes the prior preparation of documents was intended to forward more selfish ends. In 1627, Robert Mason wrote to the secretary of the Duke of Buckingham that the statutes of his college would not permit him to take his degree without a dispensation 'wch I have sent up by my man fitt for ye Kings hand wch I would desire yo^{w} to move my lord to procure speedily'.[30] Neither were academics ignorant of the ease or the means by which the all-important royal signature that initiated prerogative action could be obtained.[31]

In 1621/22 our old friend Robert Creighton had been in competition with Robert Metcalfe for the professorship of Hebrew. On that occasion Lord Keeper Williams – an old hand at Cambridge politics – had written to his friend, Samuel Collins, Provost of King's. Williams assured Collins that he would deal with the King if Metcalfe was elected, and if Creighton 'or any other shall procure his Maties l[ett]res'. Equally well versed in Court practices, Williams added that to obtain such letters 'is an easy thing surrepticiously to be effected'.[32] Similarly, in 1631, Thomas Bainbrigg, Master of Gonville and Caius, remarked to Viscount Dorchester that 'if y^{r} Ho^{r}: had procured (as easily I know you might) y^{t} great hand' for a dispensation from the college statutes, then he would be obliged to admit an importunate aspirant to a fellowship.[33] As Secretary of State, Dudley Carleton, Viscount Dorchester, was, of course, advantageously placed to obtain the royal signature.

I will now outline my third argument with regard to the changes in the use and availability of the prerogative during this period, and look in particular at the relationship between the prerogative and corporations. From the mid-1620s it is possible to see a positive effort to control the indiscriminate 'private enterprise' invocation of the royal prerogative in university elections.[34] In part – and after 1628 – this was the result of a more rigorous attitude on the part of central government to all such grants. In part it was the outcome of a positive policy of religious discrimination.[35] Moreover, there are indications at this time of attempts to make *systematic* alterations to the statutes of local limitations of a number of colleges as an alternative to the individual waivers employed hitherto.

The initiative for this latter development appears to have come from interested groups within the colleges,[36] but the response was in keeping with attitudes prevalent at the Caroline Court. Perhaps more significantly, the modifications to local limitations that followed these representations were effected by an exercise of the royal prerogative powers under the lesser seals. The Peterhouse statutes were altered in 1629 to redistribute the counties as between the northern and southern divisions, and to permit Middlesex and London, and Cambridge and the Isle of Ely, a maximum of four fellows per county.[37] A petition to the King from Jesus College resulted in a modification of their statute of local limitation in 1635 similar in its effect to the changes made at Peterhouse some six years earlier.[38]

That alterations such as these were not welcomed by all can be seen in the opposition that arose to similar modifications attempted at Emmanuel and examined by a committee of the House of Commons in 1640 appointed at the instigation of the descendants of its founder, Sir Walter Mildmay, to examine what violations there had been to the laws and statutes of the College.[39] Both then and earlier, in 1627–29, when the matter had been examined within the University, there was considerable feeling against tampering with the wishes of founders and benefactors as expressed in the statutes.[40] Primarily, these moves had arisen from attempts to ease the statute requiring men to quit the College after due time and to go forth to preach the word. In addition, by the 1640s some of the fellows were also hankering after a change in the statute imposing local limitations.[41] It is not without significance that the Committee to examine the violation of the statutes at Emmanuel had been appointed at the beginning of the Long Parliament at a time when the Commons was also investigating John Cosin's 'Popery', both as Master of Peterhouse since 1635 and as secretary and chaplain to the Bishop of Durham.[42] Later, a more comprehensive committee was instituted to investigate abuses in both religious and civil government in the universities.[43] The two were closely associated in the eyes of contemporaries.

In 1627 the King had given a conditional general dispensation from the statute requiring a fellow of Emmanuel to leave his fellowship one year after gaining his doctorate.[44] This permitted the fellows to continue to live in a manner appropriate to their academic status and the new sacramentalist view of the dignity of the clergy.[45] But no longer would Emmanuel continue to spew proselytising preachers out into the provinces as had been its founder's intentions. Additionally, it was represented at this time that the paucity of livings available made it necessary for men to take up lectureships 'and to seeke meanes of Livelyhood from the benevolence and favour of the people'.[46] This was not only at variance with a view of the dignity of the clergy; as is well known it made them less amenable to clerical control.

The alteration at Emmanuel took place over the same years in the later 1620s that the proposals for the relaxation of the statute of local limitation at Peterhouse were being contemplated. These proposals coincided with the appointment as Master of the arminian, Mathew Wren, in 1625/26.[47] Initially, the proposals were referred for examination to the Bishops of London, Durham, Winchester, Ely and St Davids or any three of them.[48] That is, George Montaigne, Richard Neile, Lancelot Andrewes, Nicholas Felton (Visitor of the College) and William Laud; all men of a similar doctrinal persuasion. In fact, other business and the deaths of Andrewes (25 or 26 Sept. 1626) and Felton (5 or 6 Oct. 1626) and then the continued vacancy of the latter's see of Ely meant that the matter was not actually considered until April 1629[49] when the referees were Laud, Neile, John Buckeridge (Bishop of Ely and Visitor) and Francis White. Again, with the possible exception of the latter, all members of the Durham House group. Not unnaturally, these close associates of Wren reported in favour of the proposed changes on 20 April, and by 15 May the instrument embodying them had passed the great seal.[50] The similar changes instituted at Jesus in 1635[51] coincided with the mastership of Richard Sterne, made a chaplain to Laud in 1633,[52] and were refereed by Laud, William Juxon and Francis White.[53]

There were good rational grounds for some modifications. However, in addition, the effect of both these changes in local limitations was to create greater flexibility in the choice of fellows. Given the effective power of the masters on these occasions it permitted them the more easily to mould the colleges to their doctrinal wishes. At the same time, in the way the balance between north and south was altered at Peterhouse, it threatened to reduce the opportunities for likely lads from those very dark corners that an earlier generation of proselytising academics and benefactors had set out to illuminate. Such moves could not but alienate benefactors and their descendants on the one hand, and on the other those members of the local communities with close connections with the colleges whose vested interests were touched by these alterations. Moreover, the doctrinal beliefs of the majority of the local aristocratic and intellectual elites are likely to have been at variance with the doctrine that masters could now more readily introduce into their colleges. In addition to the modifications to the statutory local limitations at some colleges there were arbitrary alterations to other statutes.

In the 1620s the King suspended the statutes at St John's that permitted only two fellows to study civil law.[54] In 1635 he permanently converted two fellowships from theology to civil law.[55] These moves inevitably affronted the principles of 'practical theology' on which the College had been founded.[56] Moreover, they were moves that afforded support for that branch of the law that was most closely associated with the imposition of discipline through the Church courts.[57]

The formal means by which these systematic changes to college statutes were implemented did not fail to carry implications for a larger context. Nor were those implications lost on a wider audience.

The modification to the statutes of Emmanuel in 1627 were made by a royal letter that was to be treated as an authoritative instrument of record; as the King said, it was to be committed 'to safe custodie among other the Escriptes and writinges of o^{r} said Universities'.[58] Little wonder, then, that in 1640, following inquiry into this procedure, the lineal descendants of its original founder took the precaution of seeking to base Emmanuel's statutes on the firmer ground of parliamentary sanction rather than leaving them within the vulnerable territory of a corporation by royal patent.[59]

Peterhouse's statutes were amended by letters patent in 1629.[60] Those at Jesus by a signet letter in 1635. It was ordered that the letter was to be 'transcribed into yor Book of Statutes, & obtain ye force of a Statute wth ye rest forever, this being our expresse pleasure'.[61] As we have noted at St John's, in the same year, the King converted two fellowships from theology to civil law and nominated one of the first occupants.[62] The signet clerk recorded the instrument by which this was done as 'An ordinaccon or Statute in latin under ye Signet' and especially noted that this was to be 'entred at large in the privat booke'. The change was said to be grounded on the powers given to the King by the college statutes.[63] This was a claim that had been expressly refuted by Lord Keeper Williams in 1625.[64] The high-handed procedure evident in the 1620s and 1630s may be compared with the far less authoritative tone adopted by the Privy Council in 1575 when it 'enjoined' the acceptance by the University and City of Oxford of orders designed to settle disputes between the two bodies. Moreover, this earlier order was the outcome of a careful process of arbitration and elucidation of *existing* 'charters and privileges', mutually agreed between the parties, and not, as later, modifying existing local university or college statutes.[65]

Now, it is arguable that these were legitimate exercises of the royal prerogative; that Williams was wrong and that technically Charles did have the rights he claimed at St John's. That, as the King had said in a rebuff to Parliament in 1626 when it questioned the election of the Duke of Buckingham as Chancellor of the University, it and 'all Corporations derive their right and privilege from him'.[66] It was certainly a view supported and, indeed, extended by some within the University.

William Beale had been Master of St John's when its statutes were altered in 1635. Some months later he preached a sermon to the effect 'That all we had was ye Kings. He might command all[,] wifes, children, estates and all'.[67] But it was at Oxford in the following year that this principle was most fully articulated with reference to the universities and to all other corporations.

During the mid-1630s Cambridge was desperately fighting off Laud's attempt at archiepiscopal visitation.[68] Ultimately they were successful, but their sister University was not. On 22 June 1636 Oxford's new statutes were delivered to the University in Convocation. They were accompanied by a speech that was intended to leave the audience in no doubt as to their dependence on the authority of the Crown. 'But for universities and colleges, they are the rights of Kings in a most peculiar manner. For all their establishments, endowments, privileges, and orders, by which they subsist and are maintained are derived from regal power.'[69] Three generations of private benefactors might not have agreed. This was offensive enough, but no doubt what was more disconcerting for contemporaries was the way in which the remodelling of university statutes, it was asserted, was only a particular example of a general principle of regal rights. For, 'not only particular men and families, but all corporations, societies, nay counties, provinces and depending kingdoms, have all their jurisdictions and governments established by him; and by him (for public good) to be changed or dissolved'.[70] Surely what we see embodied in this statement is the notion of a prerogative that answers to a higher purpose than the specific needs of particular private men. It appeals to a concept of 'public good' and 'reason of state', ultimately only determinable by the King and his ministers, and which is increasingly invoked from the 1620s.[71]

But then, the speaker on this occasion was Sir John Cooke, secretary of state, and therefore keeper of the signet, the initiatory seal. In this capacity the daily round of business furthered under the seals and his auspices may well have persuaded him to think that the king was not only supreme governor of the Church, but also of the 'commonwealth, over all causes or persons'. Here, there is no explicit mention of parliament. 'This then we must build upon, as an axiom and fundamental rule of government: that all our laws and statutes are the King's laws, and that none can be enacted, changed or abrogated without him.' True, and in itself an unexceptionable claim, but is it the King-in-Parliament that is being spoken of here, or is Cooke recalling those exercises of the royal prerogative under the seals that as secretary he daily facilitated? Was the experience of the increasingly multifarious activities of the executive encouraging some of its agents to feel that their actions made 'law' as much as did the deliberations of brief and infrequent parliaments? Cooke is clearly thinking not only of an undisputed dispensing power – 'and no pardon or grace proceeds from any but from the king' – but also of a unique power of initiation as 'he [is] the source of honour; all dignities, all degrees, all titles, arms and orders, come originally from the King, as branches from the route'. Moreover, there is reference to those spheres in which, at least in theory, the King was not hampered by a shared authority: 'So his power reacheth to foreign plantations, where he may erect principalities, and make laws for their good government, which no man may disobey.'[72] Here, we surely have one manifestation of the problem of 'multiple kingdoms' that plagued early modern Europe.[73] The speech includes a positive side-swipe at parliamentary pretentions to concurrent authority in the Church, where 'his regal power by ancient right extendeth to the erection of bishoprics, deaneries and cathedral churches, and to settle orders for government in all churches, by the advice of his own clergy, without any concurrence of foreign usurping power'.[74] Clearly an allusion to the notion of a medieval 'Ecclesia Anglicana'. But in the 1620s it had been Parliament, not the papacy, that had threatened to intervene, and the University's Chancellor, Laud, seated next to Cooke on this occasion at Oxford, who was insistent upon the Church's status as a separate estate under the Crown.[75]

Here also we may detect an awareness of, and distaste for, the independent corporatism so evident in continental Europe. Bacon had disparagingly alluded to the danger that 'this monarchy would have the corporation in it, like unto the cities of Holland'.[76] Hobbes was also aware of the dangers inherent in any 'great number of corporations; which are as it were many lesser common-wealths in the bowels of a greater, like wormes in the entrayles of a naturall man'.[77] This aversion to semi-independent corporations in their various forms had a long pedigree.[78] It also had its advocates, culminating in Milton's proposal for a federation of county communities.[79]

In the speech as a whole, in the words of a leading courtier, delivered to a university audience, the constitutional status of those institutions is swept up in a broader reach of constitutional thinking. Here, the notion of a dispensing power and a regulatory authority within defined spheres appears to teeter on the brink of grander claims to an initiatory power, perhaps cognate with that of parliamentary statute. After all, three years earlier the chief amongst Cooke's audience, Laud, was reputed to have said in the case of the soap-makers in Star Chamber that he would 'make a proclamation as available as an act of parliament', urging Matthew 21:44 ['And he who falls on this stone will be broken to pieces; but when it falls on any one, it will crush him'] – 'this he Applyed to the Power of the King'.[80]

In this – if in nothing else – Laud seems to be a precursor of Hobbes. Hobbes was to provide a definition of law in terms of command and prohibition, specifically with reference to proclamations.[81] What appears to lie behind this feeling on the part of both men and, I would venture to suggest, of other men such as Secretary Cooke, was the conviction that executive action defined sovereignty. In the early modern State executive action lay with the King, and, so this belief went, it was the sovereign power that made law. This had certainly not been the Tudor view, as interpreted by Professor Elton,[82] nor the view expressed by James I in 1614.[83]

What we also seem to have in Cooke's remarks is a strict interpretation of 'the concession theory' of corporations. That is, in Maitland's words, that 'the corporation is, and must be, the creature of the State. Into its nostrils the State must breathe the breath of a fictitious life, for otherwise it would be no animated body but individualistic dust'.[84] Whilst English lawyers had long accepted this theory, in practice they acknowledged the reality of a form of corporate existence embodied, for example, in their own unincorporate Inns, and they also accepted the alternative route to the benefits of incorporation provided by the trust.[85]

Here, these two ideas are combined: the notion of the executive roots of sovereignty and the strict interpretation of the concession theory of corporations. The concession theory says in effect that a corporation is a franchise, and a franchise is a portion of the state's power in the hands of a subject.[86] If, also, sovereignty resides, and resides only, in the executive power of the state, and the King is the executive power, then, only the King may grant incorporation.

Nor was it inappropriate that Cooke should express these thoughts in a university context, for those institutions had played their part in the development of the practices that lay behind his words. As Cooke made plain, the universities were not the only spheres for intervention by the prerogative. Nonetheless, because of their often asserted royal connections, and the clear disjunction between their local statutes and the changing social demands made upon them, they had positively invited frequent interventions by the prerogative, specifically by means of signet letters. The universities had helped to induce a habit of mind and action. By the late 1620s they were reaping the harvest of their own importunity, as piecemeal and opportunist intervention was re-shaped by a positive and systematic policy, not limited to, but certainly keenly felt within the universities.

But Sir John Cooke's claims were unlikely to have won wide acceptance. Indeed, Professor Elton has cited contemporary authorities to prove the continuity into the early seventeenth century of the restricted, Tudor view of the prerogative.[87] Certainly, most contemporaries did not respond to the actions of Charles in relation to the universities as if they were unexceptionable or legally well-grounded. If it had been so, the King's *ex post facto* intervention in the election of the Master of Gonville and Caius, in 1626, would not have alarmed Joseph Mede to the point of asserting that it was likely to bring about 'the utter overthrow of all elections of masters for ever'.[88] If it had been so the descendant of the founder of Emmanuel would not have instituted an investigation into the modification of that College's statutes when Parliament at last met in 1640.[89] If it had been so, Pym would not have cited Beale in the Short Parliament for his sermon at St John's five years earlier.[90] If it had not been so the signet office clerks might not have been so punctilious – either on their own initiative, or under instruction – in recording *in extenso* the instruments of the King's actions in modifying college statutes.[91]

Moreover, these remarkable and unacceptable constitutional innovations were inextricably linked with the entrenchment of a minority group of doctrinal innovators. At his trial, Laud's accusers were as anxious to press as he was to refute the documentary evidence to be found in the signet office docquets. These were held to prove his responsibility for procuring the appointment of chaplains to the King and of bishops – all former or current members of the universities – who were tainted with arminianism.[92] Furthermore, Laud was accused of engineering the election of an arminian, Thomas Jackson, as Master of Corpus Christi College, Oxford, and of slighting the days of King Edward and extolling the time of Queen Mary in the preamble to the new statutes of Oxford University of 1636.[93]

These *systematic* uses of the royal prerogative in the universities were employed on behalf of, approved, implemented and justified by a religious faction at Court and their associates in academe. But, clearly, they had implications beyond those unquiet groves.

The broader constitutional and political implications of practices in the Church or the universities were not lost on a wider audience. In 1637, Laud had harangued the soap-boilers in Star Chamber. At the Archbishop's trial they recalled the occasion, deposing that Laud had said he would continue to complain 'till men were brought to obey such things as were enjoined by authority'. At this, they and others recollected thinking this 'to be a sad presage of blind obedience which would be required of all men in matters of liberty and estates, as we saw it was then too forward in matters of the church'.[94]

The parallel could as well have been drawn with the universities, especially with regard to the King's treatment of them as corporations. For even though a number of the colleges had close associations with the Crown they were still essentially *private* corporations. Their corporate existence often derived *from* the Crown,[95] but so did that of an increasing number of charitable foundations, of the recently established trading companies, and of the great municipal corporations.[96] But this did not make them possessions of the Crown, accessible to detailed intervention and regulation. If the King was to interfere in the universities as he had done on behalf of courtier-clerics and his great favourite, Buckingham, in 1626, might he not do so in these other corporations and communities? Certainly, secretary Cooke, in his speech at Oxford, had linked together 'all corporations, societies ... counties, provinces, and depending kingdoms'.[97] Neither were contemporaries unaware of the parallel.

For example, whatever the individual politicking may have been that went on behind the scenes, in 1623/24 contemporaries had seen the charter of the Virginia Company withdrawn through an action on a writ of *quo warranto*.[98] Amongst other things, it was this, it has been suggested, that prompted the Massachusetts Bay Company to remove its charter from under the hands of the King.[99] The caucus that engineered this move had signed a compact to this end at a meeting held in August 1629 at Cambridge,[100] the University of which the signatories had been members, which their sons were attending at the time of the signing, and for at least one college of which the Winthrops – amongst the signatories – had served as auditors for many years.[101] This familiarity with the University can have left them in no doubt of the Crown's attitude to corporations – like the University, like their Company – that derived their existence from the royal prerogative.[102]

Or, again, when in 1638 Henry White attempted to gain entry *gratis* to the Company of Eastland Merchants he obtained a letter in his favour from the King, and took his brother-in-law Charles Farbench along to their Assembly.[103] The latter subsequently deposed as to the irate response elicited from the Master of the Company, Sir Christopher Clitherowe, who 'wth some vehemency alledged. That if his Ma^{ts} Lettres should prevaile in that kynde, they knewe not where nor of whome to raise moneys or contribucon for defraying the expence of their Assemblies adding that such admittances were contrary to their oath and ordes'.[104] Farbench can hardly have endeared himself to the Company when, at what he thought was the opportune moment, he pointed out 'the respect wch the universities shewed to satisfy his Maties Missives &

requests' and directed attention to the favours the King seemed to promise in the letter, 'implyeing a requitall or good turne'. Sir Christopher clearly had more guts than many a college master and by the late 1630s had been frustrated more than once by broken royal promises. He responded 'in an unseemly slighting manner "that they all know well inough what the Kings good turnes were when they came to seek them".[105] Neither did they require reminding of the extent of successful Crown intervention in other corporations such as the universities; as members of the metropolitan elite, with relations at Oxford and Cambridge, and with benefactions linking their livery companies to the universities they could hardly remain ignorant of the inroads into the autonomy of those institutions.[106]

Neither would all lawyers and parliamentarians have agreed with Sir John Cooke's assertions. The inferences to be drawn from a number of his judicial pronouncements makes it clear that another Coke, Sir Edward Coke, did not.[107]

Sir John was to claim in his speech at Oxford that 'all corporations, societies, nay counties, provinces and depending kingdoms, have all their jurisdictions and governments established by' the King.[108] But in the case of Sutton's Hospital (a charitable educational endowment), Sir Edward had enunciated *four* lawful means of incorporation; by common law, by authority of Parliament, by the King's charter [i.e., by an exercise of the prerogative] or by prescription.[109] Later in the seventeenth century Sir Mathew Hale was to opine that '*Counties* in England are, some by prescription, some by charter. The power of a charter is in their erections, divisions and unions'.[110]

Sir John Cooke was to assert that the King could alter corporations. But in the City of London's case, Sir Edward Coke had cited an incident in 32 Edward III to prove that, in this instance, there were three methods of entry to the freedom of the City, and the King could not make a freeman by patent.[111] That is, the royal prerogative acting through the seals could not modify the form of a pre-existent corporation.[112]

Sir John was to assert that the King could dissolve corporations. But in the case of the Dean and Chapter of Norwich Sir Edward and others had held that Henry VIII's letters patent had re-incorporated the Dean and Chapter, but subsequently 'all those who pretend any Title by any Letters Patents of Concealment, are for ever barred of all Pretences and Claims which they can make to any of these Possessions'.[113] Contemporary opinions differed as to whether the surrender by a corporation of its property extinguished its corporate identity, and this was the main point in this case,[114] but in addition Coke also seems to be saying that the subsequent devolvement of the prerogative by letters patent to searchers for concealed lands cannot be employed to impeach the integrity of the corporate existence erected by the same means. In the King's Bench in 1628, Whitelocke even remarked, 'Et coment le Roy create & grant un corporation, uncore il ne poit dissolve ceo'.[115]

The irony is, of course, that this final assertion is the result of the growth in the notion of 'corporate personality' in this period, in which the King had shared.[116] But, if the King might dispose at will of the *persona ficta* of corporations, might he not do likewise to natural persons? In objecting to the untrammelled exercise of the prerogative in the sphere of corporations it was not only corporate privileges but ultimately also personal freedom that was being defended; not merely liberties but liberty.

The converse of a situation in which the Crown increasingly intervened in the affairs of corporations was one in which the King withheld the corporate legal status imparted by the great seal. In the 1580s Elizabeth might not altogether havc approved of the puritan seminary created by Mildmay at Emmanuel.[117] Nevertheless, the radical interests embodied by Mildmay had been represented at Court, and had been able to obtain the necessary royal instruments for the establishment of the college. The universities had shared in the creative ferment of these years, as men sought institutional form for their ideals and aspirations. *Pace* Dr Hinton and Dr Hassell Smith, the increase in instruments under the seals is not only an indication of the increasingly interventionist desires of central government; it is also an index of initiatives from individuals in the country at large.[118]

By way of contrast we may compare Mildmay's success in the 1580s with the problems encountered by the Feoffees for Impropriations in the 1620s and 1630s. Their aims were similar: the creation of a preaching and proselytising ministry. The difference was that by the time the Feoffees came into existence political circumstances had changed and they were unable to seek incorporation by royal charter. Thus politically incapacitated from achieving formal corporate status, ultimately the Feoffees were brought to Court by Attorney-General Noy on the grounds that they had acted as a pretended corporation.[119]

In those same decades of the 1620s and 1630s even the leaders of corporations that owed their existence to an exercise of the prerogative were becoming disillusioned with the Crown. During the 1590s and early 1600s there had been a distinct antagonism on the part of the Commons and the outports towards the great chartered trading companies, effectively controlled as they were by the financial magnates of the City of London. As heads of these companies, and in their other capacities as Crown concessionaires and city fathers, the interests of these men were closely associated with those of the Crown. However, by the 1620s there is evidence for greater discrimination by their critics between the different elements in this interest group and between their various corporate enterprises.[120] At the same time the inconsistent treatment meted out to these interests by the Crown served only to create a sense of insecurity, and dissipated any sense of loyalty they may once have felt. The cynical realism of Sir Christopher Clitherowe's remarks in 1638 – already quoted – is but one instance of this process of alienation.[121]

In part the exploitation of these concessionary interests by the Crown was achieved by further exercises of the prerogative, but now to their disadvantage. Alternatively, they might be coerced on the grounds that corporations, such as the East India Company, were dependent on the royal prerogative for their continued existence. For example, in 1617 it had been asserted that 'Without his Majesty's usinge his prerogative power, the said Companie and theire stock are at his Majesty's grace and pleasure to require of them what his highnes thinketh meete for his honner and proffit, which, as their case standeth, they nether may nor will deny'.[122]

During the 1620s there was an evident rapprochement between on the one hand the concessionary interests and their corporations, and on the other, the House of Commons.[123] On the part of the former group this may have owed something to a growing realisation that parliamentary statute might ultimately provide a more secure basis for corporate stability than the all-too-variable royal prerogative. At the least, parliaments were relatively brief and infrequent events that did not pose the constant threat of unwelcome intervention now found in the prerogative. Unfortunately, during the 1620s parliamentary statute was also becoming less available for private purposes.

For the moment, we may accept the rather unsatisfactory classification into public and private Acts provided by *The Statutes at Large*. On this rough-and-ready basis it is evident that Elizabethan parliaments always passed more public than private Acts. During James' first Parliament this balance was reversed, while at the same time there was a substantial increase in the absolute number of private Acts.[124] On the basis of this experience the legislative debacles of 1614 and 1621 were all the more disappointing to individuals with private ends to pursue in parliament. The legislatively abortive Parliament of 1621 was yet more unsatisfactory because of the long intermission since the last legislatively satisfactory parliamentary session, in 1610.[125] It was only in James' last Parliament that there was a reversion to something like the pattern and volume of legislation that had characterised the first seven years of his reign. Again by way of contrast, only one session of a Caroline Parliament during the 1620s (that of 17 March 1627/8 to 26 June 1628) produced anything like an Elizabethan volume of legislation, let alone the successful legislative achievement of James' early years.

During the sixteenth and first two decades of the seventeenth century the prerogative had served as an adjunct, if ultimately inferior, tool to that of parliamentary statute. Yet at the very time, in the 1620s, when the exigencies of ill-managed politics meant that the alternative means of achieving private ends via parliamentary statute was no longer available the prerogative powers were also becoming less readily accessible and less amenable to the needs of a wide variety of groups in society. Even amongst those on whose behalf it had earlier been exercised in order to confer corporate status there was a progressive alienation from the Crown, as that same prerogative was used in such a way as to undermine the stability that had originally been sought through the means provided by incorporation.

During the 1620s Buckingham may not have wholly monopolised patronage at Court, but it was certainly less plural than it had been even in Elizabeth's latter years. The Durham House group sought to impose a new sacramentalism and a revised doctrine through the manipulation of the prerogative.[126] In the thinking of men such as Beale and Cooke that prerogative was coming to be seen first and foremost as an instrument of royal policy, rather than as a tool available to both King and subject. By the late 1620s the prerogative had become the vehicle for advancing a sectarian religious policy, and the seals were the instruments for imposing both this and a new and grander view of kingly power. Through the manipulation of college elections, through the imposition of Buckingham as their Chancellor,[127] through the modification of college statutes, through the pronouncements of Beale in Cambridge in 1635 and Cooke at Oxford in 1636, this doctrine was enforced and this grander view was expounded within the universities. The prerogative became the tool of the argument from 'reason of state'; the means of pursuing that higher policy that was *arcanum imperii*. What had been a royal prerogative available to all had become the King's prerogative and an instrument of his policies. It was the latter that Sir John Holland was criticising in the early 1640s.

NOTES

1. Bodl. Tanner MS. 321 fol. 4.
2. R.W.K. Hinton, 'The Decline of Parliamentary Government under Elizabeth I and the Early Stuarts', *Cambridge Historical Journal*, XII (1957), pp. 116–32. See also, *idem*, 'Government and Liberty under James I', *Cambridge Historical Journal*, XI (1953), pp. 48–64; *idem*, 'English Constitutional Theories From Sir John Fortescue to Sir John Eliot', *English Historical Review*, 75 (1960), pp. 410–25. See also A. Hassell Smith, *County and Court: Government and Politics in Norfolk, 1558–1603* (Oxford, 1974), pp. 246–7, 334; J.P. Cooper, 'Differences Between English and Continental

Governments in the Early Seventeenth Century', in *Britain and the Netherlands ... 1959*, ed. J.S. Bromley and E.H. Kossman (London, 1960), pp. 63–4. Apart from the interpretation placed on them, Dr Hinton's figures ('Decline', pp. 131–2) are not always accurate. In particular he seems not to have realised that the published index which he uses for the statistics on the use of the signet systematically *omits* all references to letters missive (Hinton 'Decline', pp. 119, 130–2). I hope to deal with the workings of the signet office and its surviving records in another paper.

3. 'The prerogatives of princes may easily and do daily grow; the privileges of the subject are for the most part at an everlasting stand', wrote the author or authors of the abortive 'Form of Apology and Satisfaction to be presented to his Majesty', compiled during the first session of James' first English Parliament of 1604 (quoted in J.R. Tanner, *English Constitutional Conflicts of the Seventeenth Century 1603–1689*, Cambridge, 1928, p. 19). For Tanner's misuse of this document see G.R. Elton, 'A High Road to Civil War?' in *From the Renaissance to the Counter-Reformation: Essays in honour of Garrett Mattingly*, ed. Charles H. Carter (London, 1965), pp. 325–47. To my mind this particular comment embodies a view of Continental experience as much as, in Tanner's reading, it is used to misinterpret the parliamentary history of the Tudor period. For the awareness of foreign precedents see Hinton, 'Government and Liberty', p. 62; Cooper, 'Differences', p. 90; J.R. Tanner, *Constitutional Documents of the Reign of James I, 1603–1625* ... (Cambridge, 1930), pp. 261–2.
4. The most important recent discussion of the prerogative has revolved around two issues: whether the Tudor monarchs, or their ministers, intended to use it as an instrument of their supposedly despotic intents, and the extent to which contemporaries believed and acted as if the prerogative was within or beyond the common law. See Joel Hurstfield, 'Was There a Tudor Despotism After All?', *Transactions of the Royal Historical Society*, 5 ser., 17, 1967, pp. 83–108 and *contra* Hurstfield, G.R. Elton, 'The Rule of Law in Sixteenth Century England', in *Tudor Men and Institutions*, ed. A.J. Slavin, (Baton Rouge, La., 1972), pp. 265–94, reprinted in G.R. Elton, *Studies in Tudor and Stuart Politics and Government* ..., (Cambridge, 1974) pp. 260–84. For some pertinent remarks on the prerogative and parliament see Kevin Sharpe, 'Parliamentary History 1603–1629: In or out of Perspective?' in *Faction and Parliament: Essays on Early Stuart History* ed. Kevin Sharpe (Oxford, 1978), p. 15, and on the fiscal uses (or misuses?) of the prerogative, G.L. Harriss, 'Medieval Doctrines in the Debate on Supply, 1610–1629' in Sharpe, *Faction*, pp. 76, 80–9.
5. One aspect of this complexity is that although some modern historians have tended to treat the prerogative as a unitary entity it was, in reality, a highly complicated phenomenon (Elton, 'Rule' in *Studies*, p. 265, cf. Margaret Attwood Judson, *The Crisis of the Constitution: An essay in constitutional and political thought in England 1603–1645*, 1949; repr. New York, N.Y., 1971, pp. 23–5); S.B. Chrimes, *English Constitutional Idea in the Fifteenth Century*, 1936; repr., New York, N.Y., 1965, pp. 41–3). One reason for this treatment is that there was what might be described as a 'demonstration effect' from one area of the prerogative to another – an effect of which nervous contemporaries were not unaware (cf. the argument employed by Edward Crawley JCP, in the Exchequer Chamber in the cause of Ship Money; Hampden's Case, 1637 *Cobbett's Complete Collection of State Trials* ..., ed. J.B. Howell, London, 1809, col. 1083). However, learned contemporary commentators certainly recognised the great complexity of the prerogative. Camden remarked that to express the whole prerogative was 'a thing not so hard to do as [to] treat of the deity, though I know it is a very hard thing' (Frank Smith Fussner, 'William Camden's "Discourse Concerning the Prerogative of the Crown"', *Proceedings of the American Philosophical Society*, 107, 1957, p. 207b). Staunford alluded to 'an infinite number of prerogatives more, which were too tedious here to recite' (quoted in Franklin Le Van Baumer, *The Early Tudor Theory of Kingship*, New Haven, Conn., 1940, p. 186 n. 223). For Lord Chancellor Ellesmere's note of the prerogative 'Mandatorye ... Prohibitorye ... Declaratorye and Explanatorye ... Dispensatorye ... etc'. See Huntington Library Ms. El. 2562 (I owe this reference to Dr J.A. Guy) and Harvard Law Library Ms. 4006. See in particular the 'Tabulae Prerogativae Regis' in Sir Matthew Hale's *The Preroga-*

tives of the King ed. D.E.C. Yale (Selden Society, xcii, London, 1976) pp. xii–xx, and quotation at p. xxi, cf. p. xlii. In its ramshackle complexity the prerogative shared a characteristic with the law as a whole: it has been said that in the seventeenth century 'the idea of systematic law did not exist ... the whole body of the law was plural; it was a congeries of isolated and unrelated rules' (Francis D. Wormuth, *The Royal Prerogative 1603–1649: A Study in English Political and Constitutional Ideas*, 1939; repr., Port Washington, N.Y., 1972, p. 48, and see p. 49).

6. Professor Youngs has noted that even in the case of proclamations – often treated as the epitome of prerogative action – the initiative for two types of proclamations (or, more strictly, re-proclamations) rested with local officials (F.A. Youngs, 'Additional Marian and Elizabethan Royal Proclamations', *Bulletin of the Institute of Historical Research*, xlvii, 1974, p. 236).
7. Samuel E. Thorne, 'Tudor Social Transformation and Legal Change', *New York University Law Review*, xxvi (1951), pp. 10–23.
8. Cf. Hinton, 'Government and Liberty', p. 52.
9. Victor Morgan, 'Country, Court and Cambridge University, 1558–1640: A Study in the Evolution of a Political Culture' (UEA–Norwich Ph.D., 1983).
10. For Creighton see DNB; John Venn and J.A. Venn, *Alumni Cantabrigienses* ... (Cambridge, 1922), I, p. 416b [hereafter cited as *Al. Cant.*]. He had obtained his fellowship at Trinity College in 1619 by means of a royal mandate nominating him to the office (PRO. S.P. 38/11, 22 Sept. 1619).
11. Cambridge University Archives, Lett. 12A 24 [hereafter cited as CUA.].
12. *Al. Cant.*, III, p. 106b.
13. CUA. Lett. 12. A.24 and A.26.
14. CUA. Lett. 12. A.26, A.20, A.21 (sworn version of A.20).
15. CUA. Lett. 12.A. 26.
16. *Al. Cant.*, IV, p. 670. Entered Trinity 1611; Fellow 1618–44.
17. CUA. Lett. 12. A.26.
18. CUA. Lett. 12. A.24.
19. CUA. Lett. 12. A.26.
20. This latter phrase is added to the deposition in Creighton's own hand.
21. CUA. Lett. 12. A.20.
22. CUA. Lett. 12. A.26.
23. CUA. Lett. 12. A.20.
24. CUA. Lett. 12. A.26.
25. CUA. Lett. 12. A.19.
26. CUA. Lett. 12. A.24. That is, the Duke of Lennox.
27. Morgan, 'Country, Court and Cambridge', pp. 377–382.
28. CUA. Lett. 12. A.18.
29. CUA. Lett. 12. 11A.C.3.c. See also CUA. Lett. 11A.C10.a. It had long been a practice to prepare a 'bill' or 'book' ready for the royal signature. See the comment of John Husee in 1536 (*The Lisle Letters*, ed. Muriel St Clare Byrne, 6 vols., Chicago and London, 1981, III, pp. 469–71).
30. PRO. SP. 16/95/47.
31. There has been very little discussion of the role of the monarch, and of those surrounding him, in this context. However, see David Starkey, 'The King's Privy Chamber, 1485–1547' (Cambridge Ph.D., 1973), pp. 309–56 and Morgan, 'Country, Court and Cambridge ...' pp. 700–12. I hope to deal more fully elsewhere with the passage of instruments under the signet seal in the late sixteenth and seventeenth century.
32. J.E.B. Mayor, 'Letters of Archbishop Williams with Materials for his Life', *Cambridge Antiquarian Society Proceedings*, III (1865–66), p. 67. On this occasion he was not successful in obtaining the position. In 1620 the King himself had recognised the ease with which his signature could be obtained surreptitiously (*Acts of the Privy Council, 1619–21*, p. 323). For the implication that the King might be misled in the matter of grants see William Hyde Price, *The English Patents of Monopoly* (Harvard Economic Studies, I; Boston, Mass., 1906), p. 173. The literary complexity of documents meant that the Crown often did not know that it had already granted (Hinton,

'Government and Liberty', p. 54, n. 18). For an example of the latter type of difficulty see the petition of Paul Thompson, complaining that the King had granted to him the advowson of Somersham, Hunts., in January 1604, and then, in August, granted it to Cambridge University for augmentation of the stipend of the Divinity Reader (House of Lords Record Office, Main Papers (Supplementary), H.L., 26 Feb. 1605/6). Such examples could be multiplied many times.

33. PRO. SP. 16/19/8.
34. Morgan, 'Country, Court and Cambridge ...' pp. 484–92.
35. *Calendar of State Papers Domestic, 1641–3*, p. 535. In 1635 the officers of the Crown were instructed not to permit the drafting or passage of the seals of any matter of an ecclesiastical nature that had not first received the approbation of the Archbishop, Laud.
36. That from Peterhouse was from 'the young Schollers, Students' in the College *Documents Relating to the University and Colleges of Cambridge*, (3 vols., London, 1952), II, p. 97.
37. *Op.cit.*, pp. 66, 103–5.
38. *Op.cit*,. p. 102; James Bass Mullinger, *The University of Cambridge* (3 vols., Cambridge, 1873–1911) II, p. 634, n. 1; Cambridge University Library [hereafter, CUL], MS. Dd. iii, 42, fol. 21; *VCH Cambridge*, p. 424.
39. Charles Henry Cooper, *Annals of Cambridge* (5 vols., Cambridge, 1842–53), III, pp. 306–7.
40. BL. Harl. MS. 7033 fol. 101 *et. seq*; CUL. Baumgartner MS. 23 fol. 16; CUA. Lett. 12.A.7 – A.10, D.4.
41. BL. Harl. MS. 7033 fol. 101.
42. *Commons Journals*, II, p. 35a; *Proceedings of the Short Parliament of 1640*, ed. Esther S. Cope and Willson H. Coates (Camden Soc. Fourth Series, 19, London, 1977), pp. 280–2.
43. *CJ*, II, p. 55b (22 Dec. 1640).
44. CUA. Lett. 12. A.10.
45. CUA. Lett. 12. A.9.
46. 349. *ibid.*
47. Although the petition came from the students it is clear from its subsequent history that it had Wren's approbation.
48. *Cambridge Documents*, II, p. 98 (21 May 1626).
49. *Op.cit.*, pp. 101–2.
50. *Op.cit.*, pp. 103–5.
51. Above, note 38.
52. *DNB*.
53. CUL. MS. Dd.3.42 fol. 21.
54. Or rather, to treat their fellowships as sinecures. John Thompson, 'in the King's service' had a mandate exempting him from taking orders, 15 June 1627 (Thomas Baker, *History of the College of St. John the Evangelist, Cambridge*, ed. J.E.B. Mayor, 2 vols., Cambridge, 1869, pp. 293, 493, where it is wrongly ascribed to temp. Charles II). Thompson was M.P. for Cambridge in 1625/6, and nephew of Lord Keeper Coventry's wife. Robert Mason (8 March, 1627), employed on state affairs in France, leave of absence, and income during leave of absence. Disputed by some of the junior fellows, but granted at the request of Conway, and the Duke of Buckingham, whose servant he is. Mandate for Mason in this cause 27 June 1627 (op.cit., p. 494). On Mason see *Cambridge Antiquarian Society Proceedings*, II, p. 34ff.
55. For the conversion of fellowships from theology to civil law see *Fifth Report From the Select Committee on Education etc. Appendix B: Documents* (Parliamentary Papers, 1818), p. 464.
56. The phrase is that of Edward Miller, *Portrait of a College: A History of the College of St John the Evangelist* (Cambridge, 1961), p. 11.
57. Morgan, 'Country, Court and Cambridge ...' ch. X.
58. CUA. Lett. 12. A.10.
59. Cooper, *Annals*, III, p. 707n.

60. *Cambridge Documents*, II, pp. 103–5.
61. CUL. MS. Dd. 3.42. fol. 29.
62. Allen Henman (and also John Wentworth), recorded as having been admitted by the Master and major part of the seniors (Baker–Mayor, I, p. 294) 27 Jan. 1635. Ejected in 1650 by order of the Committee for the Reform of the Universities, for refusing the Engagement (*op.cit.*, p. 297).
63. PRO. SP. 38/16/19 June 1635; SP. 16/291/1. It was duly entered at the end of the Elizabethan statutes, on 23 June (*Fifth Report of the Select Committee on Education... Documents*... pp. 463–4), but is attributed to the statutes of Henry VIII and Elizabeth by those of Victoria (*Cambridge Documents*, III, pp. 256–7).
64. SP. 16/2/96, 96I.
65. G.R. Elton, *The Tudor Constitution: Documents and Commentary* (Cambridge, 1960), pp. 112–13.
66. *Parliamentary History*, VII, col. 235; *HMC* 33:13R. VII, *Lonsdale*, p. 32, 'all corporations were derived from him'.
67. *Short Parliament* ..., p. 204.
68. *The Works of the Most Reverend Father in God, William Laud* ... V, ii, pp. 555–82.
69. Printed in Laud, *Works*, V, i, pp. 126–32, quotations at p. 128. These sentiments are in keeping with Sir John Cooke's long-held opinions. In 1628 he had told the House of Commons that 'the wrath of a King is like a roaring lion, and all the laws with his wrath were of no effect' (*Parliamentary History*, VIII, col. 79).
70. Laud, *Works*, V, i, p. 127.
71. 'Reason of State' originated in the notion of those areas of government, especially the conduct of foreign affairs, that were considered to be the sole province of the prince. 'Public good' derived from the need for discretionary powers residing in the executive, in particular the *non obstante* power of dispensation from statute. During the 1620s resort to these ideas seems to have increased (Wormuth, *Royal Prerogative*, p. 74ff). I hope to deal with this development more fully elsewhere.
72. The basis for this assertion is surely the incorporation of boroughs and colonisation in Ireland, as much as in North America (see Martin Weinbaum, *The Incorporation of Boroughs*, Publications of the University of Manchester, no. ccxlix, Historical Series, no. lxxii, Manchester, 1937, p. 114). Seven Irish boroughs were incorporated before 1552, twelve under Elizabeth, fifty-eight under James, and eight under Charles (*op.cit.*, pp. 135–6). It is worth noting that Cooke appears to have been the secretary of state with whom Strafford preferred to correspond. The Lord Deputy wrote of him as a friend and 'a servant that goes the same way to my Master's ends that I do' (quoted in Dorothea Coke, *The Last Elizabethan: Sir John Coke, 1583–1644*, London, 1937, p. 199). It is however, necessary to avoid oversimplification; while Cooke was an advocate of the prerogative, and worked with Strafford and Laud, by the 1630s he was an old man who had been brought up in the Elizabethan calvinist tradition. In 1639 he can be found expending considerable effort to obtain a calvinist incumbent for a living in his presentation (Margaret Rosemary O'Day, 'Clerical Patronage and Recruitment in England in the Elizabethan and Early Stuart Periods, with Special Reference to the Diocese of Coventry and Lichfield', London Ph.D., 1972, p. 157).
73. The King of England was King of more than England (for a discussion of one aspect of the legal dimension to this problem see Brian P. Levack, 'English Law, Scots Law and the Union, 1603–1707' in *Law-Making and Law-Makers in British History: Papers presented to the Edinburgh Legal History Conference, 1977*, Royal Historical Society Studies in History Series, no. 22; London, 1980, pp. 105–19, esp. p. 116ff. More generally, see J.H. Elliott, 'The King and the Catalans, 1621–1640', *Cambridge Historical Journal*, xi, 1955, pp. 253–71). In theory the common law could not take cognizance of mercantile disputes originating outside the country. However, by the middle of Elizabeth's reign the common law courts had begun to issue prohibitions to the Admiralty Court, and thereby to extend the common law beyond the bounds of England (Sir Charles Ogilvie, *The King's Government and the Common Law 1471–1641*, Oxford, 1958, p. 123). In the Commons in 1610 one MP argued that 'The common lawe extends as farre [as] the power of the Kinge extends. It is as the soule in

the body. The liberty of the seas is parcell of the liberty of the subject' (*Parliamentary Debates in 1610* ..., ed. Samuel Rawson Gardiner, Camden Society, o.s., 81, 1862, p. 89).

74. Laud, *Works*, V, i, pp. 127–8. Although somewhat ambiguously, in this Laud differed from Hooker who had written that 'to define of our churche's regiment the Parliament of England hath authority' (J.W. Allen, *English Political Thought 1603–1643*, 1938; repr. Archon Books, 1967, pp. 187–8).
75. For subsequent parliamentary criticism of Laud's attempt to erect a rectory *de novo*, see *CSPD 1641–3*, p. 527. It was said at the time that the common lawyers 'have held it impossible to be done without a Parliament'.
76. *The Letters and Life of Francis Bacon including all his Occasional Works* (7 vols., London, 1861–1874) VI, p. 304, and see H.G. Koenigsberger, *Dominium Regale or Dominium Politicum et Regale: Monarchies and Parliaments in Early Modern Europe* (Inaugural Lecture ... at University of London King's College, 25 Feb. 1975), pp. 19–20 and E. Lousse, *La société d'ancien régime: organisation et représentation corporatives* (1943; repr., Louvain 1952).
77. Thomas Hobbes, *Leviathan*, ed. C.B. Macpherson (1651; Harmondsworth, 1968), p. 375 (pt.ii, ch.29).
78. See the attack on town corporations, probably written in the late 1580s (*Tudor Economic Documents* ..., ed. R.H. Tawney and Eileen Power, 3 vols., London, 1924, III, esp. pp. 273, 275–6).
79. John Milton, *The Readie and Easy Way to Establish a Free Commonwealth* (1660) in John Milton, *Selected Prose*, ed. C.A. Patrides (Harmondsworth, 1974), pp. 354–5.
80. *The Manuscripts of the House of Lords*, N.S. XI, *Addenda 1514–1714*, ed. Maurice F. Bond (London, 1962), p. 368; *CSPD 1641–3*, pp. 551, 552–3; Robert Ashton, *The City and the Court 1603–1643* (Cambridge, 1979), p. 142. Laud's threat appeared to be a realisation of fears expressed in Parliament in 1610 (J.R. Tanner, *Constitutional Documents of the Reign of James I 1603–1625*, Cambridge, 1930, pp. 154–5). The phrase 'Act of State' became a common name for proclamations (Wormuth, *Royal Prerogative*, p. 81, n. 23, and above, note 71). Strafford was alleged to have told the Irish that 'the King's little finger would be heavier than the lines of the law' and that they 'must expect lawes as from a conqueror, and an act of state should bee as binding as an act of parliament' (*Verney Papers. Notes on Proceedings in the Long Parliament, temp. Charles I* ..., ed. John Bruce, Camden Society, o.s., xxxi, 1845, p. 63). Earlier, Camden's opinion had been that proclamations 'are law so far as they take not away other written laws or received customs; the right use of them is to turn away a mischief which is not provided for by law' (Camden, 'Discourse concerning the Prerogative ...', p. 212a), and those of Coke in the Case of Proclamations in 1610 (*Cobbet's Complete Collection of State Trials* ..., ed. J.B. Howell, *et.al.*, 33 vols., London 1809–1826; II, *1602–1627*, cols. 725–6).
81. D.E.C. Yale, 'Hobbes and Hale on Law, Legislation and the Sovereign', *Cambridge Law Journal*, 31 (1972 B), p. 138.
82. Elton, *Tudor Constitution*, pp. 20–33; *idem*, 'Rule of Law', pp. 263–70; Baumer, *Early Tudor Theory of Kingship*, pp. 184–7.
83. Quoted in Cooper, 'Differences between English and Continental Governments ...' p. 66, cf. *Certaine Considerations Upon the Government of England by Sir Roger Twysden*, ed. John Mitchell Kemble (Camden Society, o.s., x1v, 1849), p. 66.
84. Otto Gierke, *Political Theories of the Middle Age*, translated with an introduction by Frederick William Maitland (1900; repr., Cambridge, 1938), p. xxx.
85. Gierke, p. xxxi.
86. Gierke, *ibid.*
87. Elton, 'Rule of Law', pp. 267–9.
88. *The Court and Times of Charles the First* ... compiled by Thomas Birch [ed. R.F. Williams], (2 vols., London, 1849), I, p. 169.
89. Above, note 39.
90. *Short Parliament* ..., pp. 204–5.
91. Above, note 63; *CSPD 1641–3*, p. 535.

92. *CSPD 1641–3*, pp. 546, 548. From the phraseology it is not clear whether the allusion is to the clerks' signet office docquet books, or to the docquets on signet warrants.
93. *Manuscripts of the House of Lords ... 1514–1714*, pp. 438–46.
94. *CSPD 1641–3*, p. 531.
95. But not always: Sir Edward Coke remarked on 'every corporation or Incorporation, or Body politick and incorporate, which are all one' (10 Co. Rep. p. 29ᵛ in *The Reports of Sir Edward Coke ...*, London, 1727 edn.) and alluded to 'certain companies erected by assent, without any corporation' and referred to 'any body incorporate', citing 15 Richard II, c.5. (1 Co. Rep. 22b–24a, Porter's case, in *English Reports*, 76, pp. 50–3). The statute 23 Henry VIII c.10 (1531) had recognised the existence of 'bodies', 'erected and made of Devotion, or by common Assent of the People without any corporation'.
96. In the seventeenth century and later the distinctions between different types of corporations were not always clearly drawn. For a discussion of the emergence, means of creation, and common characteristics of corporations see Sir Frederic Pollock and Frederick William Maitland, *The History of English Law Before the Time of Edward I* (2 vols., 1895; 2nd. edn. 1958, with new introduction and select bibliography by S.F.C. Milsom, Cambridge), I, pp. 486–511, 669–88; Sir William Holdsworth, *A History of English Law* (16 vols., 5th. edn., London, 1942), III, pp. 469–90, VIII, pp. 192–222, IX, pp. 45–71; *Select Charters of Trading Companies A.D. 1530–1707*, ed. Cecil T. Carr (Selden Society, xxviii, 1913), pp. xi–xiv; Martin Weinbaum, *British Borough Charters 1307–1660* (Cambridge, 1943), pp. xxiii–xxviii; *idem.*, *The Incorporation of Boroughs ...*, *passim.*; Shelagh Bond and Norman Evans, 'The Process of Granting Charters to English Boroughs, 1547–1649', *English Historical Review*, 91 (1976), pp. 102–20; Robert Tittler, 'The Incorporation of Boroughs, 1540–1552', *History*, 62 (1977), pp. 24–42; Samuel Williston, 'The History of the Law of Business Corporations Before 1800' in *Select Essays in Anglo-American Legal History* ... comp. and edited by a committee of the Association of American Law Schools (3 vols., repr., London, 1968), III, pp. 195–235. See also William Robert Scott, *The Constitution and Finance of English, Scottish and Irish Joint-Stock Companies to 1720* (3 vols., 1912; repr., New York, 1951), I, p. 227 and Armand Budington DuBois, *The English Business Company after the Bubble Act 1720–1800* (1938; repr., New York, 1971), pp. viii–ix. George Peacock has some pertinent remarks placing the universities in this broader context (*Observations on the Statutes of the University of Cambridge*, London and Cambridge 1841, pp. 63–6). However, his narrowly constitutional viewpoint ignores the prime social facts of increasing involvement by very many of the elite in a proliferating number of corporations, of which the universities were only one type. For example, over 6,300 investors were involved in corporate trading ventures between 1575 and 1630 (see Theodore K. Rabb, *Enterprise & Empire: Merchant and Gentry Investment in the Expansion of England, 1575–1630*, Cambridge, Mass., 1967).
97. Laud, *Works*, V, i. p. 127.
98. Charles M. Andrews, *The Colonial Period of American History I: The Settlements* (1934; New Haven, Conn., 1964 ed. cit.), pp. 177–8; Wesley Frank Craven, *Dissolution of the Virginia Company: The Failure of a Colonial Experiment* (1932 repr. Gloucester, Mass., 1964), esp. pp. 292–336.
99. Samuel Eliot Morison, *Builders of the Bay Colony* (1930; rev. edn., Boston, Mass., 1958), pp. 65–6.
100. Morison, *Builders*, p. 69.
101. *Winthrop Papers 1498–1628* (Massachusets Historical Society, Boston, 1929, repr. 1968), I, *passim*.
102. For an ironically re-directed exploitation by the colonists of these royal pretensions in their disputes with later Parliaments see C.H. McIlwain, 'The Transfer of the Charter to New England and its Significance in American Constitutional History' in his *Constitutionalism & the Changing World: Collected Papers* (Cambridge, 1939; repr. 1969), pp. 231–43.
103. White was a purveyor of timber for building the King's houses, but no 'mere' merchant

(R.W.K. Hinton, *The Eastland Trade, and the Common Weal in the Seventeenth Century*, Cambridge, 1959, p.82).

104. SP. 16/395/2. For Clitheroe's substantial mercantile interests and aldermanic status see Valerie Pearl, *London and the Outbreak of the Puritan Revolution* ..., pp.296–7; T.K. Rabb, *Enterprise and Empire* ..., p.266 and *DNB* (the latter is incorrect, and does not agree in every point with the other sources cited in this note). Farbench's remarks can hardly have endeared him to a man such as Clitheroe. His father (of the same name) had been a benefactor of the universities. In 1625 he had firmly established the educational functions of Christ's Hospital by conveying to the Governors capital intended to generate rents to fund two exhibitions from the Hospital to Oxford, with a preference for St John's (W.K. Jordan, *The Charities of London, 1480–1660: Aspirations and the Achievements of the Urban Society*, London 1960, pp.213, 385). Clitheroe himself had been a student at St John's in the 1590s. (For the family's connections with Oxford see Joseph Foster, *Alumni Oxonienses* ..., Oxford, 1891–2, I, p.292b.) They had substantial estates in the county (*CSPD 1637–8*, p.520). Concurrent with his problems as a member of the Eastland Company he was being hounded in both his private and aldermanic capacity over ship money (*CSPD 1637–8*, pp.165, 520). He had also incurred Crown displeasure through his part in the manipulation of the sale of Corporation of London Bonds (Robert Ashton, *The Crown and the Money Market 1603–1640*, London, 1960, pp.145–6). Farbench was clearly speaking from his experience of Cambridge, having taken his BA and MA from Magdalene in 1616 and 1620 respectively (John Venn and J.A. Venn, *Alumni Cantabrigienses*: ..., Cambridge, 1922, II, p.158b).

105. SP. 16/395/2. Clitheroe's own experience suggests why he responded in this manner (see preceding note).

106. In the 1650s the common corporate status of colleges and municipalities was again manifested. In this instance the parallel was drawn in the opposite direction to that adopted by Farbench, whom we have seen arguing from university to company. Charles Hotham, a disgruntled former member of Peterhouse, submitted a series of petitions to Parliament. He argued that the negative voice of the masters of colleges (Morgan, 'Country, Court and Cambridge ...', pp.296–8) should be abolished 'by some provision of a parallel Nature to that made for the City of London' (*A true stating of the Case of a Negative Voice* ..., n.d., copy in BL. Harl. MS. 7032. Not recorded separately in *The British Library Catalogue*, or *Catalogue of the Thomason Tracts*. For Hotham's career, see *DNB* and *Al. Cant.*, I, p.412).

107. This paper was written and delivered at short notice when another speaker had to withdraw from the conference. At that time I had not had the opportunity to read David Little, *Religion, Order and Law: A Study in Pre-Revolutionary England* (New York, 1969). It is gratifying to see that we have both come to similar conclusions on the importance of ideas of corporation in this period, and of the significance of Edward Coke's pronouncements on the subject. However, it seems to me that the work of Professor Little, and of others who have written on Coke, has been vitiated by their preoccupation with the consequences of Coke's judgements for the economic organisation of society. This leads them to write of corporations as if they were only monopolies or commercial companies, and to ignore the broader context of corporate bodies of which Coke was very much aware (Little, p.190, n. 2, and pp.215–17). A further deficiency is that Little's discussion of the theoretical roots of Coke's law is ignorant of the parliamentary procedures and the political realities within which it was formulated. See, for example, his explanation of the apparent inconsistencies in the Statute of Monopolies (21 Jac. I, c.3, 1623) as 'an article of faith' (p.217). These inconsistencies are far more likely to be the outcome of the exigencies to which many Bills were subject in their passage (the classic description of this process is S.T. Bindoff, 'The Making of the Statute of Artificers', in *Elizabethan Government and Society: Essays Presented to Sir John Neale*, ed. S.T. Bindoff, J. Hurstfield and C.H. Williams, London, 1961, pp.59–94). Moreover, as Brooks and Sharpe have pointed out, the preponderant influence of Coke's view of law and history during the 1620s and 1630s was an outcome of the political uses to which those views were being put at that

time (Christopher Brooks and Kevin Sharpe, 'History, English Law and the Renaissance', *Past & Present*, 72, 1976, pp. 141–2). It is this which helps to explain the quite manifest changes in Coke's attitudes during his career, and his cavalier approach to evidence. The outstanding description of what at its kindest could be described as Coke's myopic a-historicism is J.G.A. Pockock, *The Ancient Constitution and the Feudal Law: A Study of English Historical Thought in the Seventeenth Century* (Cambridge, 1957), pp. 30–69, however psychologically appropriate this view may have been to its moment in time (cf. William J. Bouwsma, 'Lawyers and Early Modern Culture', *American Historical Review*, 78, 1973, p. 327).

108. Laud, *Works*, V, i. p. 127. *cf.* Weinbaum, *Boroughs* ..., p. 92, and Alan Harding, *A Social History of English Law* (Harmondsworth, 1966), p. 248; Coke 2 *Inst.* 330.

109. 10. Co. Rep. p.29^{v}. Here, Coke means the King as a corporate institution, the notion of which underwent a marked development during the late sixteenth and seventeenth centuries. On this I agree with Holdsworth, rather than with Elton's subsequent criticisms. See below, note 116. Holdsworth (IX, p. 55) has some perceptive comments on the extent to which the clarification resulted from the development of the notion of the corporate personality of Kingship.

110. *Sir Matthew Hale's 'The Prerogatives of the King'*, ed. D.E.C. Yale, Selden Society, xcii for 1975; London, 1976), p. 246. He also noted that 'An honour cannot be but by prescription or by act of parliament and cannot be created by letters patent' (p. 249), and that 'a manor cannot be created at this day by the King's grant' (p. 250). More generally, Hale opined that 'The commencement then of every legal corporation is either by prescription or custom or charter' (p. 241). Blackstone was to accept the concessionary theory, but to enlarge the means by which it might be applied. He assumes that the King's assent may be *implied* by the recognition at common law of corporations, or *presumed* in the case of prescription, where they have existed time out of mind. Blackstone saw the King's *express* consent as given either by act of parliament or by charter (Sir William Blackstone, *Commentaries on the Laws of England: in four books; with an analysis of the work*, ed. Thomas Lee, London, 1829, I, p. 472).

111. 8 Co. Rep. p. 126^{v} (Hilary 7 Jac., 1610).

112. In practice, although informally, Charles was to attempt precisely this in the case of Henry White and the Eastland Merchants in 1638 (above, note 103). This clearly had implications for Parliament. At the end of James' reign, the House of Commons Committee on elections reported that no local by-law could vary the right of election, and that the King's charter was equally inoperative for that purpose (Henry Alworth Merewether and Archibald John Stephens, *The History of the Boroughs and Municipal Corporations of the United Kingdom* ..., 3 vols., London, 1835, p. 1549). The report was presented by Sir John Glanville, both a lawyer and MP and Recorder for Plymouth (*DNB*). The extent to which the typical municipal employments of most successful lawyers as recorders of boroughs influenced their attitudes to the notion of corporation requires further investigation – as Dr Hirst has shown, having won the right to determine electoral disputes, after 1603, the Commons consistently favoured the extensive franchise, thus making more difficult the manipulation of elections by the Crown (Derek Hirst, *The Representative of the People?: Voters and Voting in England under the Early Stuarts*, Cambridge, 1975). Cooke's theoretical claims on behalf of the King might, if put into practice, have undermined this victory and placed control of the personnel or even the very existence of a large proportion of Commons seats in the hands of the King by permitting him to manipulate borough charters.

113. 3 Co. Rep. pp. 74^{v}–75 (40 & 41 Eliz., 1590).

114. Hale was of the opinion that surrender of lands 'doth not extinguish the corporation. Yet, it was admitted that by apt words the corporation itself might have been surrendered and dissolved, the dean and chapter having the full fee and disposal with the King's consent as well of their corporation as their lands' (Hale, *Prerogatives*, p. 244); Holdsworth, IX, pp. 62–3.

115. Palm. Rep. p. 501 (Hayward v. Fulcher) Hilary 3 Car., in *English Reports*, 81, p. 1191. In the Commons in 1610, James Whitelocke had argued that 'if the King made a grant by his letters patents out of parliament, it bindeth him and his successors: he cannot

revoke it, nor any of his successors' (*State Trials*, II, *1603–1627*, col. 482). The speech is there attributed to Yelverton, but see *Parliamentary Debates in 1610*..., ed. Samuel Rawson Gardiner, Camden Society, o.s. 81, 1862, p. 103, where, however, the sense of the speech is garbled. For its part, internal evidence makes plain that the version printed in *State Trials* is a later elaboration of the speech as delivered.

116. F.W. Maitland, *The Constitutional History of England*, ed. H.A.L. Fisher (1908; Cambridge, 1961 *ed. cit.*), p. 54; Holdsworth, IX, pp. 4–5; Weinbaum, *Boroughs*, p. 2; Chrimes, *Constitutional Ideas*..., p. 38; Gareth Jones, *History of the Law of Charity 1532–1827* (Cambridge, 1969), pp. 66–7; Wormuth, *Royal Prerogative*, pp. 50–53; Hale, *Prerogatives*, pp. 84–7; Camden, 'Discourse concerning the Prerogative', pp. 207, 429. Maitland observed that it was during Coke's lifetime 'when men first called the King a corporation sole, though many had called him the head of a corporation' (*The Collected Papers of Frederic William Maitland*, ed. H.A.L. Fisher, 3 vols., Cambridge, 1911, III, p. 219). For a recent summary of this development see Mary Axton, *The Queen's Two Bodies: Drama and the Elizabethan Succession* (Royal Historical Society, Monograph Series, no. 5; London, 1977), pp. 11–25.
117. *VCH Cambridge*, p. 474, no. 10.
118. R.W.K. Hinton, 'The Decline of Parliamentary Government under Elizabeth I and the Early Stuarts', *Cambridge Historical Journal*, XIII (1957), pp. 116–32. I am indebted to my colleague, Dr A. Hassell Smith, for discussion of this point. On 'the rise of the interventionist state' see Victor Morgan, 'Maps, Government and Society, 1500–1640', an unpublished paper presented to the British Library Colloquium on Tudor and Stuart Map-Making (London, 1981).
119. Gareth Jones, *History of the Law of Charity 1552–1827* (Cambridge, 1969), pp. 77–81; Christopher Hill, *Economic Problems of the Church from Archbishop Whitgift to the Long Parliament* (1956; London, 1971 *ed. cit.*), pp. 245–74; Hale, *Prerogatives*, pp. 240–1.
120. Robert Ashton, *The City and the Court 1603–1643* (Cambridge, 1979), *passim*.
121. Above, note 105.
122. Quoted in Ashton, *City and Court*, p. 103.
123. Robert Ashton, 'Conflicts of Concessionary Interests in Early Stuart England' in *Trade Government and Economy in Pre-Industrial England; Essays Presented to F.J. Fisher*, ed. D.C. Coleman and A.H. John (London, 1976), pp. 113–31.
124. Ranging from a difference of one to a difference of seventeen or eighteen more public than private Acts for some parliamentary sessions. See the remarks of G.R. Elton, 'Parliament in the Sixteenth Century: Functions and Fortunes', *The Historical Journal*, 22 (1979), p. 260.
125. As contemporaries recollected (Twysden, *Considerations Upon the Government of England*, pp. 144, 173). For the other problems that arose in the sphere of Public Acts as a result of the abortive nature of these Parliaments see W.J. Jones, *Politics and the Bench: The Judges and the Origins of the English Civil War* (London, 1971), pp. 80–3, 157–9.
126. A wide range of appointments could be described as 'ecclesiastical', including those at the universities. In 1635, Laud's stranglehold in this sphere was formalised when the King authorised a letter missive admonishing the Attorney General and other officers neither to draft, or permit to pass the seals, any cause, grant or gift of an ecclesiastical nature without it first receiving the Archbishop's approbation (*CSPD 1641–3*, p. 535). In the 1640s, those responsible for Laud's indictment were anxious to establish proof of his monopoly of ecclesiastical patronage from 1628 onwards (*op.cit.*, pp. 546, 548). For the evidence they used, and its relationship to letters mandate, see note 92. The arminians also managed to alienate influential groups such as the lawyers of Lincoln's Inn by complaining that they were 'not incorporate, neither by Act of Parliament nor by any Letters Pattents from the King's Matie'. The complainant was Richard Montague, the arminian Bishop of Chichester (*The Records of the Honourable Society of Lincoln's Inn: The Black Books*, ed. W.P. Baildon, 2 vols., [London], 1897, 1898, II, pp. 333, 334, 337).
127. Examined in Morgan, 'Country, Court and Cambridge', pp. 1–44.

Judicial Review in the House of Lords (1640–43)

J.S. HART, Jr.

In his extended study of the High Court of Parliament, published in 1910, Professor McIlwain made the following claim:[1]

> Parliament, up to the time of the Tudors, was hardly thought of primarily or principally as a legislature; it was still in reality the 'High Court' of parliament. That Court retained the functions of the old Curia . . . but the judicial functions bulked larger in men's minds than the legislative. So long as the law was a thing fundamental and immutable . . . Parliament's functions must have been conceived to be in large part the enforcing and applying of this law. Parliament must have been thought of first as a court rather than as a legislature. This I believe to have been the view prevailing, among lawyers at least, as late as the assembling of the Long Parliament.

McIlwain's statement, as an expression of popular attitudes toward Parliament, contains nothing particularly surprising or unusual. It was only meant to suggest that contemporaries did not, in the first place, recognise what we now see as clear-cut distinctions between Parliament's legislative and its judicial functions; that Parliament was still seen as equally responsible for declaring the law as for making it; and that despite its growing preoccupation with purely legislative concerns, it still retained, in men's minds at least, its original medieval power and authority to act as the ultimate arbiter of the law, both in general legal disputes, by issuing what Lambarde called 'decisions in Controversies'.[2] and in individual party to party cases, where ordinary courts had been unable or unwilling to offer appropriate remedy.

The evidence to support McIlwain's claim was readily available from the writings of a number of early-modern lawyers and legal scholars, from Lambarde and Smith in the sixteenth century to Coke and Ellesmere in the seventeenth, all of whom had, in one way or another, paid tribute to the essential judicial character of Parliament, to its special legal jurisdiction, and to its pre-eminent stature as 'the Highest and most Authentical Court of England'.[3] McIlwain was clearly aware that in practical terms Parliament had, by the close of the Tudor regime, ceased to function, other than in the most exceptional circumstances, as a conventional court of law, and he only went so far as to suggest that the view prevailed among leading antiquarians and members of the legal profession. What was important, in his view, was the fact that despite the real decline in parliamentary judicial proceedings, and the seemingly inexorable march towards legislative sovereignty, the notion of Parliament as a court, as the ultimate court of last resort in all cases, had endured and remained an integral part of contemporary constitutional theory.

Paradoxically, McIlwain's exploration of this idea stopped at precisely the point, chronologically, where it should have begun: in the Long Parliament of Charles I. Had he examined the proceedings of that parliament in any depth, he would have discovered that the 'prevailing view' which he described had been even more widely and firmly held than he had imagined; that it had been an article of faith, not just with legal scholars and constitutional theorists, but with the public at large. He would have discovered, in fact, that members of the general public had, in November 1640, put the notion to the test, by calling on Parliament, and the House of Lords in particular, to resume operations as a court of law.

From the opening of the Long Parliament, individual litigants began to flood into the House of Lords with petitions seeking legal remedy in private civil disputes. By any measure, their numbers were unprecedented. At the end of December 1640, barely seven weeks into the session, the Lords had received over 120 separate requests for review of private party suits. By the end of February the number had climbed to 310, by the end of June to 540, and by the close of the calendar year to almost 650. Despite the repeated and concerted attempts made by the House to halt the flow of petitions, well over 100 new cases were brought in 1642, and half again as many in 1643. Certainly by comparison with the levels of litigation in the other central courts during this period, those numbers are not particularly impressive. In the context of parliamentary judicial proceedings, however, they represent a very dramatic increase, and it is fair to say that by the close of 1641, the House of Lords was facing something of an administrative crisis. In addition to its very considerable legislative tasks, and its equally important responsibilities in the conduct of major state trials, the Lords were being asked, indeed compelled, to revive and exercise, as they had not done since the fourteenth century, an extraordinary remedial jurisdiction in civil litigation. They were being asked, once again, to act, in the words of Denzil Holles, as 'the Supreme Court to which all persons aggrieved might apply themselves for relief'.[4]

What I would like to do in the course of this paper is to provide a brief and very general introduction to the litigation brought before the House of Lords in this Parliament (using for the purposes of discussion, the main body of 643 cases brought in 1640–41), to offer some suggestions as to why and how it found its way into the House, and finally, to give some indication of how the Lords responded to it.

As the numbers cited above suggest, the nature of the complaints presented in these petitions varied to an extraordinary degree. However, sufficient documentation exists in the majority of cases – in 593 of the 643 – to allow at least some preliminary lines of demarcation to be drawn. From a purely technical point of view, the litigation as a whole divides almost evenly between straightforward appeals against proceedings and decrees in inferior courts, of which there are 303, and cases brought effectively in the first instance, of which there are 290. The cases brought on appeal from other tribunals originate in a wide variety of venues. The list includes literally every major court in the legal system (see Table I).

TABLE I

COURTS OF ORIGIN

Chancery	(62)	Exchequer (Equity Side)	(12)
Star Chamber	(40)	Requests	(11)
High Commission	(37)	Admiralty	(10)
Privy Council	(23)	Common Pleas	(9)
Diocesan Courts	(21)	Council of the North	(7)
Wards and Liveries	(21)	Court of Arches	(6)
Irish Privy Council	(20)	Exchequer	(4)
Kings Bench	(17)	Prerogative Court of Canterbury	(3)

It has also been possible to identify, in the majority of cases, the principal issue in contention between the parties, and accordingly to divide the litigation into relatively familiar topical classifications (see Table II).

TABLE II

CLASSES OF LITIGATION

Real Property	(138)
Debt	(101)
Disputed Ecclesiastical Livings and Advowsons	(50)
Alleged Abuse of Judicial Procedure	(50)
Testamentary Disputes	(47)
Local Parish Disputes	(41)
Accusations of 'Unjust Imprisonment'	(39)
Domestic Disputes	(24)
Complaints against Crown Officers	(21)
Ship Money and Coat and Conduct Money Disputes	(15)
Disputed Offices and Reversions	(17)
Complaints against Patents and Proclamations	(12)
Maritime Disputes	(9)
Miscellaneous	(21)

On their own, neither of these lists is particularly helpful in explaining the revival of legal proceedings in the House. They are offered here primarily for the purposes of identification. A more useful, if admittedly rather unconventional, starting point, is to see all of the cases falling, initially, into two major groups which reflect general causes, rather than specific types of complaints. The first of these two groups is composed principally of those cases which can be said to have arisen directly out of disagreements over the content, administration, and/or enforcement of specific Crown policies imposed in the decade prior to 1640, complaints which were, in effect, peculiar to the Personal Rule of Charles I, and to the political and religious disequilibrium which accompanied it.

Cases falling under this general heading include, as an example, those listed collectively as 'Disputed Ecclesiastical Livings'. Plaintiffs here included individual clerics who had been deprived or suspended from their livings through proceedings in the Court of High Commission; lay impropriators whose right of presentation had been denied by the Bishop of the diocese, and then effectively superseded through the institution of another cleric; and administrative officers in the church courts who had been summarily dismissed from their positions. The two complaints common to all of these litigants were, first, that they had been denied their right and title to the particular living or office through summary or improper proceedings, either in the church courts, or at the hands of senior church officials; and secondly, that the actions in question had been taken because of their expressed or demonstrated disagreement with the Laudian church reforms imposed by the Crown during the 1630s. In all cases, the individual had been unable to obtain effective remedy, either because, as in the case of deprived ministers, there was no appellate recourse from decrees in High Commission (the provisions for a Board of Review having been removed from the Commission's Letters Patent in 1625)[5] or because subsequent attempts to recover possession at common law had been circumvented, stayed altogether, or simply ignored by the party in question.[6] These complainants appealed to the House of Lords to be restored to what they considered their rightful freehold property, and where appropriate, to gain compensation for lost profits.

The cases listed under the heading 'Local Parish Disputes' were another manifestation of the same problem. Plaintiffs here were normally churchwardens who had been prosecuted and summarily excommunicated for their refusal to implement the alterations to their churches required by the new Laudian rubrics. Alternatively, they were individual parishioners who had likewise suffered excommunication, and often imprisonment, for their refusal to attend and participate in the newly ordered ceremonies, where those changes had in fact been successfully imposed. In either case, the individual had been unable to obtain an unbiased and independent rehearing of his case within the existing appellate structure of the church court system, and consequently petitioned the House of Lords seeking some means of gaining absolution, and in many cases, seeking damages for the penalties suffered as a result of prosecution and/or excommunication. Together, these two sets of cases account for the high number of appeals brought from High Commission, and the local consistory courts. They testify, generally, to the concerted effort made by the Church in the 1630s to secure conformity with its new official orthodoxy, and its willingness to employ the extensive judicial powers at its command to meet that end.

Another example of cases which were clearly indigenous to the 1630s were those relating to the administration of the Crown's twin financial expedients; Ship Money and Coat & Conduct Money. Plaintiffs in this group were, for the most part, local magistrates, notably sheriffs and constables, who had suffered for their refusal to collect one or the other of the levies, or for their refusal to distrain the goods of those individuals who had themselves refused to contribute to the tax. Their refusal had led to prosecution in Star Chamber, or to proceedings before the Privy Council, to fines of various degrees, and in some cases, to extended imprisonment. They petitioned the House seeking, in appropriate cases, release from confinement, or recompense for their fines, and on occasion, damages for their troubles. They did so because they remained unconvinced of the legal propriety of the original writ and instructions issued by the Privy Council to collect the tax, and therefore questioned the punitive legal proceedings which had followed from their refusal to comply with it. The general uncertainty about thc two levies produced another kind of complaint as well; this from individual magistrates whose diligent services in collection and distraint had exposed them to numerous suits for illegal seizure of goods. They, conversely, appealed to the House to be indemnified against any future or pending legal actions, arising from their previous services to the Crown.

In other less conspicuous ways, Crown-sponsored programmes in the 1630s had led to conflicts between citizens which had resulted in litigation before the House. The Crown's attempts to generate revenue through the sale of patents and reversions to a host of minor administrative offices, particularly in the central courts, caused a number of problems; between the new patentees and the existing office holders who claimed the right of reversion, between new patentees and senior courts officials who claimed the right of presentation as part of the traditional privileges of their office or, on a couple of occasions, between individuals who had, at different times, been sold the rights to the same office. The rights of patronage in office holding were not always clearly defined, but were always keenly felt.[7] Public offices of administration were traditionally considered freehold property, and the issue of new royal grants, to offices that had long been held and disposed of under other arrangements, was seen by these complainants to be an unjustifiable interference with the ownership and possession of that property. It was felt that Parliament was the only appropriate place where a successful challenge to the legal validity of those individual patents might be lodged.

Similar complaints were presented against a number of patents and proclamations issued during the 1630s granting corporate monopolies to a variety of commercial enterprises. Petitioners in this group normally appealed to the House seeking relief from prosecution which had been threatened, or actually initiated against them, usually in Star Chamber, for trading or producing in violation of the terms of a given monopoly, or alternatively seeking relief from the extortionate fees or taxes being imposed by the monopolists. Common to both was the belief that the monopolies unfairly restricted their right to trade (certainly not a new complaint in 1640) and the conviction that the restraint itself was 'against law' because, as one plaintiff expressed it, 'regulation of this kind alters law by patent, and not by Parliament'.[8]

In a sense, that remark expresses the dilemma which is at the heart of all of the complaints in this group. The churchwarden who had been excommunicated by his local church court, the constable who had been imprisoned by the Privy Council for failure to collect Ship Money, and the soapboiler who had been heavily fined by Star Chamber for violating the Soapmakers monopoly, were all attempting, in their appeals to the House of Lords, to challenge, in the first place, the legal propriety of those decisions. But they were also attempting, if only implicitly, to question the general authority under which those actions had been taken; to question the Crown's de facto legislative powers which had been used to impose important and often disruptive changes in policy; and to question, moreover, the legal means which had been used to enforce them.

The cases in the second of the two major groups were, on balance, far more disparate in nature. They relate less to the administration of any specific government programmes or political initiatives, than to the existence of a number of serious problems inherent in the legal system itself – problems which had, in fact, been raised and discussed repeatedly in earlier parliamentary debates on law reform.[9] Initially, these cases point to at least three major 'administrative' issues: the absence of effective appellate remedy from the central courts of equity – and, most particularly, from the court of Chancery; the absence of clear jurisdictional boundaries between individual courts (and the consequent proliferation of jurisdictional conflicts) and the ever-present matter of cost.

Each of them had generated petitions to the House by a more or less direct route.

In the first case, litigants had simply found the existing methods of appeal against equity decrees wholly ineffective and unsatisfactory. Bill of review procedure, available in the courts themselves, had proved to be altogether too restrictive in scope to meet the needs of most complainants, and the process of securing a Royal Commission of review – the only other viable option – was, by its nature, too costly and impractical to be of any immediate use. Since errant decrees in the courts of common law were relievable in the Upper House, through writ of error procedure, logic held that the same ought to be true of decrees in equity, and in the absence of any alternative legislative remedy (promised, but not produced by Parliament) complainants began, by way of petition, to seek reconsideration in the House of Lords.[10]

In the second instance, appeals were most frequently generated by a standoff between two courts and their respective clients, arising from collateral proceedings undertaken by one or more parties to a suit. Inevitably, both courts involved had claimed an 'exclusive' right to adjudicate the matter in dispute, and each had issued countervailing injunctions to stay proceedings in the other, thereby leaving neither party with a satisfactory solution. Litigants caught in the deadlock looked to the House of Lords to intervene, and make a clearcut determination on where the matter ought best to be tried.[11]

The needs of petitioners in the third category were more straightforward. Aside from those litigants just mentioned, who arguably needed a final determination from the House, if only to avoid the debilitating expense of maintaining a continuing interest in multiple suits at law, the majority of these complainants had simply found, in the first instance, that the cost of proceeding through normal channels was too prohibitive to be undertaken. They requested assistance from the Lords, either in the form of a determinant hearing in the House itself, or in the form of a directive issued to a lower court to waive its customary fees, and admit the petitioner to writ process and representation free of charge.

In addition to these more general complaints, the Lords were also asked to consider a number of specific procedural and jurisdictional abuses peculiar to individual courts; notably, to Chancery, the court of Wards, and the court of Exchequer. The complaints were, again, familiar ones. Chancery, for example, was accused, time and again, of having violated the presumptive bounds of equity jurisdiction by adjudicating matters properly relievable at common law – most often by deciding matters of title.[12] Appellants from the court of Wards complained, alternatively, of unwarranted protections granted to wards and their sureties against actions of debt, or, in other cases, of illegal or irregular proceedings in inquisitions post-mortem. Those from the court of Exchequer focused, instead, on the abuse of Quominus procedure which had allowed notional 'officers' of that court to collect their personal debts in the name of the Crown.

It should be stressed that none of these grievances were new, or in any way unusual. Each of them had been clearly outlined at some stage in the Commons' debates of 1621 and 1624.[13] Numerous bills were suggested to deal with them, but none had been carried forward with any evident conviction. To that extent, Parliament's failure to carry through the specific remedial measures proposed in the 1620s had more or less guaranteed that those issues would be raised – indeed they now had to be raised – in a more immediate practical way by individual litigants on a case by case basis. That had already begun to happen, on an admittedly small scale, during the 1620s, as increasingly frustrated suitors began to apply directly to the House of Lords for various kinds of special relief. By 1629, those proceedings had established enough of a pattern, and a sufficient number of precedents, to ensure that the subsequent intermission of parliaments would only interrupt the process temporarily. In fact, the abrupt and extended demise of parliamentary remedy of any sort (and doubtless, the growing acuity of the problems themselves) during the 1630s, only made it more certain that similar complaints would proliferate once Parliament reconvened in 1640.

The attraction of the House of Lords as a court of law lay primarily in the ease and flexibility of its procedures; that is, in its general accessibility, and in the powers which it was able to exercise in the litigant's behalf. The process of judicial review got underway in each case once the plaintiff had presented his petition of grievances. In the organisational scheme devised by the new clerk of Parliament, John Browne, each petition was to be delivered into his office, where it was registered, with the date of receipt recorded on the back. From there it would be taken into the House, read, and then referred to one of the two judicial committees appointed to handle civil litigation; the Lords Committee for Petitions, and the ad hoc Committee for Abuses in Imprisonments and Courts of Justice. The Clerk's system was clearly predicated on the assumption that the intake of petitions would be small, and that the House as a whole would be both willing and able to hear a preliminary reading of each case, and make a considered judgement on its intrinsic merits, before referring it to commitee. That quickly proved not to be the case. When the petitions began to arrive at the rate of a dozen or more a day, the initial reading in the House which was to follow its registration in the Clerk's office, became entirely impractical, and had to be abandoned. Instead, the Clerk was instructed to forward the petitions directly to the appropriate committee. They were then given the responsibility for the preliminary vetting of each case, on the understanding that their findings would be subsequently, and regularly, reported to the whole House.

Specific guidelines for accepting or rejecting any given case were never formally established. When this change took place, in early February 1641, the Committees were simply instructed to 'meet and peruse petitions, reject those that are fit and proper to be relieved at the Common Law or courts of Equity, and retain such as are fit for their Lordships' consideration'.[14] The wording of the instruction was amended in a significant way in June when the Committee for Petitions was ordered to retain 'only those petitions that are without any other remedy but in Parliament'.[15] Both orders were clearly designed to discourage inappropriate or indiscriminate litigating in the House. On the other hand, the failure to impose specific guidelines, or clearer definitions of what was 'fit' for the consideration of the House, was equally deliberate. What that reflected was the Lords' insistence that their ability to offer remedy as a court of last resort could not, and ought not to be constrained in any case by preconceived notions about its jurisdiction. It is perhaps worth noting in this context that the open-ended criteria suggested by both of the above orders is almost identical to that set down periodically by the late Elizabethan and early Stuart Privy Councils in their attempts to establish general guidelines for the adjudication of private legal disputes.[16]

Despite the absence of precise criteria, the House was, in practice, neither careless nor indiscriminatory. Cases were, on occasion, dismissed from the House on grounds that the suit ought, in the first instance, to be tried elsewhere, or that it was, in substance, 'too meane for their Lordships' recognizance'.[17] Moreover, the committees were specifically empowered to punish plaintiffs who brought frivolous suits. The Committee for Petitions was authorised to tax costs, at their discretion, against any petitioner who complained 'without just cause' of proceedings or decrees in inferior courts. Individuals suing out a writ of error, in an attempt to delay execution of judgement in King's Bench were subject to the same penalties.[18] In their initial review, the Lords were only concerned that the plaintiff be able to demonstrate a genuine need for parliamentary remedy.

To a large degree, that depended on the skill with which the plaintiff or his attorney presented his case in the initiating petition. In their basic outlines, the petitions to the House of Lords resembled the standard English Bill of Complaint in the Court of Chancery, in so far as they were, in West's words, 'a declaration in writing showing the plaintiff's grief and wrong, which he supposes to be done to him by the defendant, and what damages he sustaineth by occasion thereby, praying process against him for redress of the same'.[19] The Lords required as well that the plaintiff carefully explain why the special jurisdiction of the House was being sought. For that reason, the opening address was normally followed by a lengthy account of the history of the dispute and, where appropriate, an account of any prior proceedings in other courts, all of which was designed to identify the 'griefs and wrongs' done, and the specific ways in which justice had been unfairly denied. If the plaintiff was successful, and his case was accepted for review, his petition would be returned to the Clerk's office, copied, and then forwarded to the defendant. The defendant would then be ordered to appear within a specified period of time, to answer the charges set forth by the complainant, or to show 'good cause' why the plaintiff's requests should not be granted. That summons carried the force of a formal subpoena, and the defendant ignored it at his peril. Failure to appear rendered the individual 'in contempt of Court', for which he could be fined and/or imprisoned at the pleasure of the House.[20]

Once the defendant had responded – usually by submitting his own equally elaborate petition – the preparations for the hearing were initiated. In a number of cases, the House was called upon to issue its own 'special injunctions' in order to protect the material interests of the plaintiff during proceedings in the House – orders to secure possession of property, to prohibit specific actions being taken, such as laying waste to crops or woods, or to sequester the profits of a particular office in the hands of a third party. Usually, however, the first expedient needed was a warrant for witnesses. As a matter of course, both parties were granted warrants, directed to the witnesses named, commanding them to appear at the appointed hearing to testify. In cases of hardship, where the witnesses were, for some reason, unable to attend the hearing itself, the House would appoint a special commission to examine them locally, on the basis of interrogatories submitted by both parties, and approved by the House. The resulting depositions would then be sealed and returned to the Clerk's office to be kept until the hearing. It was also necessary, in many cases, to summon documents from the court where prior proceedings had taken place. This was easily accomplished with a straightforward order from the House to the Register of the court in question, directing him to bring the cited materials into Parliament.

In the hearings that followed, the House was, to a large extent, dependent on the advice and support of what might fairly be called its judicial 'personnel' – a large group of Crown legal officers who were summoned to attend the House by Writs of Assistance.[21] These officers included the justices of King's Bench and Common Pleas, the Barons of the Exchequer, the Master of the Rolls, the Attorney General, the Solicitor General, and four King's Serjeants. In addition, the House commanded the services of four Masters in Chancery, who were summoned not by writ, but by special order of the House, and who served officially as 'Attendants'. Two of the senior members of the Bench were permanently assigned to the Committee for Petitions, and it is clear that the Committee relied heavily on their expertise. Cases involving exceptionally difficult or complex legal issues were frequently referred to the judges, on the understanding that they would review the case independently, and subsequently report their findings and recommendations by way of a formal certificate. The Committee's final decision was often guided by those findings.

The actions taken by the House in any given case obviously depended on the individual circumstances and needs. In those cases where the petitioner had suffered from purely punitive measures, the House could act with considerable speed and directness. Often, the most immediate requirement was to secure the complainant's freedom from confinement. This could be accomplished either by virtue of an order of the House itself, directed to the keeper in question, instructing him to release the plaintiff into Parliament's custody, or by virtue of a standard writ of Habeas Corpus, issued through the Crown Office in Chancery at the behest of the House.[22] Once the individual had been brought before the Committee, the Lords could hear his complaint in more detail. If, as in most cases, the imprisonment proved to have been arbitrary, or in the Lords' view, unwarranted, the individual would be allowed his liberty on a permanent basis, and the hearing would then be given over to establishing his right to damages. In many of these cases, in fact, remedy took the form of a simple declaratory order; as, for instance, an order to a consistory court official to grant absolution to an excommunicate,[23] to the Attorney General to withdraw a criminal information in King's Bench lodged against a constable and his fellow townspeople for their refusal to pay Ship Money[24] or, as happened in one case, to two J.Ps to repay the costs and fees expended by the petitioners as a consequence of unwarranted proceedings before Privy Council.[25] The issues were not always clear-cut, however. In those cases involving disputed ecclesiastical livings, offices, or advowsons, a rather different approach was needed. The Lords generally took the view that these disputes involved, in the first instance, the question of title, and in consequence, would refer the two parties to a trial at common law on that issue, before taking steps to settle possession, or award compensation for lost profits. That particular procedure was in fact used in all cases where the primary issues at stake appeared to require a prior determination at law. The Lords would direct the parties to proceed to trial on those specific points, on the understanding that the case as a whole would then be returned to the House for a determination on the remaining matters of equity.

For the most part, however, the actions taken by the House were more administrative in nature. The Lords were often asked, as an example, to override claims of privilege which had protected prospective defendants from legal action. Standard procedure here was simply to require the named defendant to show good cause why the plaintiff's suit should not be answered. If he could not, he would then be ordered to appear and plead to the action 'forthwith'. In other cases, simple procedural limitations had forestalled or impeded normal proceedings. In one case, for example, a petitioner wishing to sue for recovery of an advowson had been prevented from doing so because he had been unable, through no fault of his own, to sue out the appropriate writ of Quare Impedit within the six months required by statute.[26] In his case, the hearing was given over to a review of the extenuating circumstances which had led to his default. On the basis of the evidence produced, the Lords then decided that the litigation ought to be allowed to proceed, and accordingly ordered that the relevant prohibition be waived.

In a sense, the 'judgements' required in cases involving conflicts between two inferior court jurisdictions were administrative as well. In most instances, the Lords were simply being asked to determine whether the injunction which had stayed proceedings in the plaintiff's court had issued forth on legitimate grounds. In order to do that the Lords had only to ask the judges responsible to certify their reasons for issuing the stay, and on the basis of that report, and subsequent discussion, the appropriate action could be taken, either to order the injunction removed or, where it had been clearly justified, to dismiss the petitioner's complaint. In the latter case, the Lords normally admonished the defendant to proceed to trial expeditiously, in order that the matter might be settled without delay.

Where the principal object of the plaintiff's petition was to gain a rehearing of his case after judgement, the Lords generally attempted to make possible an appeal in the original court, rather than hear the case in the House itself. A number of appeals from the court of Chancery, as an example, had been brought into the House simply because the plaintiff had been unable to fulfil the stringent requirements imposed by Bill of Review procedure in that court. In these cases, the Lords could direct the Lord Keeper to waive those requirements altogether, and admit the plaintiff to a rehearing on the merits of the case as a whole. The hearing in the House was then limited to a prior determination on whether appeal itself appeared to be warranted.

Perhaps not surprisingly, given the implicit authority attached to proceedings in the House, the Lords were often able to effect a settlement between the parties through the simple process of arbitration, conducted either in the House itself, or by a specially appointed commission of referees. This was true in the majority of domestic disputes, for instance, where close familial relationships could facilitate a compromise agreement. It was true as well in any number of cases involving debt and commercial accounts, where the Lords were able to prevail on both parties to accept a more realistic and equitable schedule of payments for the outstanding obligations.

In general, it is fair to say that the Lords employed, in all of these cases, whatever means or methods would best ensure a proper and speedy resolution to the dispute. They exercised what might be fairly called a 'supervisory jurisdiction', in so far as their primary responsibility, as they saw it, was to provide effective remedy in those cases where normal judicial proceedings had proved, for any number of reasons, to be inaccessible, inadequate, or inappropriate to the needs of individual litigants. They served in this capacity in order to guarantee what one litigant called 'the Right and Inheritance of every Free Born subject', which he described as 'the free course of Justice according to the good Laws and Statutes of England'.[27] The House of Lords was seen, and came to see itself, during this Parliament, as a court which, in the words of Denzil Holles, could provide 'ordinary remedy in extraordinary causes'.[28]

NOTES

1. C.H. McIlwain, *The High Court of Parliament*, New Haven, (1910), p. 109–10.
2. William Lambarde, *Archeion* (1635), p. 272.
3. Thomas Smith, *De Republica Anglorum*, Book II, c. 4.
4. Denzil, Baron Holles, *The Case Stated Concerning the Judicature of the House of Lords in Point of Appeals* (1675), p. 65.
5. Roland G. Usher, *The Rise and Fall of High Commission*, 1913, pp. 242–3.
6. Actions to recover possession at Common Law were the Assize of Novel Disseisin in the case of offices, and the writ of Quare Impedit, in the case of disputed advowsons.
7. Michael Hawkins, 'The Government; Its Role and Aims', in C.R. Russell (ed.), *The Origins of the English Civil War* (1973), p. 46.
8. HLRO, 'Main Papers', 24 Feb. 1641 (Speckard v. Weolly).
9. For a full discussion of law reform generally, see S.D. White, *Sir Edward Coke and the Grievances of the Commonwealth*, Manchester, 1979, and D. Veal, *The Popular movement for Law Reform 1640–1660*, Oxford, 1970.
10. Even Sir Matthew Hale, who was ill-disposed to recognise the 'legality' of the Lords' jurisdiction in equity appeals, admitted to the logic of these arguments. See Hale, *The Jurisdiction of the Lords' House*, London, 1796.
11. An appeal of this kind was in fact brought before the House of Commons in 1621, in the case of Hall v. Fuller. On that occasion the Lower House studiously avoided the fundamental question of jurisdiction. See Robert Zaller, *The Parliament of 1621*, Berkeley, 1971, p. 91.
12. For a fuller discussion of the Lords' role in these cases see J.S. Hart, 'The House of Lords and the Appellate Jurisdiction in Equity, 1640–1643', *Parliamentary History* ii, 1983.
13. S.D. White, *Sir Edward Coke and the Grievances of the Commonwealth*, pp. 46–85.
14. *Lords' Journal*, iv, p. 155.
15. Ibid., p. 126.
16. J.P. Dawson, 'The Privy Council and Private Law during the Tudor and Stuart Period', *Michigan Law Review*, 1xvii (1950), p. 69.

17. See, for example, HLRO, 'Main Papers', 23 Dec. 1640, 'Orders on Private Petitions' (Browne v. Marten) (Weoly v. Weoly).
18. *L.J.* iv, pp. 263 & 270.
19. William West, *The Second Part of Symboleography* (*Of the Chancerie*) (1594), p. 71.
20. See, for example, HLRO, 'Main Papers', 23 Dec. 1640, 'Orders on Private Petitions' (Cope v. Fisher) (Gerrard v. Pitts).
21. The writ reads as follows:

    Whereas, by the Advice and Assent of our Council, for certain affairs concerning us ... We have ordered a certain Parliament to be holden at our City of Westminster on the XX day of XX next ensuing, we strictly enjoining, command you (waiving all excuses) to be at the said day and place present with us and the rest of our Council to treat and give advice upon the affairs aforesaid; This in no wise do you omit. (See PRO C 231/5 p. 425)

22. The Lords used the former method considerably more often than the latter. On one occasion, the Keeper of Ludgate Prison indirectly questioned the validity of their order in law, by requesting to be indemnified against possible proceedings which might arise for an 'escape' as a consequence of executing the release at the Lords' command. The Lords referred his petition to Justices Crawley and Heath, who subsequently reported as follows:

    While it would have been more formal and warrantable if a writ of Habeas Corpus had issued directing the sheriffs to bring the prisoner before your Lordships, yet seeing that your Lordships are not tied to such regularity of proceedings as inferior courts are, and must be ... we are of the opinion that your Lordships' order is sufficient warrant in this case. (HLRO, 'Main Papers' 3 Dec. 1640)

23. HLRO, 'Main Papers' 22 Dec. 1640 (Garfield v. Clarke).
24. HLRO, 'Main Papers', B2, 'Book of Orders and Judgements' 1 Dec. 1640 (Francis Freeman's case).
25. *L.J.* iv, 137 (Waters v. Powell).
26. HLRO 'Main Papers', 8 Feb. 1641 (Riddington v. Crofte). The statute in question was the Statute of Westminster II, c. 25 (1285).
27. Ibid, 15 Jan. 1641 (Walker v. Lambe).
28. Denzil, Baron Holles, *The Grand Question Concerning the Judicature of the House of Peers* (1669), p. 99.

Criminal Equity in Restoration London and Middlesex

VALERIE C. EDWARDS

The aim of this paper is to consider whether such a process as 'criminal equity' did operate in London and Middlesex during the Restoration period, and if so, in what way?

Perhaps I should begin with a few definitions, principally of 'criminal equity'. As far as I know, the phrase was coined by Jerome Hall in his book *Theft, Law and Society*, in the following passage:

> there is represented in the history of the criminal law from the seventeenth century to the present day a process roughly analogous to that described by Maine in his *Ancient Law*. There is first the formal body of rules which, with changes in conditions and passage of time, lag behind the needs of the community. There results in the civil law, the growth of equity, a superior body of rules. In the criminal law the absence of a dual system of courts confines the change in the case-law to the narrow limits of judicial redefinition of this law. Accordingly, practices analogous to equity in civil proceedings develop in the trial of criminal cases which, in effect, supersede and are superior to the rules of law. Finally, the legislature takes cognisance of what is being done and what has in fact been established, and enacts legislation which directs these practices into expressly legal avenues. Whereupon a new cycle sets in.[1]

What I interpret Professor Hall as saying is this: that alongside the blackletter criminal law, particularly with respect to those crimes known as felonies for which capital punishment was the typical penalty, there existed another process whereby that blackletter law was unofficially moulded, modified and generally mitigated so as to keep it in line with some parallel body of norms as to what was just in the particular circumstances. Hall identified various elements as being part of this process, beginning with the extension, by means of legal fiction, of the escape route of benefit of clergy from the original narrow category of clerks in holy orders to the entire male population by accepting as proof of being a clerk in holy orders the mere ability to read the so-called 'neck verse'.[2] Parallel with benefit of clergy, perhaps coeval, or perhaps only developing as Parliament began from Tudor times to enact legislation gradually curtailing the availability of benefit of clergy in certain offences, were other devices for preventing the blackletter law from being enforced in its full vigour. There was the discretion which, in fact if not in theory, lay with private prosecutors whether or not to prefer charges at all, and if so, as to the form in which the charge was couched. There was the practice of grand juries of throwing out presentments as 'ignoramus' bills, in cases where in fact there was objectively sufficient prima facie evidence to justify a return of 'billa vera'. Petty juries also followed a practice of outright acquittal or of returning what Beattie[3] has called partial verdicts in effect substituting a lesser offence with a similar actus reus for the actual offence committed. Judges, in cases of conviction, awarded reprieves in order that the convicted person might sue for a pardon whether unconditional or conditional on agreeing to transportation to the colonies. Other variants no doubt also existed.[4]

While in the original paragraph quoted above, Hall referred to the process as having taken place since the seventeenth century, it is clear from other remarks that he saw it as primarily an eighteenth century phenomenon, tacitly linking its development with the spate of legislation in the eighteenth century, restrictive of the availability of benefit of clergy. Thus he says 'What in fact happened was that, beginning in the early part of the eighteenth century, the persons . . who administered the criminal law, invented and indulged in practices which almost nullified the capital penalty in most non-clergable [sic] felonies'.[5] Cockburn, however, in his work on the English Assizes from 1558 to 1714, identified many of the processes singled out by Hall as being part of criminal equity as operating in the early and mid-seventeenth century.[6] Also, Professor Green has shewn the operation of a parallel set of extra-legal considerations, in the case of grand jury manipulation of fact verdicts in homicide cases, in a much earlier period still,[7] although the difference may be that in Professor Green's period the two systems conflicted whereas Professor Hall would argue that the two systems operated together in an institutionalised fashion.

The main thrust of my paper is a consideration of empirical data culled from the Latin indictments in the sessions of the peace and gaol delivery rolls for the two jurisdictions of London and Middlesex.

By London I mean the City of London proper, the square mile within the walls over which the justices of the peace and the justices of gaol delivery appointed for the City had criminal jurisdiction. Although for many practical purposes by the latter part of the seventeenth century, as Brett-James has shewn, the 'metropolis' (a word, incidentally, coined for it by Dryden in his 'Annus Mirabilis')[8] extended beyond the original city to the so-called 'Liberties' on the north bank of the Thames, to the adjacent City of Westminster further along the river, and to Southwark on the south bank, as far as local government administration and criminal jurisdiction was concerned, the City justices of the peace and justices of gaol delivery had no jurisdiction there. With Southwark I am not concerned at all, since it lay in Surrey, but Westminster and the suburbs on the north bank are my concern since they were part of Middlesex for the purposes of criminal jurisdiction, as were the still rural parishes of the county.

By Restoration I mean the period between 1660, when Charles II returned from exile and the monarchy was reinstituted in England after the experiments of the Commonwealth and Protectorate, and 1688 when James II fled the kingdom.

The data which I shall be using have been drawn from all the sessions rolls for London and Middlesex (including Westminster) for five years chosen at random over the Restoration period: 1662; 1667; 1675; 1682 and 1688. Usually where statistical evidence is concerned here, I have averaged the figures for the years because in respect of criminal equity there do not seem to be dynamic trends so much as a stable pattern of behaviour.

Perhaps the first thing to remark upon is the question of perspective and context. Criminal equity as seen by Cockburn and Hall operated in respect of capital felonious offences and Hall's thesis seems to suggest that without this process English criminal law in the eighteenth century would have been a very sanguinary and draconian affair. By modern standards he is probably correct, but the matter should be put into perspective. The cases which I have considered are those prosecuted before quarter and gaol delivery sessions – the more serious offences. Of these on average only 28 per cent were felonious offences carrying any risk of capital punishment. The majority 72 per cent were misdemeanours mainly dealt with by quarter sessions and were punished by means of fines, imprisonment and corporal punishment.[9] So even on the basis of the offences of which I have cognisance, the operation of criminal equity to mitigate capital punishment has to be seen as applying only to a minority of cases involving breach of the criminal law. Additionally, in the background is the dark figure – dark because records do not exist concerning it – of very minor transgressions which would have been dealt with by individual justices of the peace in petty sessions. For instance, on average the quarter sessions and gaol delivery records reveal only 12 prosecutions per annum of petty larceny (theft of below 12d) in the whole of the metropolitan area (which had a projected population of 500,000 in 1700):[10] many such prosecutions and other minor offences must have been dealt with outside the quarter sessions and gaol delivery system. So, in reality, compared with the operation of the criminal law as a whole, the impact of criminal equity as a means of mitigating capital punishment affected only a tiny minority of cases.

To return to the prosecutions at quarter sessions and gaol delivery, on average 1,624 of these occurred each year for misdemeanours and 627 for felony.[9] Within the 1,624 misdemeanour prosecutions the discretion allowed to justices in levying of fines, imposition of corporal punishment or imprisonment, requirement of sureties and so forth gave an overtly recognised place to a criminal equity in the sense of modifying the principle (punishment for transgression) to fit the particular instance (what type of punishment in this particular case). Therefore the scope for the operation of practices such as those referred to by Hall is narrowed, and it is also difficult, relying purely on indictment evidence in run-of-the-mill cases without political overtones such as to have brought them to the attention of contemporaries and thus to have occasioned remark, to detect whether acquittals and ignoramus returns were expressions of criminal equity rather than authorised performances of the function in question.

One area in the field of misdemeanour prosecution, where a criminal equity of a type may be discerned, however, is in a situation which is the converse of the usual perception of criminal equity as mitigating the law in favour of the defendant. During the Restoration period over the years a number of prosecutions were brought and were treated as misdemeanours by the Bench, relating to obtaining goods by deception in circumstances not amounting to cheating by means of false tokens. According to Hawkins writing in the early eighteenth century, these were not offences at all at common law.[11] For a time, therefore, one may argue that a kind of criminal equity operated which led prosecutors to present such conduct as criminal (on the basis that that was what they thought it should be in law) and the bench and juries in many cases accepted these attempts.

To proceed however to felony prosecutions and criminal equity in its prime sense of mitigation of the severity of the criminal law, I will look at the empirical data in more detail.

Of the 627 defendants on average prosecuted for felony 358 or 57 per cent of them were indicted for straightforward larceny.[12] Only 12 on average were cases of petty larceny and therefore in theory the vast majority of the larceny defendants ran the risk of a capital sentence, since the prescribed penalty for grand larceny was hanging.[13]

In fact in 60 per cent of the larceny prosecutions no conviction occurred – either because of an acquittal (28 per cent) or an ignoramus bill (18 per cent) or for some other unknown factor (14 per cent), perhaps an abandoned prosecution or death in prison of the defendant or the fact of the defendant's being at large. So only 40 per cent were convicted: 143 out of the 358 concerned.[14] Even they were not in any certain danger of hanging, however, because of the availability of the most institutionalised of the factors enumerated by Hall, the 'defence' of benefit of clergy.

It was available in certain circumstances and in fact generally proved effective. The conditions varied depending on the sex of the offender. If he were male (99 out of the 143) then he would be entitled to benefit of clergy if (i) he could convince the court that he could read – because this was the fiction upon which the court was satisfied as to his being in holy orders; and (ii) he had not been granted the privilege before on a previous conviction – branding on the thumb was the method used to advertise the granting of benefit of clergy.[15]

For the 44 women convicted there was an additional hurdle, (iii) the amount involved needed to be less than ten shillings. For from the Henrician Dissolution until 1623 women, since they could not be in holy orders, could not claim benefit of clergy. An Act of James I in 1623[16] gave them the defence but only in larceny cases where the amount was less than ten shillings.

What then of those men who, convicted of larceny, either could not read or had already received benefit of clergy on a previous occasion, or those women who either fell into those categories or were convicted on an indictment involving goods worth more than ten shillings?

In theory they were subject to a mandatory capital penalty. However, in various ways, particularly in the case of those who had not previously been granted the privilege, this eventuality was generally avoided. Firstly, in respect of 22 of the 44 women convicted, i.e. 50 per cent, the conviction was on what Blackstone, one hundred years later, called a 'pious perjury'[17] and what Beattie today calls a partial verdict.[3] The jury found them guilty of theft but to the value of five or eight or nine shillings only, not to the amount specified in the indictment as being the value of the goods. These may have been genuine attempts at revaluation by the jury if it was of the opinion that the prosecutor had overvalued the stolen property. The fact, however, that round figures such as those quoted above are invariably chosen by the jury would tend to discount this interpretation. One isolated indictment from the August gaol delivery for 1661[18] indeed would seem to buttress the general deduction very strongly. In this indictment one Mabel Tracie was found guilty of theft of goods from Henry Osbaston, gentleman, and claimed the privilege of benefit of clergy. The body of the indictment is written in one hand and one type of ink apart from a few words in the middle, obviously inserted later in a different coloured ink. These few words were those giving the value of the goods stolen: namely, nine shillings. It would seem that this was an instance of an exercise of discretion by the prosecutor who was reluctant to proceed on an indictment that would be for a non-clergyable offence. It lends credence to the supposition that jury verdicts reducing the value of property in indictments were motivated by the same reluctance to put the defendants concerned in jeopardy of a capital sentence.

Occasionally both women and men were convicted of petty larceny only on an indictment originally of grand larceny: the jury convicted to the value of 12d only. This may be because it was known to the jury that benefit of clergy would not be available (perhaps because it had been observed that the defendant had been branded on the thumb as a sign of having already received the privilege, or because it was clear that the defendant was illiterate) or it may have been that the notion of criminal equity had much finer graduations still and operated where the jury thought a deterrent or reformative flogging might be a juster penalty in the circumstances – perhaps reserving benefit of clergy for another occasion if the defendant should prove recidivist?[19]

Secondly, both with regard to men who had failed to read and women who were nevertheless convicted of theft of more than ten shillings, in many cases judicial and executive intervention prevented the capital sanction from being carried out. Thus occasionally a defendant would be reprieved and in some cases transported to Barbados as a condition of being granted a pardon.

The anomalous position of women in particular is highlighted by four cases[20] where two or more defendants were jointly prosecuted for grand larceny, both (or all) being convicted, but the male defendant was able to claim benefit of clergy while the female was theoretically liable to capital punishment because the amount involved was more than ten shillings. In all these cases the women concerned were reprieved and probably pardoned (two at least were pardoned on condition of transportation).

In respect of benefit of clergy and the practices connected with it, the penultimate stage of Hall's cycle can be seen, for in the post-Revolution period legislation was passed (a) providing that one did not actually have to read in order to claim benefit of clergy[21] and (b) removing the ten shilling limit from benefit of clergy in the case of women.[22] To quote Hall again, the legislation embodied in 'expressly legal avenues' the combined effect of the practices of (i) reducing the amount concerned and (ii) reprieving those who technically fell foul of the law by being unable to read. It may very well be that consideration of prosecutions in the early part of the seventeenth century would shew that women were very frequently acquitted or found guilty of petty larceny only because of their inability to claim benefit of clergy; that the norm behind this practice was formalised in the Jacobean statute of 1623, and that Hall's cycle set in again after the 1623 statute to work to remove the ten shilling limit thus introduced.

In respect of other property offences such as burglary, robbery in a dwelling house or on the highway, horse stealing or theft from the person which were non-clergyable offences by statute,[23] a similar though not so clear-cut process can be discerned. Non-clergyable property offences accounted for 139 out of 627 felony prosecutions (22 per cent). Of these, 36 per cent resulted in convictions. Of these convictions, however, 19 (38 per cent) were on a reduced charge allowing of benefit of clergy – generally a finding that, on a charge of burglary, there had been no breaking and entering; or on a charge of theft from the person that in fact it had been a straightforward larceny with no pocket picking involved.[24]

Finally, in respect of property offences, what was the combined effect of abandoned suits, ignoramus bills, acquittals, partial verdicts, benefit of clergy and reprieves?

Of the 543 people on average prosecuted for property felonies (this includes approximately 46 people per annum accused of harbouring property offenders, another clergyable offence), 63 (12 per cent) were actually given a capital sentence and of these 27 received reprieves. Many of those reprieved may have ultimately been pardoned, sometimes on condition of transportation.[25] It is possible then that only thirty or so (6 per cent) capital sentences for property felonies were actually carried out as a result of the operation of various processes described above – barbaric by twentieth century standards, but in the context of more than 500 potentially capital prosecutions indicative of a greater degree of leniency than could be envisaged from a mere perusal of the blackletter law.

The property felonies with which I have been concerned so far comprised 88 per cent of all the felony prosecutions – the remaining 12 per cent involved felonies against the person: 75 defendants per annum on average.[26] All but one or two of these 75 defendants per annum faced a homicide charge: there were but one or two prosecutions for rape or sodomy or cutting of the nose with intent to disfigure under the so-called Coventry Act of 1672[27] which was the only non-fatal non-sexual assault to be made an indictable felony rather than a misdemeanour. (Mayhem was a felony but one subject to prosecution by the archaic procedure of appeal of felony, not by indictment at the King's suit[28] and stealing an heiress[29] was, as the word 'stealing' indicates, more of a property offence than an offence against the person). This is not to suggest that only 12 per cent of all indictments related to offences against the person: in fact, overall, at quarter sessions and gaol deliveries together, about one third of prosecutions were for such offences but the vast majority were misdemeanour prosecutions for assault, not felony prosecutions.[30]

The context of Hall's thesis on criminal equity (a book after all on theft, law and society) limited the operation of the process tacitly to felonies against property. It is possible, however, to discern to a lesser degree the same sort of process at work with regard to offences against the person, particularly with regard to the substitution of verdicts of manslaughter (an offence which like grand larceny was clergyable) for the original indictment of murder malice aforethought.

It must be admitted, however, that because of the paucity of information contained even in homicide indictments made on a coroner's inquest, it is far from easy to decide which manslaughter verdicts were true (in the sense of reflecting distinctions drawn by the substantive blackletter law) and which were 'pious' (in the sense of reflecting what the jury thought should be the law or of achieving a just result in the instant case).

The rate of conviction on homicide charges was not significantly different from that for property felonies as a whole – on average 32 per cent as compared with 36 per cent.[31] Forty-four per cent of cases resulted in an acquittal, 5 per cent in ignoramus bills and 19 per cent were not fully prosecuted, usually because the offender had fled abroad, although occasionally for other reasons such as death in prison from gaol fever or from wounds sustained in the course of perpetrating the homicide.

Approximately half of the guilty verdicts related to murder – on average 10 capital sentences per annum were ordered. Approximately 14 cases per annum were manslaughter verdicts where the defendant was given benefit of clergy.[32]

In some of the manslaughter verdicts we know from other sources that these are inconsistent with the result that should have obtained from the state of the law at the time, which should have been a murder verdict. These generally involve the internecine activity so often depicted in for instance the Verney papers[33] as occurring between members of the gentry or upper classes. Some we know from contemporary sources were premeditated duels, technically murder, but returned as manslaughter on the doctrine of 'heated blood'.[34] Others, equally premeditated assassinations, were also returned as manslaughter under the 'heated blood' rubric. For instance, in 1662 Charles Dillon and Thomas Howard, gentlemen, were convicted of manslaughter for killing Giles Rawlings in a brawl as he emerged from the tennis court in Pall Mall.[35] The doctrine of 'heated blood' hardly seems appropriate when considered in the light of the fact that the assailants, according to other evidence, wore padded armour under their clothing and lay in wait for Rawlings outside the court.[36]

There may be numerous alternative explanations for these cases, to which I will return later. There are, however, some prosecutions, numerically very small, where the issue of criminal equity operating through acquittal or ignoramus bills is a little clearer. These involve prosecutions under two Jacobean statutes – the Statute of Stabbing[37] which attempted to oust the jury's ability to use the 'heated blood' doctrine to negative malice aforethought, and the statute concerning the murder of bastard children[38] which in effect attempted to reverse the burden of proof. Under this statute a mother who had concealed the birth of such a child had the burden of establishing that it had been born dead, otherwise she was to be convicted and treated as if she had murdered it.

Notwithstanding the fearsome burden in this latter offence, the rate of conviction was no higher than that for offences against the person as a whole: five out of 15 cases across the five years considered. Only six prosecutions under the Statute of Stabbing occurred in the records which I have used – none of these resulted in conviction. Significantly in this latter instance, however, each of the six defendants was also indicted on a common law murder charge and four out of the six were convicted on the common law presentment.[39] They were convicted of manslaughter because of lack of malice aforethought, the very eventuality which the Statute of Stabbing sought to obviate.

One last point I would like to make with regard to offences against the person before proceeding to the final section of this paper is that here, as in offences against property, there does seem to be some evidence of redressing the balance between man and woman, but by judicial or executive intervention rather than by the jury. In 1688[40] one Henry Jeane killed Samuel Moore in a rapier fight. He was convicted of manslaughter (despite the fact that it may very well have been a premeditated duel) and was able to claim benefit of clergy. One Anne Crispe, however, found guilty of being an accessory after the fact to Jeane, was sentenced to hanging – a man in her position, like the principal himself, could have claimed benefit of clergy. Women in 1688, however, had only the limited entitlement to benefit of clergy under the Jacobean statute of 1623: in cases of larceny of goods worth less than ten shillings. It is probable that the pardon granted to Anne Crispe was so granted because of the glaring injustice which the peculiarities in the law relating to benefit of clergy would have created.

When the reform in the law of benefit of clergy occurred in the 1690s,[41] the anomaly highlighted by this case was removed by equating a woman's entitlement to benefit of clergy to that of a man in similar circumstances.

So much then for empirical data. All of the conclusions which I have reached have been merely deductive and to construct a process of criminal equity purely on deduction may be rather rash. There may be other explanations for the phenomena which I have observed. Certainly, in the case of the homicide verdicts, since most of them involve members of the aristocracy, the alternatives of bribery, jury packing, intimidation and access to legal advice (though not representation in court) on how to present the evidence may all be alternative explanations. This was almost certainly so in the case of the acquittal in 1682[42] of Count Konigsmarck on a charge of complicity in the murder of Mr Thynne (over the long-standing dispute concerning the conquest of an heiress): three foreign desperadoes, Vratz, Boroski and Sterne, were convicted. Konigsmarck, however, whom contemporary extra-judicial sources indicate as the instigator of the affair[43] and at least an accessory before the fact, was not.

However, with regard to the phenomena in the case of offences against property, the likelihood of bribery or jury packing is slim – most of the defendants are described as labourers who would not have had the wherewithal to effect this. Some may have been professionals, with gang solidarity behind them and some expertise at manipulating the situation to their advantage,[44] but this would not explain the extensive occurrence of the phenomena in cases where no signs of professionalism or of criminal networks can be discerned.

Even if, for the majority of straightforward felonies against property, we dismiss the alternative explanations, how justifiable is it to refer to the phenomena as manifestations of a criminal equity? May they not simply be coincidental occurrences indicative of genuine doubts of guilt on the part of prosecutors, juries and judges? Is there anything in contemporary sources to support the deduction here made, rather than any other interpretation of the data?

If one looks behind the empirical data to what is known about attitudes to the criminal law and to punishment in the seventeenth century, one can discern an undercurrent of dissatisfaction. This undercurrent seems to have two intermingled and overlapping themes: one, that the law was too severe and discretion with regard to punishment of felonies too limited, seems to spring from a genuine unease that offences against property should be capital; the other, that too severe a law was inevitably laxly enforced and therefore was self-defeating as far as deterrence was concerned, was voiced on the whole by more sophisticated and less humanitarian critics.

Barbara Shapiro[45] has shewn that concern with the criminal law's harshness was not purely an isolated phenomenon of the civil war and interregnum period: it was, after all, in the reign of James I that the first step towards statutory equalisation of the position of men and women with regard to benefit of clergy occurred.[16]

Both Veall[46] and Christopher Hill[47] have expounded the views of Levellers and Diggers on the perceived iniquity of capital punishment for offences against property and of the role of the jury in redressing the balance in favour of the common people. Peter Chamberlen's rhetorical question 'Is that law to be valued by Englishmen that values an Englishman at but thirteen pence halfpenny?'[48] puts the reactions of the common people to the law relating to property felonies in a neat epigram.

While the views of the Levellers and of Gerard Winstanley and his ilk may be perhaps not regarded as typical of those of the juries and prosecutors of Restoration London and Middlesex (particularly after the introduction of the twenty pound property qualification for jurors in 1665),[49] the same may not have been true of the views of the Hale Commission chaired by Matthew Hale himself, which recommended abolition of the capital penalty for simple larceny for both men and women.[50]

From the early seventeenth century (if not earlier still) there had been those like Bacon who had suggested a reduction in capital penalties for property offences not from the humanitarian point of view because of their cruelty and excessiveness, but from the standpoint that overly harsh penalties led to a breakdown in law enforcement and frustrated the purpose of the offence.[51]

This point was echoed in the relatively few instances of vocalised dissatisfaction with the criminal law that survived from the Restoration period. Thus Edward Chamberleyne, writing in 1667, after saying that changes in the value of money and passage of time had made the law more severe than had been originally intended by the law makers, went on to recommend hard labour rather than a capital sentence as being of a more deterrent effect. Thus he said that it was 'much more suitable to the ends of Government that a criminal should live in perpetual ignominy, slavery or misery, rather than be taken quite away, because a living condemned wretched criminal will be a spectacle in others' eyes, will in time be convinced of his crime, will justifie his judg [sic] and ultimately repent his own folly'. He also refers to pious perjury (although not in those words) and confirms Bacon's view (and the empirical data) that the law was frequently not enforced.[52]

Ten years later, W.G., in his *Proposals for Building Almshouses*[53] thought it would preserve more lives if poverty could be alleviated by provision of work and thus lead to a 'great abatement of felons'. Moreover, he suggested that it would be more Christian to suppress criminals by setting them on work than branding them after benefit of clergy or sentencing them to transportation; he remarks that in practice those sentenced to be transported were often pardoned and let loose without any punishment by way of reformation, because the plantations of America and the West Indies refused to receive them.

The same theme occurs in Sir William Temple's *Of Popular Discontents*. After observing[54] that the English character was known to 'be more fearless of death . . and more impatient of labour or of hardships' than any other, he recommended hard labour rather than the death penalty, at the discretion of the Bench, since such a punishment would be better than 'short easy deaths' as the defendants would find hard labour 'much harder to bear and [would] be more unwilling and afraid to suffer [it]'.

Sir Matthew Hale nowhere in his *Pleas of the Crown* indicated that dissatisfaction with the capital sentence for offences against property which the eponymous Hale Commission's recommendations reflected.[55]

This is probably because the book was an exposition of the law as it was rather than a critique. However, in his list of eighteen *Things necessary to be continually had in remembrance*[56] he continually reminds himself against being swayed too much in the defendant's favour, as if tacitly recognising that this was likely to happen. Thus in Consideration VIII he says 'That in business capital, though my nature prompt me to pity, yet to consider that there is also a pity due to the Country'. Yet later in Consideration XIII he says 'If in criminals it be a measuring cast, to incline to mercy and acquittal'. Clearly he was ambivalent about the issue.

Likewise Lord Guildford, according to his brother Roger North, although not openly expressing dissatisfaction with the Law, was 'infinitely scrutinous' in capital cases wherever there was any doubt.[57]

One last remark of Sir William Temple's leads me into my penultimate suggestion. After making his recommendations, Temple wryly observed that he recognised that such laws were not likely to be passed until Parliament 'was at leisure from the necessity and urgency of more pressing affairs'.[58] May it have been that the demands for reform were not reiterated after the Restoration not because the disquiet was not there, but because such demands would have received little sympathy as they would have been dismissed as tarred with the republican and democratic brush of the Commonwealth and Protectorate? In fact, many of Temple's notions, though it is not known if his proposals with regard to the criminal law were being specifically referred to, were chidingly denounced by Charles II as too 'popular'.[59] Moreover, it may well be that the political climate – the religious question, the plots real or imaginary, the Exclusion Crisis, Monmouth's Rebellion and the events leading up to James II's flight, not to mention the Great Plague and the Great Fire – made concern with criminal law reform of secondary importance. This may particularly have been the case if it were tacitly recognised by those who might otherwise have advocated reform that in fact, if not in theory, the inequity of the law was mitigated by the various practices with which we have been concerned here.

One line of research which I have not yet pursued with any vigour is the question of the development of penal theory in the seventeenth century, and in particular, the views of the Natural Lawyers such as Locke (who was clearly uneasy on the issue of the death penalty for offences against property)[60] on the function of punishment. That is another story – but surely the affinity of the Natural Law position (the existence of the identifiable body of Natural Law behind the positive laws of domestic governments) and the apparent operation of a parallel body of criminal equity behind or alongside the positive criminal law of Restoration England is something that needs further exploration.

NOTES AND REFERENCES

Middlesex records in Greater London Record Office: referred to by reference prefix 'MJ/...' London records in Corporation of London Record Office: referred to merely by date of session, no reference prefix.

1. J. Hall: *Theft, Law and Society*, 2nd Ed. Bobbs-Merrill Co. Inc. (1952), p. 149.
2. Ibid., pp. 110, 111.
3. J. Beattie: 'Crime and the Courts in Surrey 1736–53', in *Crime in England 1550–1800* ed. J.S. Cockburn, Methuen (1977), p. 171.
4. Hall, op. cit., p. 141.
5. Ibid., p. 118 – emphasis mine.
6. J.S. Cockburn: *A History of English Assizes from 1558 to 1714*, c.u.p. (1972), pp. 125–33.
7. T.A. Green: 'The Jury and the English Law of Homicide 1200–1600', in *1976 Michigan Law Review*, Vol. 74, pp. 414–99.
8. N.G. Brett-James: *The Growth of Stuart London*, George Allen & Unwin (1935), p. 21 and passim.
9.

FELONIES AND MISDEMEANOURS

Year	*Total*	*Felonies*		*Misdemeanour*	
		No.	%	No.	%
1662	2859	766	27	2066	72
1667	1518	477	31	1037	68
1675	2592	850	33	1738	67
1682	2240	468	21	1766	79
1688	2099	575	27	1514	72
Average	2262	627	28	1624	72

Discrepancies are accounted for by a very small incidence of treason offences not dealt with here.

10. Penelope Corfield: 'Urban Development in England and Wales in the 16th & 17th Centuries', in *Trade, Government and Economy in Pre-Industrial England*, ed. D.C. Coleman and A.H. John, Weidenfeld & Nicolson (1976), pp. 217–18.
11. W. Hawkins: *Pleas of the Crown*, London (1716) Vol. I, p. 188. See for instance the prosecution of J. Reynolds and H. Stephenson at the May Sessions of the Peace for Middlesex, 1688 (MJ/SR 1726) for obtaining property from one J. Shaw on pretext of having been sent to collect it for inspection by a regular customer. They were fined 12d each and sent to the House of Correction.
12.

FELONIES

	1662	*1667*	*1675*	*1682*	*1688*	*Average*	
	No.	No.	No.	No.	No.	No.	%
Larceny	453	300	463	287	288	358	57
Burglary *	168	81	249	82	115	139	22
Harbouring	52	29	75	39	37	46	7
Homicide #	84	58	54	47	130	75	12
Others +	9	9	9	13	5	9	2
Total	766	477	850	468	575	627	100

* includes robbery, theft from the person, horse stealing etc.
\# includes rape, sodomy, theft of an heiress etc.
\+ e.g. bigamy etc.

13. M. Hale: *Pleas of the Crown*, London (1736), Vol. I, p. 504.

14.

LARCENIES

	1662	1667	1675	1682	1688	Average	
	No.	No.	No.	No.	No.	No.	%
Ignoramus	147	91	124	62	72	99	28
Acquittal	78	61	75	59	46	64	18
Conviction	176	100	184	126	128	143	40
Unknown	52	48	80	40	42	52	14
Total	453	300	463	287	288	358	100

15. Hale, op.cit., Vol. II, pp. 371–3; 381.
16. 21 Jac. I, Cap. 6.
17. W. Blackstone: *Commentaries on the Laws of England*, 5th Ed. Dublin (1773), Vol. IV, p. 239.
18. August Gaol Delivery, Middlesex, 1661 (MJ/SR 1237).
19.

PARTIAL VERDICTS

	1662	1667	1675	1682	1688	Average
Partial *	34	16	53	26	52	36
% Larceny #	19	16	29	21	41	25

* partial verdict: charge reduced to clergyable or non capital offence.
\# partial verdicts as a percentage of all larceny convictions.

20. Mary Jessop & Henry Gray, convicted at June Gaol Delivery, Middx. 1662 (MJ/GBB 6/146); Brian Sweete, Mary Wexam & Jane Jarvis, convicted at October Gaol Delivery, Middx. 1667 (MJ/SR 1341): Wexam and Jarvis pardoned on condition of transportation; Edward Wells & Margaret Morris, convicted at April Gaol Delivery, London 1675; Robert & Martha Huckle, convicted at January Gaol Delivery, London 1682.
21. 5 Anne Cap. 6.
22. 3 & 4 W. & M. Cap. 9. It is significant that whereas the proportion of male to female defendants is generally constant at approximately 65% male, 35% female, the proportions are reversed in the case of partial verdicts. This I believe highlights the tendency to right the inequality between the sexes of the substantive law.

PROSECUTIONS FOR LARCENY

	1662	1667	1675	1682	1688	Average	
	No.	No.	No.	No.	No.	No.	%
Male	317	178	287	187	187	231	65
Female	136	122	176	100	101	127	35

IGNORAMUS

	1662	1667	1675	1682	1688	Average	
	No.	No.	No.	No.	No.	No.	%
Male	58	28	41	37	24	38	60
Female	20	33	34	22	22	26	40

ACQUITTAL

	1662	1667	1675	1682	1688	Average	
	No.	No.	No.	No.	No.	No.	%
Male	90	60	74	37	46	61	62
Female	57	31	50	25	26	38	38

CONVICTION

	1662	*1667*	*1675*	*1682*	*1688*	*Average*	
	No.	No.	No.	No.	No.	No.	%
Male	136	63	123	86	87	99	69
Female	40	37	61	40	41	44	31

CONVICTION ON PARTIAL VERDICT

	1662	*1667*	*1675*	*1682*	*1688*	*Average*	
	No.	No.	No.	No.	No.	No.	%
Male	12	3	18	15	24	14	39
Female	22	13	35	11	28	22	61

23. Hale, op.cit., Vol. I, chaps. XLIV, XLVI, XLVIII.

24.

BURGLARIES ETC

	1662	*1667*	*1675*	*1682*	*1688*	*Average*	
	No.	No.	No.	No.	No.	No.	%
Ignoramus	23	5	23	12	8	14	10
Acquittal	56	37	88	28	25	47	34
Conviction	53	23	84	38	54	50	36
Unknown	36	16	54	4	28	28	20
Total	168	81	249	82	115	139	100

PARTIAL VERDICTS

	1662	*1667*	*1675*	*1682*	*1688*	*Average*
Partial *	14	10	23	12	33	19
% Burglary #	26	43	27	32	61	38

* partial verdict: charge reduced to clergyable or non capital offence.
\# partial verdicts as a percentage of all burglary etc. convictions.

25.

CAPITAL SENTENCES

	1662	*1667*	*1675*	*1682*	*1688*	*Average*
Sentences	78	35	107	55	41	63
Reprieves	39	23	40	18	13	27

It can again be seen by looking at the sex distribution that reprieves & pardons seem to have been used to redress the balance, for while the proportion of capital sentences passed on men & women is in line with the overall proportions (see 22 above), the number of women reprieved far outweighs that of men. Most of these women were convicted of larceny of above 10/–.

CAPITAL SENTENCES

	1662	*1667*	*1675*	*1682*	*1688*	*Average*	
	No.	No.	No.	No.	No.	No.	%
Male	62	11	82	33	26	43	68
Female	16	24	25	22	15	20	32

REPRIEVES AND PARDONS

	1662	1667	1675	1682	1688	Average	
	No.	No.	No.	No.	No.	No.	%
Male	25	1	19	7	1	11	41
Female	14	22	21	11	12	16	59

26.

FELONIES

Year	Total	Person		Property		Other	
		No.	%	No.	%	No.	%
1662	766	84	11	673	88	9	1
1667	477	58	12	410	86	9	2
1675	850	54	6	787	93	9	1
1682	468	47	10	408	86	13	3
1688	575	130	23	440	76	5	1
Average	627	75	12	544	87	9	1

27. 22 & 23 Car. II, Cap. 1. There were in fact two earlier statutes relating to the cutting off of tongues or putting out of eyes (5 H. 4, Cap. 5) and to the cutting off of ears (37 H. 8, Cap. 6) but these appear to have fallen into desuetude.
28. Hawkins, op.cit., Vol. I, p. 112; Vol. II, pp. 157–8.
29. 3 H. 7, Cap. 2.
30.

ALL PRESENTMENTS

Year	Total	Person		Property		Other	
		No.	%	No.	%	No.	%
1662	2859	800	28	967	3	1092	38
1667	1518	527	35	568	37	423	28
1675	2592	831	32	1092	42	669	26
1682	2240	885	40	683	30	672	30
1688	2099	829	39	689	33	581	28
Average	2262	774	34	800	35	687	31

31.

HOMICIDES ETC

	1662	1667	1675	1682	1688	Average	
	No.	No.	No.	No.	No.	No.	%
Ignoramus	4	3	5	3	5	4	5
Acquittal	41	27	28	17	51	33	44
Conviction	22	15	17	23	44	24	32
Unknown	17	13	4	4	30	14	19
Total	84	58	54	47	130	75	100

32. CAPITAL SENTENCES

	1662	*1667*	*1675*	*1682*	*1688*	*Average*	
	No.	No.	No.	No.	No.	No.	%
Cap. Sentences	5	9	9	14	13	10	42
Manslaughter	17	6	8	8	28	14	58
Total	22	15	17	22*	41#	24	100

* discrepancy of one caused by a conviction of unlawful sexual intercourse substituted for rape charge.

\# discrepancy of two caused by (a) an outlawry; (b) one man's conviction on 2 charges, capital sentence counted once only.

33. Historical Manuscripts Commission (HMC), 7th Report (Verney Papers), passim, but see e.g., p. 486 (Danby), p. 465 (Scroope) and p. 479 (Glover) etc.
34. M.M. Kaye: 'The Early History of Murder & Manslaughter', Vol. 83, *L.Q.R.* pp. 365–95; 569–601.
35. October Gaol Delivery, Middx. 1662 (MJ/SR 1259).
36. HMC 7th Report (Verney Papers), p. 484; S. Pepys: *Diary*, 19 Aug. 1662, Everyman Edition, Dent Dutton (1953), Vol. I, p. 286.
37. 1 Jac. I, Cap. 8.
38. 21 Jac. I, Cap. 28.
39. Convictions under 21 Jac. I, Cap. 28: Elizabeth Burnsham (Dec. 1662 MJ/SR 848); Anne Penney (London, Apr. 1675); Mary Roblin (Oct. 1682 MJ/GBB 241); Sina Jones (London Jan. 1688); Elizabeth Dumas (London Dec. 1688). Prosecutions under 1 Jac. I, Cap. 8: Cropton (Apr. 1662 MJ/SR 1249) unknown outcome; Everard (London Dec. 1662) acquittal on statute, manslaughter at common law; Wells (Dec. 1662 MJ/SR 848) outcome as for Everard; Hodgkins (London Dec. 1662) outcome as for Everard; Crofts (Dec. 1675 MJ/SR 1498) outcome as for Everard; Brereton (Apr. 1688 MJ/GBB 237) acquittal on both.
40. October Gaol Delivery, Middx. 1688 (MJ/SR 1735). A similar case, involving conviction for rescuing a felon, resulted in a pardon for the woman: Rose Gwynne's case Dec. Gaol Delivery London 1662.
41. 3 & 4 W. & M., Cap. 9.
42. Feb. Gaol Delivery, Middx. 1682 (MJ/SR 1609).
43. HMC Report on the Mss of the Duke of Buccleugh at Montagu House, Vol. I, p. 336; HMC, Report on the Mss of Mrs Frankland-Russel-Astley, p. 49; Calendar of State Papers Domestic, 1682, passim.
44. A fictional example, probably drawn from true experience, is Gibbet, the highwayman in G. Farquhar's *The Beaux' Stratagem* (1707) who says, in Act IV Scene II 'I must reserve £200 to save my life at the sessions'. (Le Flemyng Papers), p. 108, records an instance where a special commission for immediate trial of five highwaymen was ordered by the King in 1674 to obviate the possibility of witnesses being tampered with before the regular Gaol Delivery.
45. Barbara Shapiro: 'Law Reform in 17th Century England', in *American Journal of Legal History*, Vol. 19, p. 286.
46. D. Veall: *The Popular Movement for Law Reform*, Oxford (1970) passim but especially chapter 5.
47. C. Hill: *The World Turned Upside Down*, Penguin Books (1975) passim but especially Chaps. 7 & 12.
48. Quoted in Veall op.cit., p. 128.
49. 16 & 17 Car II. Cap. 5. It is, however, clear that juries were on occasions empanelled from those technically unqualified – see e.g., D. Ogg: *England in the Reign of Charles II*, Oxford (1934), Vol. II, p. 519; K.H.D. Haley: *The First Earl of Shaftesbury*, Oxford (1968), pp. 658 & 676. It is not clear whether this only occurred in politico–religious trials such as that of College, or whether it was a general phenomenon. Certainly the composition of the Grand Jury in Shaftesbury's case, of very wealthy jurors, seems to have been the exception rather than the rule: see Haley, op.cit., loc.cit.

50. *Somers' Tracts*, 2nd Ed. (1809–1816), vol. VI, p. 236, section IX.
51. Quoted in Shapiro, op.cit., p. 286.
52. E. Chamberleyne: *England's Wants* (1667), pp. 16–18: see *Somers' Tracts*, op.cit., Vol. IX.
53. W.G.: 'Proposals for Building Almshouses' (1677), *8 Harl. Misc.*, pp. 126, 124.
54. Temple: 'Of Popular Discontents', in *Miscellanea* (1701), Part III, pp. 63–5. This was published by J. Swift in 1701 but he says in the preface that the essays were written many years before Temple's death.
55. Hale's statement that indictments in capital felonies should be very strictly construed (Vol. II, p. 168) can be seen as tacitly disapproving the imposition of a capital penalty.
56. G. Burnet: *Lives of Hale, Bedell and Rochester* (Dove's English Classics, date unknown), pp. 29–31.
57. R. North: *Lives of Guilford* (sic) *and Others*, Henry Colburn (1826), Vol. I, p. 266.
58. Temple, op.cit., p. 66.
59. R. Faber: *The Brave Courtier, Sir William Temple*, Faber & Faber (1983), p. 50.
60. J. Locke: *Second Treatise of Government*, ed. P. Laslett, Cambridge (1960), paras. 12 & 13. He does not specifically voice any qualms concerning capital punishment for offences against property but he avoids a direct answer to his rhetorical question 'it will perhaps be demanded, with death?', which contrasts starkly with his remarks on capital punishment for homicide in para. 11.

The Norwich Court of Requests – A Tradition Continued

MICHELE SLATTER

The problems of small-debt litigation at common law in the eighteenth and nineteenth centuries are, as Professor Arthurs remarks,[1] too well known to need rehearsal at length. Many localities[2] came to establish a local Court of Requests to alleviate the problems and, if these courts have been slow to attract researchers' interest, nevertheless the work to date has now given us a vivid picture of the later phase of their institutional development.[3] Their earlier history, however, remains relatively unexplored.[4] In particular, no previous writer has considered why the 'Requests Model' was originally chosen as a solution to the problem of small-debt claims. Was it adopted in desperation, from inertia, as a gamble or with some confidence that it could be artificially grafted onto existing court structures by statute and would successfully take root? Was the choice influenced by Interregnum notions of law reform[5] or was it determined by more pragmatic considerations? An examination of one of the earliest provincial Requests may throw some light on these questions, since we may assume that it was these 'vanguard' courts which served as the precedent for the later proliferation of Courts of Requests and provided the model from which the later courts evolved. The Norwich court was established in 1701,[6] and was the third[7] provincial Court of Requests. It was based directly and, we may think, consciously on the original precedent of the City of London court.[8] This brief paper hopes to suggest an explanation of that choice. It will indicate that, despite its statutory origin and London precedent, Norwich's new court was by no means alien to local judicial traditions,[9] and will consider the implications of this possibility.

It is not surprising to find Norwich amongst the first provincial centres trying to end the difficulties of small-debt litigation. The city was, of course, a major trading and commercial centre for the East Anglian region. During the seventeenth century its staple industry, worsted weaving, had continued to flourish, largely by adapting successfully to changing markets and, despite the occasional depressions in the latter half of the period, Norwich prospered and expanded. By 1701 it was the second city of the Kingdom and was by far the largest inland centre.[10]

Inevitably, such a buoyant economy would involve extensive credit systems which required the possibility of efficient support from the courts if creditors' confidence were to be maintained, particularly when the city had such a peculiarly large proportion of poor, but not destitute, inhabitants.[11] That existing provision for debt cases was unsatisfactory both to debtors and creditors is made clear by the city's petition to the House of Commons seeking a Court of Request:

> It is found by common experience that the erecting of a Court of Conscience in the City of London for determining all matters of debts or actions for the value of 40sh. hath been of great advantage to the poorer sort of inhabitants thereof; that the said City of Norwich is very populous and many poor inhabitants therein for want of the like good establishment there are often prosecuted in vexatious suits and imprisoned for small debts the charges whereof many times amount to more than the debt whereby whole families are ruined, the gaols filled with miserable debtors and the parish charges increased for their support.[12]

Although phrased to present the debtors' problems as paramount, the difficulties described here clearly affected both parties. It is also important to remember that at this period discrete debtor/creditor classes were unknown – most individuals played both roles in different transactions. The petition was described as from 'the Mayor, Alderman, Common Council and Chief Inhabitants of the City of Norwich and County of the same', many of whom were amongst the city's leading tradesmen[13] and we can be certain that they expressed their own needs as tradesmen and ratepayers[14] as well as a paternalistic concern for 'the poorer sort of inhabitants'.

In addition to the problem, the city's petition also details the remedy sought. Clearly the successful experience of the London Court was an inspiration in their choice. But why was it felt that such a tribunal would also succeed in Norwich? To understand this, we must consider the cause of the mischief in question and therefore turn our attention to those civic courts in Norwich which, prior to 1701, had jurisdiction over actions of debt: the Sheriffs' (or Guildhall) Court and the Mayor's Court of Equity. An outline of the Norwich cursus honorum is given in Figure 1 below.

By 1700, the Sheriffs' Court was the only court having true first-instance jurisdiction for debt. It was a local court of record deriving its authority from early city charters redefined in the 1404 charter of Henry IV.[15] Its jurisdiction included 'actions of debt and trespass between man and man'[16] and all mixed and personal actions. Its procedure followed closely the traditional common law forms, including trial by jury. Its judges were the two Sheriffs of the city for the time being, of whom no legal expertise was expected, and the Recorder or Steward who as a

Figure 1

City Officeholders in Norwich 1701

The cursus honorum

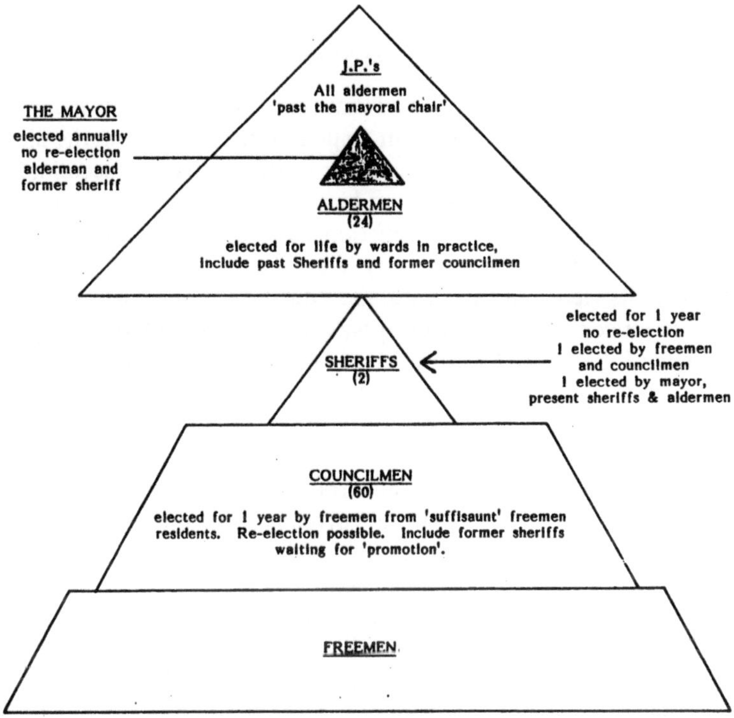

lawyer advised them as necessary. Hearings were twice-weekly on Wednesdays and Fridays in the city's Guildhall. There were two trial days per year.

This was the venue for those 'vexatious suits ... the charges whereof many times amount to more than the debt' complained of in the Petition. Apart from its geographical proximity, the Sheriffs' Court seemed to suffer from all the disadvantages of the Westminster courts both for plaintiffs and defendants. Indeed, it is possible that its only (improper) role in small debt claims was as a tool of harassment[17] and it may be supposed that this court provided the 'model' to be avoided.

The other city court which could deal with cases of debt was the Mayor's Court of Equity. The first unambiguous reference to this court as a discrete tribunal is as late as 1663, in the City's charter from Charles II, although it is clear that the jurisdiction was, by that time, well established:[18]

> Confirmation is granted of the right to hold, as held immemorially, a Court of Equity before the Mayor and Justices of the Peace, or any three of them the Mayor being one, upon bills and plaints exhibited by any citizens or inhabitants in cases where an equitable remedy may appear and none can be obtained by Common Law, and to remove such causes from the Sheriffs' Court of Pleas.[19]

It will immediately be observed that this is not a straightforward first-instance jurisdiction but rather an 'appeal' jurisdiction from the Sheriffs' Court, if we use that phrase as meaning an alternative, but second, forum for disputes rather than in its modern sense. Since debt actions were clearly within the Sheriffs' jurisdiction they were potentially within the jurisdiction of the Court of Equity, should it be invoked.

Despite its clear, and separate, identification in the Charter, it seems that in practice the Court of Equity was undifferentiated from the plenary meetings of the City's Court of Mayoralty. This body, composed of the Mayor, Sheriffs, Aldermen and Recorder met twice-weekly and had extremely wide powers and responsibilities. It has been said that it 'at once fulfilled the functions of a modern town council and a court of corrective jurisdiction',[20] having absorbed the administrative authority of the twenty-four aldermen and the corrective jurisdiction of those who were Justices of the Peace, especially the Mayor who was Chief Justice. In addition to its administrative, legislative and corrective functions, the Court of Mayoralty seems to have had an extensive original civil jurisdiction at the beginning of the fifteenth century, including cases of debt,[21] but after apparently 'a good deal of modification ... in the course of the fifteenth century',[22] no records of debt cases within this jurisdiction have been found.

The Court of Equity had no separate times or venue for its hearings. Petitions addressed to it, and accepted by it, are recorded in the city's Mayors Court Books as being presented during meetings of the Court of Mayoralty. It seems, then, that its recognition in the Charter of 1663 merely identified formally a jurisdiction which was based on the inevitable residue of discretionary powers inherent in any body with the broad powers and political control enjoyed by the Norwich Magistracy when meeting as the Court of Mayoralty. Sachse points out that 'such a development would be quite natural, for the quota of Mayor and Justices demanded by the 1663 Charter was almost invariably on hand'.[23] It is perhaps important to mention here that the 'equity' it applied was not that of the developed Chancery but rather an informal jurisdiction giving effect to 'good conscience'.

Unfortunately, relatively little material has survived to give a picture of the Court of Equity, but the few sources available are remarkably helpful to our present inquiry. The Mayor's Court Books record the presentation of petitions and, occasionally, orders made relating to those matters, until 1737, when the flow of petitions seems to cease and the jurisdiction to fall into disuse. In addition to these sources, a small number of petitions have been discovered, dating from 1664–1740.[24] From these materials we can note the following points. As the Charter indicates, litigants in the Sheriffs' Court could invoke the equity jurisdiction when they felt that justice was being thwarted by the operation of the Common Law. In fact, from the petitions available, it seems that Guildhall defendants alone invoked the equitable jurisdiction. The petitions show two grounds for seeking the intervention of the Mayor's Court. The reason most frequently given is that the petitioner 'has not such proofs as the strict rules of common law require', but has evidence or a defence which would be cognisable outside that formalistic environment, especially where no jury were involved.[25] In addition, the Mayor's Court may have been invoked where the Sheriffs' Court was being used for harassment in an unmeritorious action.[26]

Procedure in the Court of Equity seems to have been direct. Cases were accepted at any stage before issue was reached in the Sheriffs' Court,[27] although one does see petitions being postponed behind more pressing civic business,[28] indicating the priority accorded to them. The petitioners' disputes are regularly delegated to individual Aldermen or to a small group, who are enjoined frequently to use their best efforts to secure agreement (as in matters in the Court of Mayoralty) and they seem to act frequently as umpires or arbitrators rather than traditional judges.[29] Hearings could proceed in the absence of the respondent (the Guildhall plaintiff) so long as s/he had been summoned to appear[30] but naturally if the petitioner were absent without cause the matter would be remitted to the Sheriffs.

Where no settlement was achieved, an order would be made in resolution of the case. Unfortunately few orders are recorded but from those in the Mayor's Court Books we can glimpse the court's capacity to respond to individual cases and develop an orthodoxy more flexible than that of the Common Law. Orders to pay with very short periods of grace are not uncommon. Of greater interest are a number of orders made between 1664 and 1692 requiring the sum due to be paid in specified instalments.[31] Perhaps one of the best (if least typical) examples of the court's ability to make an unusual, but presumably appropriate, order is seen in 'Rose's Case', where, having moved the dispute between William Griggs and Patrick Rose concerning Griggs' daughter[32] out of the Sheriffs' Court, the Court of Equity recorded that 'it does not find that there was cause for bringing this action in the Sheriffs' Court by the said Patrick and it is ordered that the said Patrick and his family do remove from this City to Ireland whence they came within the space of a month'.[33] Such an order reflects not only the judicial and equitable powers but also those wide administrative powers of the larger Court of Mayoralty which could be used if necessary.

Finally, there is one reference to an order for the imprisonment of a party for contempt of the Court, indicating the ultimate power of enforcement which supported the jurisdiction.[34]

Having considered the two jurisdictions, the Sheriffs' Court and the Court of Equity, the reasons for the city's dissatisfaction as expressed in the petition to the Commons become clearer. Any litigation on a debt, however small, began in the Sheriffs' Court: an expensive, slow and finally ineffective tribunal, oppressive in its way to debtor and creditor alike and 'just' to neither, when a small amount was in issue. It was possible to interrupt the case by invoking the Mayor's Court of Equity which seems to have been expeditious, flexible, direct and presumably cheap for petitioners. However, petitions were not amongst the highest priorities in the Mayor's Court; it seems that its purely original jurisdiction was not interpreted by 1700 to include actions of debt and that possibly the accepted causes for invoking its help had become quite closely defined and only applicable to defendants in the Sheriffs' Court by that date. These factors limited its potential as a solution to the problems experienced with small debts. An unusual petition of 1701/2 may be evidence of an attempt to use the Mayor's Court for small debts: Anthony Water(?) petitioned that the case brought against him in the Sheriffs' Court for one shilling be removed to the Court of Equity, and pointed out that the costs of the suit far outweighed the amount sought. However, there is not sufficient information to support any hypothesis here – the petition is merely to be noted. Even if it had been constitutionally possible to introduce such cases for its decision ab initio, such a move, however, would not have been seen as practicable or desirable.

As we have seen, the solution adopted was the establishment of a new court having exclusive jurisdiction over small-debt claims. The Act of 1701 followed very closely the Act of 1605 finally establishing the London Court,[35] and taking the Petition and Act together there can be no doubt as to the model for Norwich. As in London, the jurisdiction of the Norwich Requests included 'all matters of debt or action on the case upon any assumpsit for the recovery of any debt not amounting to 40sh.' excluding 'any debt for rent . . . or other real contracts or to any other debt that shall arise by reason of any cause concerning a testament or matrimony or anything . . . properly belonging to the ecclesiastical courts, albeit the same be under 40sh.', which might arise between inhabitants of the city.

The Act included stringent penalties to discourage suits at Westminster or elsewhere in cases where Requests could be used[35] and was construed as giving Requests an exclusive jurisdiction over the debts described above.[36]

The Judges of Requests, the Commissioners, were to be the Mayor, Aldermen and Common Council men who had taken the Requests Oath, by which they promised and swore 'that all such matters and causes as I shall order and determine by virtue of the Act I will order and determine with justice and equity according to the best of my knowledge and understanding'. Three Commissioners, including either the Mayor or an alderman constituted a quorum and the Act enjoined them, in reaching their decisions, to make such orders 'as they shall find best stand with equity and good conscience in a summary way, . . . not tying themselves to the exact forms of common law or other courts of justice'. They were to be judges both of fact and law and their orders were stated to be 'final and conclusive' and expressly not subject to any 'writ of error, certiorari or process of law or equity for the removal, stay or reversal of the same'. The court could imprison for contempt and a part of the city bridewell was made over for its use.[37]

Such a court was clearly designed for the expeditious despatch of disputes without undue expense. Its success or failure, however, surely depended on the Commissioners' understanding of 'equity and good conscience'. Unfortunately, the records of the Norwich Court of Requests have not come to light.[38] However, some of the post-1701 petitions to the Mayor's Court which have been found do give some indication of litigants' confidence in the new Court. The four relevant petitions fall into two pairs. The first pair indicate the close similarity (identity?) in the procedures of Requests and the Court of Equity as perceived by the petitioners (or their advisers). In one[39] the petitioner complains of a vexatious suit in the Sheriffs' Court brought against him for 39 shillings and moneys lent and claims that he 'never borrowed or received any money from the plaintiff nor owed him one penny . . . as in a court of equity or request will appear', and continues with the familiar phrase that he 'has not such proof as the strict rules of law require but is wholly (excusable?) in a court of equity or request'. The other of this pair[40] is a petition seeking the removal of a case from the Sheriffs' Court because the petitioner is in no way indebted but 'cannot be relieved but before your worships in your Court of Equity or in a Court of Conscience'.

The second pair[41] show the jurisdictional relationship which developed as the Court of Requests took its place amongst the city courts. Both petitioners complain that the action against them in the Sheriffs' Court should properly have been brought in the Court of Requests. (Despite the Act, harassment seems to have continued.) The points of particular interest, however, are firstly that this abuse of Requests' jurisdiction is accepted as a ground for equitable intervention, and secondly that the remedy sought from and granted by the Mayor's Court is to transfer the dispute to the *equitable* jurisdiction, not, directly or indirectly, to the Requests.

It seems, therefore, that the practice of the older court informed the new court very substantially. Both Equity and Requests were courts of conscience. Their personnel overlapped considerably (see Figure 2 below), all accepting the judicial functions along with the achievement of other civic responsibilities. Evans has calculated that 'except for a handful of veterans, a complete turnover of membership of the Council occurred every fifteen years'.[42] Even a fifteen-year cycle would offer ample stability for office holders to be well trained in the traditions of the civic courts and for the practices of the one Court to thereby inform the other, where appropriate, as the actors moved from role to role. If we need evidence of this, the litigants' perceptions would seem to substantiate it. It is also particularly interesting to see the Court of Equity ordering the payment of debts in instalments before 1701, as this form of remedy has traditionally been acclaimed as an innovation of the Courts of Requests.[43] Clearly the older court had demonstrated, and developed, that same 'robust common sense' with which Harding has characterised Requests.[44]

FIGURE 2

Personnel of the City Courts 1701

COURT	Councilmen	Sheriffs	Mayor	Aldermen	JP's
Guildhall		✓			
Equity		✓	✓	✓	✓
Requests	✓		✓	✓	✓
Sessions			✓		✓

Holdsworth, writing of the local courts of a much earlier period, commented that

> If equity acts in personam and if equitable interference is grounded upon a consideration of the circumstances of the individual case, these courts, the members of which were intimately known to one another, were well fitted to exercise it. Technical difficulties did not stop them from applying that which seems to be the obvious remedy in any given case.[45]

In Norwich the city fathers seem to have built on their local equitable traditions in establishing the Court of Requests. Similarities existed between the constitutions of Norwich and the City of London and it is perhaps not surprising to see London used as a model in this instance. However, it was a model which could clearly be chosen with confidence.

Plucknett comments that the local Courts of Requests 'are interesting in many ways, notably because they embodied several legal heresies which did not become orthodox until a century or more later'.[46] In fact it may be the case that those heresies were themselves the products of traditional but local orthodoxies, which achieved a more widespread recognition as Courts of Requests proliferated. In their development, therefore, perhaps we are really seeing the slow incorporation of one orthodoxy into another?

NOTES

1. Post, p. 130
2. By 1845, 106 Acts for the establishment of Courts of Requests were in force (see schedules A and B, 9 & 10 Vict. c 95: An Act for the more easy Recovery of Small Debts and Demands in England). Of these, only nine date from before 1760, 46 more date from the reign of George III, one from George IV, 12 from William IV and 39 from the years 1837–1845. This distribution may emphasise the significance of the earlier Requests as models for the later, showing that the London model could function efficiently and successfully elsewhere.
3. The two major studies are W.H.D. Winder, 'The Courts of Request' 52 (1936) *LQR* p. 369, a most useful survey and H.W. Arthurs, post, p. 130.
4. No doubt reflecting to some extent the paucity of material.
5. Winder, op.cit., note 2 seems to imply some possible influence. For a concise discussion of such schemes see B. Shapiro, 'Law Reform in 17th Century England', *American Journal of Legal History* 19 (1975), p. 280.
6. By private Act of Parliament 12 and 13 Will 3 c7. This was the third occasion the matter had been mooted. In 1689 a Bill had passed the Commons but was rejected by the Lords: I have not yet been able to find any information about this incident. Sir W. Holdsworth in *A History of English Law*, London 1969, Vol. 1 pp. 189–90, suggests possible causes of opposition in the light of experience elsewhere.

   In 1699 the question of a Bill was raised in the City's Court of Mayoralty but it was decided not to proceed towards a Bill at that time: Norfolk and Norwich Record Office, Mayor's Court Book 20 Dec. 1969 (hereafter NNRO, MCB).

7. Courts had already been established for Bristol and Gloucester (jointly) and for Newcastle-upon-Tyne in 1689.
8. See the City's petition, p. 98 infra, and note 12.
9. The material summarised here has come to light in the course of a broader study of the Norwich Court of Requests and debt jurisdiction in East Anglia which is still in train.
10. See Penelope Corfield, 'A provincial capital in the late seventeenth century: The case of Norwich', in Peter Clark and Paul Slack, *Crisis and Order in English Towns, 1500–1700: Essays in urban history*, London, 1972, p. 263.
11. See Penelope Corfield, 'The Social and Economic History of Norwich 1650–1850: A Study in Urban Growth', unpublished Ph.D. Thesis, University of London, 1976 pp. 207–8. Dr. Corfield points out that, although poor, the large artisan population 'could earn a modest living in normal times that was above the level of mere subsistence'.
12. XIII H.C.J. 440, 27 March 1701.
13. See the analysis of office holders in John T. Evans, *17th Century Norwich Politics, Religion and Government 1620–1690*, Oxford, 1979, p. 32 Table 6.
14. Being subjected to 'higher parish charges' for the maintenance of their debtors in prison must have added insult to injury!
15. The seminal work on the civic institutions of Norwich is W. Hudson and J.C. Tingey, *The Records of the City of Norwich*, Norwich, 1906–10. Unaccountably, they do not mention the Court of Requests. For details of the other civic jurisdictions, see 'Introduction', Vol. I.
16. Hudson and Tingey op.cit., note 16 p. cxxix, quoting 'the succinct description ... as given by a nameless writer at about the close of the seventeenth century'.
17. This continued after 1701. e.g. the petitions of Wills and Tilyard infra.
18. Hudson in op.cit., note 16 p. 49 suggests the possible origins of the equitable jurisdiction in rights given to the Mayor to correct and fix the damages of any defaults or oppressions committed by the Sheriffs in 1404.
19. Hudson and Tingey op.cit., note 16, p. 49.
20. W.L. Sachse, *Minutes of the Norwich Court of Mayoralty 1630–1631*, Norwich 1943. This work gives the most complete description of the Courts' jurisdiction and practice: pp. 11–58.
21. Hudson and Tingey, op.cit., note 16 p. 101, quote the Composition of 1415, authorising the Mayor to hear, inter alia, 'pleas of debt, letters of payments and all other contracts between merchant and merchant or anyone beyond the sea'.
22. Hudson and Tingey, op.cit., note 16, p. cxxix.
23. Sachse, op.cit., note 21, p. 15. The development seems reminiscent of the medieval conciliar powers and jurisdictions.
24. NNRO case 12 Shelf e.
25. The petitions dating from 1711–1720 seem to adopt this as a standard form.
26. See for example, 'Rose's Case' infra.
27. NNRO MCB 3 Dec. 1687.
28. NNRO MCB 30 May 1674.
29. One of the best examples of the procedure is the entry at MCB Apr. 1665:

    > The difference between Henry Carver and Tho. Collyer is ordered to be called into this Court and process be issued into the Sheriffs' Court to stay proceedings in the action between them.
    >
    > The said difference was afterward referred by them to Mr Hyne(?) and Ald. Thacker who are to examine witnesses and compose the difference if they can. In the interim any further proceedings in the Sheriffs' Court are to be stayed.

    On several occasions petitioners' disputes were delegated to the determination of the Aldermen of a particular ward, as occurred with the Court's original jurisdiction.

30. NNRO MCB 15 April 1674.
31. Entries in appropriate MCB for 27 April 1664; 16 May 1664; 15 June 1672; 29 Jan. 1672; 2 Aug. 1673; 30 June 1680; 25 May 1692.
32. An extant petition, NNRO Case 12 Shelf e may relate to this same dispute. If so, it

revolved around the non-payment of an apprenticeship premium.

33. MCB 14 Mar. 1687.
34. MCB 7 Sept. 1672.
35. 5 Jac. I c. 15 repealing and replacing 1 Jac. I c. 14.
36. A copy of the Act itself is kept in NNRO.
37. NNRO MCB 21 Jan. 1701.
38. The Act required the Court to keep a record of its orders in a book, but the books seem lost.
39. Petition of Tovell, 1711. NNRO Case 12, Shelf e.
40. Petition of Dorlobe, 1717 NNRO Case 12 Shelf e.
41. Petitions of Wills, 1716; Tilyard 1717 NNRO Case 12 Shelf e.
42. Evans, op.cit., note 13, p. 47. Evans also points out (p. 51) the intermingling of officers' experience: 'some of the councilmen would later become magistrates, some of the councilmen had already been Sheriffs, and almost all the aldermen and mayors had once been councilmen'.
43. Winder, op.cit., note 3, p. 372 writes '[the payment of debts by installments] later became common to all the Courts of Requests and came to be regarded as one of their characteristic features. They appear to be the first courts to have introduced it'. In fact, they seem to be adopting an already established remedy from local courts.
44. A. Harding, *A Social History of English Law*, Harmondsworth, 1966, p. 316.
45. Holdsworth, op.cit., note 6, Vol. I, p. 384.
46. T.F.T. Plucknett, *A Concise History of the Common Law*, London, 1956, p. 207.

Brougham as a Barrister: Courtroom Dilemmas of a Notorious Radical

T.H. FORD

Henry Brougham is just the practitioner legal historians need to know more about, as Wilfred Prest recently indicated,[1] especially since the Whig barrister does not fit very well into the generalisations that Daniel Duman made about the English Bar during the Georgian era.[2] Brougham was the scion of a North Country gentry family. Brougham Hall, the family residence near Penrith, Westmorland, provided a modest income. Young Henry was given the education befitting the grandnephew of Edinburgh's most celebrated Provost, Dr Robertson, attending Edinburgh High School, and then the University. Once he graduated in 1796, he started to come out of his apolitical cocoon. While he was studying for the Bar examinations in Scots and Roman law, he joined the Speculative Society, the pillar of Edinburgh life. Thanks to his initiative, the Society started discussing political questions. When Alexander Maconochie, the conservative Professor of Public Law at the University, tried to occupy his retirement by having a colleague take down the Society's debates for reactionary purposes, Brougham moved successfully a motion that the professor had not only insulted the Society's honour, but also had assumed a function inconsistent with continued membership. The rule against political debate was even rescinded. Tory members were so alarmed by developments that they either resigned or stopped attending sessions.

While Brougham followed up these victories over the Tories by founding the Academy of Physics, Literary Society, Chemical Society, and Friday Club in quick succession, they really did not help when he was called to the Bar in 1800. As usual, when things were going badly for Brougham, he was the last to learn, as we see when he tried to explain to James Loch, his closest friend, that Loch had been premature in leaving the Scottish circuit for Lincoln's Inn:

> All is practice and seeing and knowing ye court. I never go there that I don't wish you were by me that I might advise you earnestly to consider and re-consider your London plan. For one thing, I am convinced that this bar is a better field than is generally thought.[3]

Brougham was soon reduced to wasting his eloquence, energy, and discomposing qualities for court-appointed clients before conservative judges like Lord Eskgrove, who preferred counsel who would let him determine the result. For judges who had spent the past decade in trying to expand the doctrine of constructive treason Brougham had nothing but contempt, challenging them on everything from the sex of stolen sheep to what constituted half boots. 'The Law', he complained to Loch, 'is more and more horrid every day – and the Parlt. house is still more odious than the study part of the Law. Nothing but absolute necessity can keep me at it – I mean the total want of a substitute for it'.[4] Brougham could only make the most humble ends meet by a most modest allowance from Henry Sr, and a small salary as Civil Law Examinator at the University's Faculty of Laws.

While the founding of *The Edinburgh Review*, for which Brougham was the leading writer, offered a long-term solution, it had no money for the short-term solution, and he knew it. Consequently, he started preparing for what so many North Country and Scottish barristers had done before him: moving to London. About the prospect, he wrote to Loch:

> The English Bar is in a very great degree tedious, and, to say the least of it, somewhat uncertain: I look forward with no small horror to five years' dull, unvaried drudgery, which must be undergone to obtain the privilege of drudging still harder, among a set of disagreeable people of brutal manners and confined talents.[5]

While he waited in vain for a diplomatic post, he continued to hope that more charitable solicitors would find him some more clients in Scotland, but without much success. Brougham, it seems, was so desperate to avoid a career at the English Bar that he accepted some of Lord Melville's secret service money to see if Emperor Napoleon could be assassinated in return for a suitable position.

When Brougham's mission was finished, he settled down in London, only to see Melville impeached, and Pitt die. Fox's Ministry of All Talents merely compounded Brougham's difficulties by increasing his influence without commensurate position. While he was slated for several posts, he never received one, especially because he was without a seat in the Commons. All he could show for his labours was the statute which made Englishmen subject to fine and forfeiture for engaging in the slave trade and arguing the Whig case at the Bar of the House against the subsequent Ministry's Orders in Council. The Tory Ministry not only rejected his argument but also Brougham's personal appeal to the Benchers of Lincoln's Inn to cut short his residence requirement so that he could be called to the Bar early. He had registered at the Inn during November 1803. On 30 June 1808, he petitioned for special treatment, explaining that he had 'performed all his exercises, attained the age of 21 years, and had conformed himself in every respect to the Rules of this Society, except as to his full standing of five years'.[6] Brougham had persuaded his friend, Loch, to assist his appeal, having him ask his uncle, the East India Company's counsel, to support the motion. 'I fancy', Brougham wrote with customary optimism, 'a special motion by your Uncle will be requisite'.[7] Brougham had figured without the Crown's opposition. The Law Officers showed up to make sure that the Whig troublemaker did not receive any special dispensations. Consequently Brougham had to wait until 22 November to be called to the Bar.

Once free of Lincoln's Inn, Brougham set up practice at 9 King's Bench Walk, in Southwark, near to the infamous Marshalsea and King's Bench prisons. Nearby, on Horsemonger Lane, now Union Street, stood the Surrey County Gaol and the County Sessions Hall where the assizes were held. With few briefs, Brougham satisfied himself by writing articles for *The Morning Chronicle* and the *Review*, and trying to persuade the Duke of Bedford to give him a seat in Parliament. No solicitor in the Metropolis or on the Northern Circuit was willing to give him briefs because of his radical reputation. Brougham, consequently, devoted himself to promoting such radical change that the Whigs were forced to find a seat at Camelford, a pocket-borough in distant Cornwall. Brougham took his place in the Commons on 5 February 1810, and twelve days later Henry Sr died, easing young Henry's financial burdens somewhat. The 1810 Session was an all-consuming avocation for the long frustrated barrister.

Brougham's first big case came just after the opening of the 1811 Session, the defence of the Hunts against a charge of seditious libel. During the previous summer there had been serious rioting among the military because their salaries were in arrears, and the Ministry, fearing military insubordination because of its disastrous Walcheren expedition, punished it with severe flogging. To stifle criticism of the punishment the Attorney General filed an *ex-officio* information for libel against William Cobbett for what he said in the *Courier* about similar treatment of rioting at Ely the year before. Cobbett had been particularly upset by the role of the German Legion in suppressing the rioting and inflicting punishment. Cobbett's article was especially directed towards the long-suffering troops. When the case was heard by the King's Bench Cobbett would not stoop to having a barrister represent him, and he got into repeated arguments with Lord Chief Justice Ellenborough about what was relevant to his defence. Cobbett was particularly frustrated in trying to show that during Parliament's consideration of the expedition up the Scheldt, MPs had said similar things about suffering soldiers. When Cobbett refused to throw himself on the court's mercy, as his printer and publisher had Attorney General Sir Vicary Gibbs treated his defence as a new offence 'for he had only made it the occasion for uttering new slanders against innocent and undefended persons'.[8] Ellenborough held that Cobbett had bad intentions in writing the article, and had been, indeed, guilty of seditious libel. The jury agreed, and Cobbett was sentenced to two years' imprisonment.

Brougham, if he did not actually attend the trial, read all about it in *The Times*. More important, to make up for the lack of solicitors' support, he started advertising his abilities in the *Review*. In reviewing Thomas Erskine's speeches as a barrister, Brougham showed that he was ideally suited to handle difficult cases, especially *ex-officio* informations for libel, like Joseph Stockdale's one during the impeachment of Warren Hastings. Of Erskine's defence of the printer Brougham wrote:

> for the solid and important purpose of interesting his hearers in the situation of Mr Hastings, and of his defender, the author of the pamphlet, – of leading the mind to view the prisoner as an oppressed man, overwhelmed by the weight of parliamentary resentment, and ready to be crushed, in the face of the country, by the very forms and solemnities of his trial ...[9]

Erskine triumphed over the leading Whig politicians, Stockdale's prosecutors, because he 'built on the matchless skill with which he could subdue the genius of the first rate orator to the uses of the most consummate advocate of the age'.[10] Erskine was the best instructor of the roles of juries, jurists, and judges in the courtroom.

The Attorney General, in prosecuting the Hunts, tried the case as a matter of course. Cobbett had originated the libel, according to Gibbs, and the *Examiner* had merely repeated it. Gibbs quoted from the article, contrasting the way the French and English treated refractory troops, as if the mere mention of Emperor Napoleon in a favourable way would be sufficient to secure conviction by the Westminster special jury. Brougham denied that the disputes were identical. The Hunts had not merely reprinted Cobbett's article, but had included John Scott's new research on the controversial subject. His article had first appeared in John Drakard's *Stamford News*, and had been printed in an amended version in the *Examiner*, Brougham explained. He not only quoted from qualified British professionals against the barbaric practice but also had them in court to testify. Englishmen, Brougham reminded the jury, had the right to speak and write about controversial subjects like peace, expeditions, and taxes, not to forget the abolition of the slave trade. 'Is it rebellious', he asked, stealing a page from Cobbett's defence for Ellenborough's benefit, 'to speak one's sentiments of the expeditions sent from this country?'[11] The barrister reduced the judge to telling the jury that the article was a seditious libel, but the Westminster jurors thought otherwise, declaring the Hunts innocent after little more than an hour's deliberation.

The acquittal did Brougham's legal career immense good. In fact, his growing list of clients must have reminded the Benchers of Lincoln's Inn how futile it was to try to restrain the sometime leader-writer for *The Morning Chronicle*. Before he was called to the Bar, they had 'passed a resolution, by which any person convicted of having ever written for the newspapers for hire, should be excluded from their body'.[12] Brougham responded to its 1810 repeal by turning his reportorial interests to *The Times*, and the much more secretive Barnes, the rapidly progressing assistant editor who had found the barriers to a legal career too much.

Brougham's clients had no such options. They needed him in the courtroom, and the Crown did everything it could to make his task more difficult. Gibbs instituted an *ex-officio* information for libel against John Drakard of the *Stamford News*, publisher of the parent article. 'Can that be criminal in Lincolnshire', Brougham asked, overlooking the fact that the *Examiner* piece was an abridgement of the Stamford one, 'which is innocent in Westminster?'[13] He had apparently decided that it was easier to try to overawe the jury than convince it that the more controversial article still did not constitute seditious libel. The Attorney General noted the difference between the two articles, and Baron Wood, the assize judge, told the jury that it was not bound by the Westminster decision. The packed jury found Drakard guilty, and sentenced him to eighteen months in prison and a £200 fine.

Brougham was no more successful in protecting a group of Whig activists who had libelled Canterbury's Mayor, Powlet, a case which he felt particularly responsible for. When Brougham had been directing the Whig campaign from Ryder Street during the 1807 election, he wrote to William Allen:

> Different people should at their spare hours be reading Shakespeare and Swift, with a view to selecting passages suitable to the time, as, descriptions of base courtiers, particular characters of bad ministers, hits at bishops (if safe) etc. These passages may be published in a kind of series, as quotations communicated by Jenksberry, Castlerogue, etc., on whomever they apply to.[14]

When Whigs in Canterbury translated the satires of Juvenal most liberally at Tory expense, the Attorney General filed an *ex-officio* information against them for libel. To stay conviction Brougham argued hilariously:

> But, my lords, there are other persons who fancy themselves alluded to in this publication (*The Whim*, nos. 6 & 7), and who do

> not like to go before a Grand Jury and swear that the words *jackdaw* and *cur* mean them: these parties keep in the background, and urge Mr Powlet on, puff him up, with a grand idea that his official dignity is attacked, and so completely get the better of his good-nature.[15]

The poem, Brougham reminded the King's Bench, referred to a man of fashion, and this could not mean the mayor, a former auctioneer. After a bitter exchange between Brougham and the Attorney General about what the parties would swear to, the court made the rule absolute.

Just when it seemed that Brougham was getting the reputation as a defender of hopeless libel actions, his career got another boost. In the February 1812 issue of the *Review* he reviewed some more of Erskine's speeches as counsel for his own advancement. This volume concerned Erskine's most difficult cases, like that of Hadfield who tried to assassinate George III, and the State Trials of 1794. About the assassin's insanity, Erskine said that 'such persons often reason with a subtlety which puts in the shade the ordinary conceptions of mankind'.[16] Because of Erskine's carefully marshalling the evidence on behalf of the accused, cautioning against a rash judgement to satisfy popular indignation, Lord Kenyon, the presiding judge, came round to support the defence's plea. Erskine's handling of the State Trials, Brougham added, showed the complete defence lawyer. About his defence of the Cathell libel action, Brougham wrote:

> The proper degree of punishment is not meted out to guilt. Offences totally different in kind are called by one appellation, and visited with the same penalty; and juries are obliged to violate their oaths, in order to acquit, that they may avoid a greater evil, the undue conviction, and consequent punishment, of the person accused.[17]

It was because of Erskine's courageous, independent defence of society's most unsavoury characters that Brougham singled out his activities for recognition.

As with the first review of Erskine's efforts, it immediately paid off in Brougham's practice. In the British assault on the Ile de France, an island off Africa, many British prisoners of war, some of whom had become turncoats to the French colours, were captured. Under the terms of surrender, the turncoats were given the option of either returning to France with the other prisoners, or to Britain. Many chose Britain. In due course, they were brought up the Thames, and imprisoned to await trial for high treason before a special commission, headed by the Chief Baron, Sir Archibald Macdonald. 'As attorney-general he prosecuted Stockdale for a libel in the House of Commons, and Paine for the seditious libels contained in his *Rights of Man*.'[18] Being without funds, and ignorant of how to go about making a defence, the prisoners were in desperate straits. Thanks probably to Brougham's revelations in the Commons about the droits of the Admiralty, and what they permitted the Crown to do, they appealed to its Lords for assistance, but were refused. The Home Secretary was also unresponsive to their plight. Finally the court was told that the Crown had made some special provisions for them to make their defence. It agreed to provide expenses for defence witnesses coming to court, and they were then asked who they wanted to defend them. They voted for Brougham to defend them, and James Harmer to be their solicitor.[19] Brougham's literary and parliamentary efforts, reported in papers like *The Times* and seen by the prisoners awaiting trial, seem to have landed him his biggest case yet.

Brougham immediately took charge in Erskine-like fashion. He moved for the postponement of the trials, to allow xenophobic sentiments to cool, calling for Lieutenant Fitzsimmons to come from Rio. The court said such delay could only be based upon affidavits, so Brougham moved successfully for time to prepare them. A week later, when the Crown opened its first prosecution, Brougham presented an affidavit from prisoner Cundell, calling for Captain Willoughby to come from Charing Cross, and give evidence 'that he was forced at the peril of his life to enter the service of the French at the Isle of France, and that one of his own crew was shot for refusing'.[20] When it was denied because it was irrelevant, Joseph Wath testified that Cundell had joined the French colours, and carried French arms. Under cross-examination, Brougham showed that Wath had too, and that he had turned state's evidence to save his own skin. On re-examination, Gibbs established that the prisoner had only switched sides for money, 'blood money', to wean his comrades away from British allegiance; while other witnesses were called to show that Cundell had no defence, his repudiation of Britain had been caused by fears about his own life. Brougham, in summing up the case for the jury, stated that 'the prisoner and eleven others, now indicted with him had used the first moment they were allowed a free option, and preferred surrendering themselves to the British troops. After the capture of the island, he had given himself up voluntarily, as soon as he was able'.[21] An excerpt from the *London Gazette Extraordinary* was introduced by him to show the surrender terms regarding British turncoats. While Captain Willoughby had not been able to present evidence, the court learned that he also did not want to because of how the experience had affected his health. The jury convicted Cundell of high treason, but recommended mercy because of how he had acted under the terms of the surrender.

In the subsequent cases, Brougham hammered away at the same basic facts. Prisoners and witnesses against them alike had joined the French service under difficult circumstances because of financial and personal considerations. After six more prisoners had been convicted, one where the jury 'strongly recommended mercy, on account of his having manifested much penitence at his conduct, and behaving humanely to his shipmates who were prisoners',[22] Gibbs explained dropping prosecution of the other prisoners:

> he had most studiously concealed to that moment, from his Learned Friends who conducted the defence of the prisoners, the course he intended now to pursue, lest it should be imagined that he worked under any doubt of his ability to substantiate the charges which it was his duty to bring forward, or any intimation of a lenient intention.[23]

He then broke down into tears, and the court had to go into recess so that the Attorney General could regain his composure. As in the State Trials of 1794, Gibbs realised the difficulty of applying the law to the facts in these cases. Brougham complimented Gibbs for his decision, and called upon the court to commute their sentences, stating that it 'would to the end of their lives bind them for the liveliest gratitude for the mercy they should experience from a generous country, which thus, oblivious of their past errors, opened its arms to receive them'.[24] Macdonald, while no friend of the doctrine of constructive treason, thought that Gibbs had been influenced too much by the defence in the prosecution of these cases, and he sentenced those convicted to the traitor's death. While the seven were executed, Brougham had helped the five others, and the nearly fifty others whose cases had not yet been determined, escape a similar fate.

This experience helped Brougham gain the most important brief of his life, just when Parliament was dissolved the following summer, and he was without a seat to contest. No sooner had the Government passed the Peace Preservation Bill, an alarmist piece of legislation against which Brougham spoke most effectively, than Manchester's Deputy Constable of Police, Joseph Nadin, enforced it most corruptly against some radicals. Nadin's organisation of local authorities for profitable police extended throughout Lancashire and Yorkshire. To make a meeting for political redress, culminating in a petition to the Prince Regent and Parliament, look like another Luddite conspiracy, the followers of John Buckley, the second Manchester Secret Committee, were arrested, and charged 'for felony of administering or being present at the administration of the illegal oath to Samuel Fleming'.[25] He was just the kind of spy, the 'respectable source' of alarmist magistrates, that Brougham had complained most bitterly about when the anti-Luddite measures were going through Parliament. Brougham had apparently gone to France for Lord Harrowby as a spy when he first came to London to see if Napoleon's security could be penetrated for his assassination, and he hated *agents provocateurs* usurping the title. With these credentials, it was hardly surprising that Major Cartwright should have sought Brougham's services in defending the prisoners, 'Manchester's 38'. Having nothing to lose in the case, he went all out to get the best counsel to assist him, hiring James Scarlett and John Williams, both future Barons of the Exchequer. Scarlett had a way with judges, Brougham with juries, and Williams with witnesses.

The Whig barristers tore the Crown's case apart. Fleming was exposed as a Nadin spy so interested in simply convicting the accused for financial reward that his testimony was totally rejected.[26] For example, to try to implicate John Knight, Fleming was schooled by Nadin to point him out at the appropriate time, but Knight refused to cooperate, situating himself elsewhere. Fleming, consequently, when the time came, pointed out the turnkey who was sitting where Knight should have been. The *agent provocateur* pointed out another accused, William Washington, as an oath-taker when he had an alibi for being elsewhere. This was all the more extraordinary when other oath-takers, if Fleming was telling the truth, were allowed to escape by testifying against their fellows. The prosecution's only written evidence was the petitions which, according to the defence, were being prepared for constituted authorities. Once Baron Wood said that he believed the accused, the jury had little difficulty in acquitting them, 'and the "thirty-eight bundles of Blue", as Mr Lloyd of Stockport facetiously called them, were, to the deep and unconcealed regret of the Manchester authorities, allowed to return home instead of being transported across the seas'.[27]

Brougham started getting Scottish appeals, especially to the House of Lords, and cases in the Common Law Courts, but because of the quality of his clients, and his political reputation, he did not fare well. Brougham was not dismayed by these defeats, however, despite the fact that the Hunts had fallen into new trouble with the Crown. When the *Morning Post* published a eulogy of the Prince Regent, the *Examiner* described the future King thus:

> a violator of his word, a libertine over head and ears in debt and disgrace, a despiser of domestic ties, the companion of gamblers and demireps, a man who just closed half a century without a single claim on the gratitude of his country, or the respect of posterity.[28]

The Attorney General apparently held back the prosecution of this easy case to make the most of the libel, and Brougham had a hopeless task when it finally came forward in December 1812. Garrow, the Solicitor General, not only had the libel read, as in the Drakard case, but also tried to prejudice the jury against the defence by claiming that Brougham had attempted to justify such practice in a *Review* article on the rights and duties of the people. Brougham contended that the writer of the offending article had no political purpose; he only wanted to expose the absurdity of the *Post's* rhymes, an effort which drew Ellenborough's strongest censure. Brougham was not intimidated, however, explaining that the press should print what people thought, an idea which the Lord Chief Justice thought, if put into practice, would be the end of law.[29] The jury agreed, convicting the Hunts of libel, and they were later sentenced to two years' imprisonment.

In the face of growing government repression, which had seen even the imprisonment of Daniel Lovell, proprietor of the *Statesman*, convicted of libelling the transport service commissioners despite Brougham's efforts before the King's Bench,[30] he decided that a more political approach was necessary for gaining justice in the courts. The Crown, in prosecuting such marginal newspapers, had overplayed its hand, alienating *The Times* in the process. Thanks to Barnes, the paper was no longer willing to witness silently the growing repression, as it had during the trial of 'Manchester's 38'. Brougham's renewed relation with *The Times* immediately paid off at York where a special commission was hearing the results of Nadin's provocative police work. Because of the activities by Bow-street officers, McDonald and Gosling, on special assignment against Luddites in the Huddersfield area, and the most expeditious prosecution of flagrant crimes, the Crown hoped to clear the calendar of 59 defendants in most chilling fashion. Brougham upset the plan by getting John Schofield declared innocent of the attempted murder of John Hinchcliffe. During cross-examination of Hinchcliffe Brougham made him look like another of Nadin's agents who were willing to say anything to convict Luddites. While Schofield had inquired if Hinchcliffe was interested in joining them, he had an alibi for being elsewhere when the murder was attempted.[31] After the successful prosecution of the notorious cases for face-saving purposes – and even here the Crown did not get all the convictions it wanted – it decided that prudence was the better course of action against the other 'ringleaders' of the Luddites, Crown prosecutor James Parke explaining:

> My Learned Friends and myself have examined the different causes which have not been presented to you; and, considering that many of these people have acted under the influence of other persons, we have, in the exercise of the discretion confided to us by the Crown, declined, at present, to present any other bills before you; and I hope this lenity will produce its proper effects, and that the persons on whom it is exercised will prove themselves, by their future good conduct, deserving of it.[32]

Thanks to Brougham's defence, the Crown's agents and spies had only managed to send notorious troublemakers to the gallows, a fact taken into account by the presiding judge, Justice Le Blanc, when the time came to sentence the Hunts.

Brougham's forthright defence of individual rights soon had an institutional impact upon the Commons. Thomas Creevey, continuing his fight with Liverpool for refusing his parliamentary candidacy, denounced in a speech in the House the Ministry's selection for its Inspector General of Taxes as a corrupt informer, and chose to have his remarks reprinted in the *Liverpool Mercury*. The Crown decided to institute an *ex-officio* information for libel against him, contending that the published remarks were not protected by parliamentary privilege. Brougham made a most general defence of a Member's privileges.[33] When the assize judge, Le Blanc, disagreed, and the jury concurred, finding Creevey guilty, Brougham tried to enter a bill of exceptions to limit the verdict. When he was informed that it was too late for such a motion, he called for a new trial. The proceedings of Parliament, like any court, were absolutely privileged, he argued, and the Member and his counsel risked imprisonment if they abused its privileges.[34] When Ellenborough replied that an MP could not say what he wanted to suit his constituents, Creevey's counsel corrected him. 'Mr. Brougham said that his argument was that he might publish whatever he was justified in speaking in his place in the House.'[35] The King's Bench rejected it, denying Creevey a new trial. When the time came for sentencing Creevey, Brougham had him read an affidavit, threatening constitutional conflict between the Courts and Parliament if he were sent to prison. He also had a delegation of Members in attendance to give substance to the threat.[36] Under the circumstances, the court decided that prudence was the better part of valour, fining Creevey a hundred pounds. Thanks to Brougham's persistence, an MP's right to speak freely, and an independent reporting of his remarks without fear of imprisonment, had been made more secure.

Brougham followed this up with a victory for a Member's independence outside of Parliament. In the previous General Election Burdett and Lord Cochrane had won the Westminster seats, though the former had not taken part in the campaign because of illness. The election was associated with the usual activities of the hustings. When it was over, officials sued the successful candidates for their costs, and they won a suit for them in the Exchequer. Attorney General Garrow treated High Bailiff Morris's claim against Sir Francis in the King's Bench as a matter of course: 'it was rather whimsical that, in Westminster-hall, in the city of Westminster, he should have to ask, who were the Members for Westminster? for that was literally the question which his Lordship and the Jury had to try'.[37] The prosecution used officials, especially the plaintiff's deputy, to establish the elementary facts, calling for a verdict for Morris.

Brougham answered that Burdett was not responsible for such expenditure, forcing Morris's deputy to admit under cross-examination that he had not seen the candidate throughout the campaign. The recovery action should be non-suited, Brougham concluded. The prosecution responded by getting the witness to testify further, testimony which only undermined further its action. The witness said that he had waited on the election committee, supplying the near-permanent organisation with tickets for Sir Francis's friends, evidence which only disturbed Ellenborough. When Garrow tried to introduce new witnesses Brougham objected, stating that the prosecution had closed its case. The Lord Chief Justice agreed, non-suiting the action, but giving Morris the right to open a new suit. Garrow, in moving for a new trial, repeated his argument in a most mechanical way, reiterating what he had been able to achieve before the Lord Chief Baron. Ellenborough was still unconvinced, explaining that 'a candidate *in invitum* afterwards taking his seat, was no proof that he recognised the precedent proceedings'.[38] An MP would no longer be burdened with the expenditures of an irresponsible election committee.

In November 1814 occurred Brougham's famous 'dressing-down' of Ellenborough for confusing counsel with client in a case of blasphemous libel. While Chester New in his biography of Brougham has contended that newspapers did not care to give the incident a full account,[39] *The Times* in fact gave the case full, front-page coverage. George Houston had been the object of a criminal information for libelling Christianity and established religion in a pamphlet, and he had not defended the action. At the time of sentencing, Brougham tried to have it mitigated by entering affidavits, and the Lord Chief Justice wanted to know how the author of 'Ecce Homo' had sworn to them. 'How could he be, upon the *New Testament*?',[40] the Lord Chief Justice asked testily. When Brougham tried to explain that a non-Christian could make an affidavit, Ellenborough retorted: 'Are you prepared to suggest, Sir, what belief the defendant has, by which he may be sworn?'[41] Brougham responded by stating that he was only doing his job. 'I desire that your Lordship will not mix me up with those whose causes it is my duty as an advocate to plead'.[42] Brougham got so worked up that he was soon alleging that Houston had been made a scapegoat in the action. When Attorney General Garrow tried to explain, Brougham added:

> this I will say from my own observation of these canting times, that there are many better Christians as there are truer men, than those who go bawling out their faith in high places; that we may be sincere, though quiet – devout, though charitable – nay, that a man may look forward to benefit by his piety in the way of revision, though he has not the talent of turning it to present account by making godliness a great gain.[43]

While Brougham's sarcastic invective, in response to Ellenborough's bullying, did not do Houston much good, it, coupled with his defence of Sir Henry Mildmay, did help other clients. During the past half-year, Mildmay had been having a most scandalous affair with his deceased wife's sister, the Countess of Rosebery. The case certainly had its shocking moments, particularly when the special jury learned that the Countess, who had been taken to Dalmeny Park in Scotland to get her away from Mildmay, excused herself nightly after dinner to join her disguised lover in the bedroom. The adultery was so well established that Mildmay did not even contest it in the ecclesiastical courts. He merely had Brougham represent him in Lord Rosebery's suit for damages at the Middlesex Sheriff's Office before Judge Joseph Burchall. The Attorney General went wild, however, in trying to make the case for £30,000 damages, and Brougham rose splendidly to the challenge. Garrow characterised Mildmay's most natural act of consolation with the woman who reminded him most of his deceased wife, and against whom no one had restrained him, as 'one of multiplied incest'.[44] Brougham denounced Garrow's total misrepresentation of what had happened, mistaking a most human tragedy for a most sinister crime against nature which threatened the Earl's inheritance. Contrary to Garrow's wild fantasies, Brougham concluded, the jury was confronted with 'the melancholy story of a mutual, sincere, ardent, devouring passion, overwhelming with misery two young and unfortunate persons whom accidental circumstances had placed within its reach'.[45] The jury was apparently persuaded, awarding Rosebery only half of what he wanted.

Brougham's practice before the Lords, the hearing of Scottish appeals, also improved, thanks, in part, to his growing cooperation with Romilly, especially regarding law reform.[46] They teamed up to win the big case regarding St Andrew's Golf Club. They represented its owner whose tenant stocked it with rabbits, much to the chagrin of golfers and neighbours. 'There was no foundation for this action in the law of Scotland or that of England', they complained, 'when considered with reference either to the nature of the servitude, or the character in which the Pursuers claimed.'[47] Lords Eldon and Redesdale agreed, the Lord Chancellor complaining that there had not been such a spirited contest between men and rabbits since the age of Augustus. In *Stewart* v. *Hall*, Brougham helped persuade the Lords to uphold the Court of Session's decision in favour of a shipyard whose repairs on a ship its owner refused to pay. In granting Hall £60 towards his expenses, Eldon cited the *Duke of Hamilton* v. *Rev. J. Scott*, a case Brougham had lost, for his benefit, explaining that the appeal was an unnecessary judicial experiment.[48] In an action for excessive damages, prosecuted by Romilly, Brougham prevailed, although £10,000 were involved, and improper evidence had been introduced during the trial.[49] Even the cases Brougham lost in the Lords must not have upset him all that much since they went counter to his interests and principles. In losing Montgomery's appeal to alienate the Duke of Queensberry's estate through a 97-year lease,[50] for example, Brougham also saw that Lady Hamilton, Lord Nelson's lady, against whom he railed in the *Review*,[51] did not alienate the estate further. She never got the annuity Queensberry had promised her.[52]

The culmination of Brougham's experience as a Radical barrister outside Parliament was apparently arranging the divorce of the Countess of Rosebery, something he managed so well that the Whigs found him another seat in the Commons. The adultery suit was heard before the Consistory Court, Doctors Commons, Sir William Scott presiding, and the divorce, given the case against the former Harriet Bouverie, was granted almost as a matter of course.[53] The problem was getting the divorce bill through Parliament, and Brougham withdrew to Brougham Hall, feigning illness,[54] to effect it. Brougham's task was to get the bill by Ellenborough, who was presiding as Speaker. The bill had originally provided the Countess £200 a year, thanks to Eldon's suggestion, and the Commons had increased alimony to £500. The measure also prohibited Mildmay from marrying the Countess, something ordinarily left to the ecclesiastical courts in cases of adultery. When the divorce bill was getting its second reading, Lauderdale, a Whig Lord, charged that it was 'a bill of pains and penalties against the wife'.[55] Grenville, sounding as if he was being briefed by a lawyer like Brougham, explained why the provisions against remarriage were needed. Ellenborough agreed that the measure was not a bill of pains and penalties, but was upset at the alimony. Brougham provided for this last concern by having the poor woman unattended by counsel when the Lords grilled her about the bill.[56] No sooner had the Lords given their assent to the measure than Lord Darlington found a place for Brougham at Winchelsea. This was the least the Whigs could do for Brougham for his pacification of the Lord Chief Justice who had deprived him of a seat at Westminster the previous year by his harsh punishment of Lord Cochrane for the Stock Market fraud. It had permitted the Whig Member to be re-elected.

Back in the Commons, Brougham devoted himself almost completely to his legislative duties, seeking to reduce public expenditure, eliminate the income tax, promote primary education, allow the admission of truth in libel cases, eliminate the slave trade, improve economic conditions, and prevent political reaction at home and abroad. When, thanks largely to official initiatives, these activities helped create turmoil – starting with the Spa Field riots, and culminating with the 'Pentridge rising' – Brougham concentrated on meeting the challenge through the pen rather than the plea. He became a reporter and leader-writer for *The Times*, earning, if we are to believe Fox Bourne, £100 per month.[57] Here Brougham was answering Cobbett's challenge in his *Weekly Political Register* that he meet the government's reaction with something more than a brief. Brougham covered the trial of Dr Watson, for example, rather than defend him against the charges that Spencean Arthur Thistlewood had helped invent. It was Brougham's threatened coverage of the trials of 'The Blanketeers' at Lancaster that induced Sidmouth to write to a Bolton magistrate to drop charges. Brougham's coverage of the 'Pentridge rising' helped restrict the executions to the troublemakers whom spies like Oliver had enlisted for the reactionary plot. In sum, Daniel Maclise's sketch of Brougham, 'The Editor of *The Times*', showing the barrister, in wig and gown, dashing off a column, with a copy of the newspaper on the floor, illustrates how he met the contrived, political reaction of the post-war world. As a radical barrister, pursuing his profession in court, he threatened only to compound the problems of the defenceless prisoners, and he knew it, contrary to what Holdsworth claimed in his history of English law.

Brougham saved his court performances for cases like assessments of damages for criminal conversation,[58] libel actions, and assault suits,[59] actions which concentrated the emotions of juries on the parties. The only visible exception was when Brougham sought a mandamus against the Bank of England, requiring it to give its stockholders a bigger dividend.[60] Brougham, in covering criminal prosecutions for counterfeiting and uttering, had decided that the Bank's solicitors were cooperating too liberally with Nadin's constables in granting rewards for convictions. With less money to play around with, the Bank's Directors might be forced to seek a currency which could be counterfeited less easily, rather than make an example at the expense of innocent pawns. Ellenborough, who was prepared to see almost anything Brougham complained of as a red flag, granted him a rule to show cause for the mandamus, and it was nearly granted. At the last moment, Sir Arthur Piggott, the Bank's attorney, asked for a postponement, and it was granted.[61] The full King's Bench then quashed Ellenborough's rule *nisi*, stating that Brougham must seek redress for his client from the Bank.[62]

While Brougham's prosecution of Speaker Abbot and Sergeant-at-Arms Colman for Burdett might seem another exception, it was in fact using the Chancellor's renewed antipathy towards him to try to quiet a troublesome client. No sooner had Dr Watson been declared innocent than radicals like Henry Hunt started crowing about the result being achieved without Brougham's services, since he had been asked to represent the strange Spencean, but had understandably declined. Brougham could not win an appeal in the Lords before Eldon if his life depended on it.[63] Counsel was always on the wrong side, and after reading the cases, it is hard not to think that his reputation with the Chancellor had something to do with it. Certainly, the Lords' decisions in *Newcastle Fire Insurance Co.* v. *Macmorran*, and *Towart* v. *Sellars*, reversing judgements of the Court of Session, seem arbitrary, bordering on the personal. Brougham put this sentiment surely to work when he argued *ad nauseam* Burdett's hopeless trespass actions.

The restraints on Brougham's legal career were broken by George III's death. Queen Caroline immediately made him her Attorney General, and he had his work cut out for him when the Crown deleted her name from the Liturgy. While Brougham was clearly thinking of a financial arrangement, and an exile life on the Continent, a settlement that, if it had stuck, would have resulted in his becoming King's Counsel,[64] she had other ideas, and forced him to defend her. Once the Queen arrived in England, accompanied by London's Alderman Wood, eliciting many displays of popular support, the Ministry was forced to take drastic action, and Brougham, especially because of the humiliating accounts of his behaviour in *The Times*,[65] was obliged to react in kind. With Caroline's rights and privileges as Queen Consort under unprecedented partisan attack, Brougham's abilities as a radical barrister were tested to the full. If the Queen were swept from the political scene with little more parliamentary fanfare than another Luddite scare, her Attorney General would suffer similar ignominy. In establishing the customary right of the City's Liverymen and Aldermen to do as they pleased politically, in forcing the Ministry to give up its plan of having secret committees of Parliament, furnished with yet more green bags of 'evidence', deal with the Queen's alleged adulterous conduct, and then destroying the legal basis of the Bill of Pains and Penalties, largely single-handedly, Brougham passed the test with flying colours. His subsequent prosecutions in the Queen's defence added so much to his reputation that by 1822, despite the lack of a patent of preferment, he had become one of the handful of leading barristers. By then, Brougham's radical days, at least as far as the Bar was concerned, were over.

On 29 September 1819, Lord Mayor's Day, the traditional day for electing a new mayor, the majority of officials tried to get the Common Hall to upstage the event by taking up the question of Peterloo. While Mayor Atkins and the Aldermen retired to prevent such action, Sheriff Parkins allowed the Liverymen, especially Robert Waithman, to continue discussions of critical resolutions. The Council's leadership was, of course, furious about these developments, and it got the Attorney General to open a criminal information against its majority. In defending the action, Brougham and Denman teamed up beautifully to defeat it. Denman provided evidence of Council's practice in such matters, and Brougham cautioned the King's Bench against becoming a court of last resort for disgruntled Council minorities. 'In such circumstances', he said, alluding to his dispute with the Bank, 'the Court would, as had been said by a lamented friend of his [Sir A. Piggott], in a case not quite similar to the present, appear among the other novelties of the day, a Court destined to new uses'.[66] Gifford, fearing that he would lose the case, wisely called for a postponement, and the Court agreed, despite 'Orator' Hunt's protests.

When the Lords were balloting for a secret committee to hear the Crown's evidence against the Queen, based upon the 'Delicate Investigation' and the Milan Commission, Brougham called for a decision in the City's dispute with the Liverymen. Its outcome was critical now to the Queen's cause as the Liverymen were her most prominent supporters. Brougham made the relation even more intimate by comparing what the Liverymen had done on Lord Mayor's Day with the Queen's rights upon the death of George III: the arrangement was in *eo ipso*.[67] Justice Bayley spoke of the inconvenience of the Council taking up anything that suited its fancy. Brougham said that it had done so ten times since 1769. There was concern about what selfish minorities might do on such occasions, but Brougham reminded the Judges that it was the duty of all councillors to attend elections. Brougham 'concluded by commenting upon the impropriety of granting a criminal information in a case where nothing like corrupt intention had been proved'.[68] The King's Bench agreed, preventing Copley, the Solicitor General, from trying to justify what the prosecutors had done. While the Liverymen had not been acting with legal authority, the Judges held, the Crown was wrong to try to end practice in this way. In the wake of the decision, the Liverymen, in their support of the Queen, had a field-day against the Crown.[69]

Brougham directed popular agitation for her against the proceedings in Parliament. In answer to the King's Message, announcing another secret inquiry into Caroline's conduct, Brougham presented the Queen's Message, protesting against the partial, irresponsible action.[70] While the message did not stop the Ministry from going ahead, it did help prevent the actual naming of the secret committee in the Commons. Brougham then concentrated his activities on the Lords, asking the Lord Chancellor to present her petition against its inquiry. Eldon, in keeping with his antipathy towards Brougham, turned down the request, an action that he had a hard time explaining to critical Whig Lords who knew of his exonerating role in the 'Delicate Investigation'.[71] After Lord Dacre had presented her petition, Brougham himself was heard at the Bar, calling for a six-week postponement of the *ex parte* proceedings. The Queen needed that amount of time to refute the 'wretches' whose testimony had been thrown into the sealed, green bags. Under this intense pressure, Castlereagh announced to the Commons that the Ministry had scrapped the secret inquiry, an announcement that Brougham eagerly accepted. After the Lords had carried their inquiry through to a face-saving report, they too settled for the Bill of Pains and Penalties.

In preparing for its hearing, Brougham destroyed any illusions that might have grown up about his legal abilities during his self-imposed retirement. He immediately protested at the proposal, complaining that it was neither a divorce bill nor one of pains and penalties.[72] He vowed to fight the irregular proceeding to his last breath. On the Northern Circuit he showed that this might be long in coming, defending clients right and left before favourable audiences, and seeing that *The Times* reported the results to the Metropolis. At the York Assizes Brougham won a trover action against Richard Oastler, the famous Tory Radical, portraying the bankrupt oil dealer as an operator who, like the King, used his corrupt conscience and knowledge of the law to fleece his customers.[73] Brougham also took special pleasure in winning *Boradly* v. *Fawkes*, a trespass action against a man who had torn down a poor woman's pig cot, and then tried to justify it because she and her daughter had produced bastards.[74] At Newcastle Brougham argued Jack Lambton's right to a reduced corn toll over the River Tyne for well over five hours before a packed courtroom as if it had been a case of criminal conversation.[75] Brougham did not win all his cases. He lost several to James Scarlett, the best advocate in England.[76] This could hardly have been much consolation to the Crown since he too was to represent the Queen until it was decided that his services would not be needed. When Brougham was not representing clients, he apparently wrote a column from York, subjecting the Milan Commission to devastating criticism.[77]

If ever a case had been properly prepared, Brougham's had. Short of the surprise witness of some reputation who had caught the Queen in the act with Bergami, something that Brougham had long suspected, particularly because of what his brother James had written, the Crown had no case. In recognising this, we need only note some of the high points. Given the defence's review of what witnesses had told the Milan Commission, Theodore Majocchi, the Queen's servant who had turned state's evidence, represented no challenge. In fact, while he was testifying, the Commons tried to stop the proceedings, but Brougham argued against it, stating Majocchi would now have to undergo cross-examination.[78] It was during this that Brougham and '*Signor Non-Ricordo*' became indelibly impressed upon history. After that, the Crown was just biding its time, hoping that some witness would come out of the woodwork to corroborate its case. Instead it got testimony like that of Mrs Dumont, indicating that she had not seen evidence of sexual intercourse during three years of making the Queen's bed. Brougham was ready to have a vote on the second reading of the bill after the prosecution had presented its case, so confident was he that it had failed. The Crown forced Brougham to make his defence in the hope that someone important would crack. Even here Brougham had sweet revenge on the Chancellor, getting him to force Lady Charlotte Lindsay to say why she had really quit the Queen's employ. She did it, not because of any impropriety, but because of the Crown's plot against her mistress.[79] For good measure Brougham threw in Baron Ompteda's letters, calling upon the Queen's servants to betray her. Ompteda had been the Regent's Hanoverian envoy to the Vatican.[80]

Once Liverpool gave up the bill, Brougham behaved with uncharacteristic caution. While he had been on record since 1814 about the Queen's legal rights, thanks to his article in the *Review*,[81] he did not want any new legal confrontation with the Crown. Daniel O'Connell wanted to exploit the ministerial rebuff by getting Brougham to appoint him the Queen's Irish Attorney General, but he refused. Brougham was solely interested in legislative action to improve the Queen's status and position. When the Crown forced a showdown by arranging the King's Coronation, Brougham made a most elaborate plea for the Queen to have the same, but the Privy Council rejected her claim.[82] Brougham's elaborate argument and endless efforts on Caroline's behalf in *The Times* smack of much of what he tried to do for Burdett in order to silence him.

While the Queen was not stilled by such efforts, trying to force her way into the coronation at the Abbey, death soon achieved what argument could not. Caroline's demise and funeral removed the last political shackles from Brougham's legal career. While he had already started to protect himself and his political associates from unscrupulous attacks by the Constitutional Association, instituting libel actions against former *Times* editor, Dr Stoddart, Cobbett, and Rev. Blacow, while continuing, of course, his full legal fare on the Northern Circuit,[83] it was a Brougham yet unseen who induced the 'good parson' to libels yet unheard when he was finally prosecuted at the Lancaster Assizes in September 1821. Blacow tried to justify the most outrageous libels against the deceased by claiming that her counsel used Caroline like a doll for their own expedient purposes. 'They were as ready to cast off the Queen', Blacow concluded, 'when she should have answered their purposes as that old crazy headed goat, Lord Erskine, to cast off his concubine.'[84] Blacow received a six-month sentence in prison, and a £100 fine for his trouble. Brougham followed up his victory by pursuing the Constitutional Association for its vindictive prosecution of David Ridgway for selling a libellous pamphlet by the jailed Richard Carlile, by getting *The Times* declared innocent of libel in an action which a careless attorney had instituted, and the Crown had threatened since Peterloo,[85] and by attacking Durham's clergy for failing to give proper homage to the Queen, his former mistress, when her death was announced.

While Brougham by no means won all these cases, he was no longer the radical barrister with the dock brief, living on what he could scrape up at court, Brougham Hall, and *The Times*. He was making £7,000 a year as a barrister, and he would have been making more if he had not turned down promotion to King's Counsel in deference to the ignored Denman.[86] Brougham was no longer turning down briefs for fear that he would prejudice a defence, but taking the fight to the forces of repression, as his vigorous defence of the editor, John Ambrose Williams, in the Durham clergy case showed. It is hard to imagine a more vigorous defence than his in this case against the Established Church: 'Let its members, therefore, above all let us, as well for religion as for civil policy, set ourselves to destroy the vermin which breeds in that corruption, and which stink, and sting the hand that would drive them away'.[87] Yet, for those who would take umbrage at such sentiments being expressed, there was the rebuff that Brougham and Scarlett had given Solicitor General Copley when he had tried to sue *The Times* for libelling 'attorney' Lewis. When Sergeant Hullock, the Northern Circuit's leader, was raised to the Bench, Brougham took his place,[88] which gave him a practice on a par with Scarlett's, and thereby insured a titanic struggle for the next seven years between England's two most powerful Common Law lawyers. From now on, Brougham's dilemmas would be more conventional ones, those of the barrister who had too many clients, and too little time to prepare all cases properly.

NOTES

1. Wilfred Prest, ed., *Lawyers in Early Modern Europe and America*, London, 1981, pp. 11–13.
2. Daniel Duman, 'The English Bar in the Georgian Era', ibid., pp. 86–107. For an expanded treatment of the subject, see Duman's *The Judicial Bench in England, 1727–1875: The Reshaping of a Professional Elite*, London, 1982.
3. R.H.M.B. Atkinson and G.A. Jackson, eds., *Brougham and his Early Friends: Letters to James Loch, 1798–1809*, London, 1908, 3 vols., vol. 1, Brougham to Loch, 24 June 1800, pp. 151–2.
4. Ibid.: Brougham to Loch, 6 April 1801, p. 238.
5. Ibid.: Brougham to Loch, 20 Aug. 1802, p. 344.
6. *The Records of the Honourable Society of Lincoln's Inn: The Black Books*, London, 1902, 5 vols., vol. IV, p. 113.
7. Atkinson and Jackson, op.cit., vol. II, Brougham to Loch, no date.
8. *Rex* v. *William Cobbett*, *The Times*, 16 June 1810, p. 4.
9. Art. V., 'Erskine's *Speeches*', *The Edinburgh Review*, vol. 16, no. XXXI (April 1810), p. 110.

10. Ibid., p.117.
11. *Speeches of Henry Brougham*, Edinburgh, 1838, 4 vols, vol.1, p.44.
12. Louis Simond, *Journal of a Tour and Residence in Great Britain*, Edinburgh 1815, 2 vols., vol.1, p.67.
13. *Rex* v. *Drakard, The Times*, 18 March 1811, p.3.
14. A. Aspinall, *Politics and the Press, 1780–1850*, London, 1949: Brougham to Allen, 8 April, 1807, p.453.
15. *Rex* v. *Rous, Kirby and Lawrence*, *The Times*, 27 May 1811, p.3.
16. Art. IV, 'Speeches of Lord Erskine', *The Edinburgh Review*, vol. 19, no.XXXVIII (Feb. 1812), p.343.
17. Ibid., p.352.
18. W.S. Holdsworth, *A History of English Law* (1922–1966), 16 vols., vol.13, p.557.
19. 'High Treason', *The Times*, 4 Feb. 1812, p.4.
20. Ibid., 11 Feb. 1812, p.2.
21. Ibid.
22. *The Gentleman's Magazine'*, 1812, vol.82, Part I, p.183.
23. *The Times*, 15 Feb. 1812, p.4.
24. Ibid.
25. J.L. & Barbara Hammond, *The Skilled Labourer, 1760–1832*, London 1919, p.298.
26. See 'The Trials of All the Prisoners at the Special Assizes for the County of Lancaster', commencing 23 May 1812.
27. Hammonds, op.cit., p.300.
28. *Rex* v. *John and Leigh Hunt*, *The Times*, 10 Dec. 1812, p.1.
29. Ibid., 20 Dec. 1812, p.3.
30. Aspinall, op.cit., p.36.
31. 'Special Commission', *The Times*, 11 Jan. 1813, p.3.
32. Ibid., 13 Jan. 1813, p.3.
33. *Kirkpatrick* v. *Creevey*, ibid., 2 April 1813, p.2.
34. Ibid., 8 May 1813, p.3.
35. Ibid.
36. Ibid., 21 May 1813, p.3.
37. *Morris* v. *Sir Francis Burdett*, ibid., 17 July 1813, p.3.
38. Ibid., 10 Nov. 1813, p.2.
39. Chester W. New, *The Life of Henry Brougham to 1830*, Oxford 1961, p.160.
40. *Rex*. v. *Geo. Houston, The Times*, 15 Nov. 1814, p.1.
41. Ibid.
42. Ibid.
43. Ibid., p.2.
44. *The Earl of Rosebery* v. *Sir Henry St. John Mildmay, ibid.*, 12 Dec. 1814, p.2.
45. Ibid., p.3.
46. See Brougham's articles, starting with Art. VII, 'Sir Samuel Romilly on *English Criminal Law*', *The Edinburgh Review*, vol. 19, No.XXXVIII (Feb. 1812), pp.290–317.
47. *Dempster* v. *Cleghorn* (1813) 2 Dow 47.
48. *Stewart* v. *Hall* (1813) 2 Dow 39.
49. *Macdonell* v. *Macdonald* (1813) 3 ER 789.
50. *Montgomery* v. *Charteris* (1813) 2 Dow 90.
51. Art. VII, 'Lord Nelson's Letters to Lady Hamilton', *The Edinburgh Review*, vol.23, No.XLVI (Sept. 1814), pp.398–410.
52. *The Dictionary of National Biography*, vol.8, p.1037.
53. *Earl of Rosebery* v. *Countess of Rosebery, The Times*, April 1815, p.3.
54. For Brougham's indirect explanation, see New, op.cit., p.161.
55. *Hansard's Parliamentary Debates*, 1st. ser., vol.31, p.564.
56. *Journals of the House of Lords*, vol.50, 8 May 1815.
57. H.R. Fox Bourne, *English Newspapers: Chapters in the History of Journalism*, London, 1887, 2 vols., vol.2, p.16.
58. See, e.g. *Kent* v. *Sorell, The Times*, 7 July 1817, p.3.

59. See, e.g. *Rex* v. *Lord Ranelagh*, ibid., 24 Dec. 1819, p. 4.
60. *In Re the Prosecution of the Bank*, ibid., 30 April 1818, p. 3.
61. Ibid., 2 May 1818, p. 3.
62. Ibid., 26 May 1818, p. 3.
63. For Brougham's cases, see *Newcastle Fire Insurance Co.* v. *Macmorran* (1815) 3 ER 1057; *Mucklow* v. *Attorney General* (1816) 3 ER 1069; *Maxwell* v. *Gordon* (1816) 3 ER 1165; *Steel* v. *Steel* (1817) 3 ER 1257; *MacDowal* v. *Bucher* (1817) 3 ER 1275; *Towart* v. *Sellars* (1817) 3 ER 1312; *Burdett* v. *Abbot* (1817) and *Burdett* v. *Colman* (1817) 3 ER 1289; *Gordon* v. *Marjoribanks* (1818) 3 ER 1408; *Stewart* v. *Crawford* (1819) 4 ER 58; *M'Lea* v. *Walker* (1819) 4 ER 196; and *Graham* v. *Keble* (1820) 4 ER 274.
64. *The Times*, 21 April 1820, p. 3.
65. See ibid., starting with 'The Queen', 6 June 1820, p. 3.
66. *Rex.* v. *Parkins and Others*, ibid., 11 Feb. 1820, p. 3.
67. Ibid., 9 June 1820, p. 3.
68. Ibid.
69. See ibid., starting with 'The City Address to the Queen', 16 June 1820, p. 3.
70. 'Message from the Queen', ibid., 8 June 1820, p. 2.
71. Ibid., 27 June 1820, p. 1.
72. Ibid., 6 July 1820, p. 2.
73. *Tootal* v. *Dickinson*, ibid., 25 July 1820, p. 3.
74. *Boardly* v. *Fawkes*, ibid., 29 July 1820, p. 3.
75. *Mayor and Corporation of Newcastle* v. *Lambton*, ibid, 15 Aug. 1820, p. 3.
76. New, op.cit., p. 247.
77. 'The Milan Commission', *The Times*, 28 July 1820, p. 3.
78. Ibid., 22 Aug. 1820, p. 3.
79. Ibid., 7 Oct. 1820, p. 1.
80. New, op.cit., pp. 117–18.
81. Art. X, 'Constitutional Character of the Queen Consort', *The Edinburgh Review*, vol. 23, No. XLVI (Sept. 1814), pp. 441–68.
82. 'The Queen's Right to be Crowned', *The Times*, 6 July 1821, pp. 2–3.
83. See coverage of Assizes, ibid., starting 9 Aug. 1821, p. 3.
84. *Rex.* v. *Blacow*, ibid., 17 Sept. 1821, p. 3.
85. *Lewis* v. *The Times*, ibid., 10 & 29 Jan. 1822, p. 3. For the threat, see Derek Hudson, *Thomas Barnes of The Times*, Cambridge, 1943, pp. 37–9.
86. *The Times*, 23 April 1822, p. 4.
87. *Rex.* v. *Williams*, ibid., 10 Aug. 1822, 3. Note that Brougham changed this passage when it was reprinted in his *Speeches*, Edinburgh, 1838, 4 vols., vol. 1, p. 354.
88. *The Times*, 1 March 1823, p. 3.

'Without the Law': Courts of Local and Special Jurisdiction in Nineteenth Century England

H.W. ARTHURS

1. Introduction

For the first half of the nineteenth century, civil justice in England was only to a limited extent associated with the superior courts and the common law. To a degree not often appreciated,[1] the civil disputes of most Englishmen were resolved by courts of local and special jurisdiction. In addition, justices exercising civil jurisdiction, administrative officials and tribunals, arbitrators, and domestic tribunals, usually operating under the dispensation of a special statutory, contractual or customary regime, disposed of great numbers of non-criminal matters.[2]

We need rehearse only briefly what is widely known about the superior courts to remind ourselves why people would sensibly wish to litigate elsewhere. Rules of pleading and evidence, and the participation of juries, vastly complicated and protracted the process of ascertaining facts. Substantive legal rules of ancient provenance were often unresponsive to the changing realities of social life and economic relations. The cost of litigation at Westminster or in the assize courts made it an unprofitable enterprise for everyone except lawyers.[3]

However, recourse to local and special courts – and to their special regimes of law – was not merely an act of resignation or despair. Long traditions of local justice, which have been so extensively discussed on the criminal side, were closely related to the structure of local life and political power. On the civil side, parallel traditions also reflected social and economic relations. E.P. Thompson has directed our attention to the interconnectedness of local custom, law and economic behaviour in the eighteenth century, in agricultural communities,[4] and to the tenacious survival of similar economic-based law and custom in industrial and urban contexts into the nineteenth.[5] Vestigial remnants of various mediaeval communal jurisdictions certainly persisted well into the nineteenth century,[6] and indeed they formally ceased to exist only in the 1970s.[7]

By far the most ubiquitous institutions of civil justice in the first half of the nineteenth century, however, were the courts of requests (sometimes called courts of conscience). These local courts were, in effect, absorbed into the County Courts in 1846, and have received scant notice since. It is the purpose of this paper to retrieve them from ill-deserved obscurity, to offer an account of their structure and function, and to explore their significance for our understanding of both law and social history in the nineteenth century.

2. *The Court of Requests: An Institutional Profile*

Courts of requests were established by local statutes, usually upon the petition of local merchants or municipal authorities. While the provisions of these statutes differed somewhat from place to place and from time to time, they generally exhibited certain common characteristics.[8]

Cases were to be decided upon according to 'equity and conscience'. Judges or 'commissioners' were laymen, sometimes aldermen, burgesses or mayors *ex officio*, usually appointed by local authorities, and occasionally coopted by a self-perpetuating bench.[9] Lawyers, other than 'low attorneys', seldom participated in cases, either because they were explicitly excluded, or because there was no provision for the payment of costs. Court fees were relatively low, pleadings simple, fact-finding informal; the parties had no difficulty in representing themselves.

While courts of requests did not exist in all localities, and while they did not possess unlimited powers, they did enjoy virtual autonomy in matters confided to them. Their jurisdiction was limited geographically, in terms of subject matter (usually including debts and demands, and excluding real property disputes), and in terms of amount to £2, £5 or £10. Lest the latter limitation be construed as evidence of their trivial significance, we must remember that such sums were considerable in light of then-prevailing incomes.[10] Most significantly, when the courts of requests did decide matters in their own distinctive fashion, their decisions could not be appealed to the superior courts, or reviewed on any ground, except perhaps jurisdiction.[11] Indeed a system of punitive costs discouraged recourse to the superior courts for claims which could have been pursued in a court of requests.

Some idea of the importance of these courts in the life of the community, and in the life of the law, can be gleaned from the limited statistical evidence available for the period around 1830 (see Table 1). The courts of requests largely dated from the mid-eighteenth century; by 1830, some 250 had been established; by 1845, they numbered about 400.[12] Some of these courts were very busy indeed. Ten of them, for example, each handled over 5,000 claims in 1830–31; in the London Borough of Tower Hamlets alone, the court of requests processed almost 30,000 claims. In total, of about 300,000 claims brought in local courts in 1830, well over

TABLE 1

MAJOR COURTS OF REQUESTS – 1830–31

Court	*Authority*	*Claims*	*Jurisdictional Limits*
Birmingham	47 Geo. III	7,926	£ 5
Blackheath	5 Geo. III	5,146	£ 5
Bristol			
(Conscience)	1 W & M	7,465	40s
(Requests)	56 Geo. III	1,469	£15
City of London	39 & 40 Geo. III	9,678	£5
Halifax	20 Geo. III	22,864	40s.
Liverpool	25 Geo. III	21,334	40s.
Manchester	48 Geo. III	10,364	£ 5
Sheffield	48 Geo. III*	11,518	£ 5
Southwark	22 Geo. II	16,655	£ 5
Tower Hamlets	22 Geo. II	28,624	40s.

* derived from Court Baron of Manor of Sheffield

Source: Appendix I, Fourth Report of the Commissioners on Courts of Common Law, 1831–32 (239) XXV, part V.

200,000 were commenced in courts of requests; by 1840, the number had increased to abcut 400,000.[13] By way of comparison, only some 90,000 writs were issued in all of the superior courts at Westminster in 1830,[14] and this number seems to have remained relatively constant during the period.[15]

We may say then, without hyperbole, that for most Englishmen, civil justice was the justice of courts of requests (and other local courts), not the justice of the common law and the superior courts. But so saying, we have revealed little about the differences between the two, or about the significance of those differences. To do so requires us to build a mighty edifice on a small foundation of evidence,[16] to observe the conventions of historical fiction, as much as those of historical research.

3. *A Court of Requests at Work: 1830–40*

Surviving records of the Bristol Court of Requests and Conscience appear to be unusually extensive,[17] and it is this court which will be used as the basis of a composite sketch of such institutions at work in the period 1830–1840. For several reasons, however, generalisations based upon Bristol's experience may not be warranted.

First, Bristol itself was likely not typical of urban social and economic structures elsewhere; the city was neither one of the new industrial towns nor a London borough, such as Tower Hamlets. Second, the Bristol court was unique in that it was organised into two chambers, the Court of Conscience (jurisdiction up to 40s.) and the Court of Requests (jurisdiction up to £15); an appeal lay from the Court of Requests to the Tolzey Court, another local court.[18] Third, the information presented is based upon a sample of cases only; more complete analysis might yield a different impression. Nonetheless, since the Bristol records alone offer relatively extensive information about both the nature of the claims brought, and the persons bringing and resisting them, it is to Bristol we must turn. Where possible, comparisons will be made with Sheffield for which some records exist, and to a few other courts, for which fragmentary evidence or narrative accounts are available.

During the period 1830 to 1840, the value of claims remained unchanged in the two Bristol courts (Table 2). However, the nature of those claims changed somewhat (Table 3). Throughout the decade, claims for 'goods sold and delivered', for money lent, and for promissory notes, dominated the courts' work, but to a lesser extent at the end than at the beginning. This modest decline in commercial preoccupations in Bristol may be contrasted with a significant increase in claims of the same type in Sheffield. On the other hand, claims for labour or services rendered increased somewhat in Bristol while declining dramatically in

TABLE 2
BRISTOL COURTS OF REQUESTS AND CONSCIENCE
VALUE OF CLAIMS – 1830–40

	1830	*1835*	*1840*
£ 0–5	55	55	61
£ 5–10	33	36	29
£10–15	12	9	10

Source: Proceedings books, Bristol Courts of Conscience and Requests, 1830, 1835, 1840.

TABLE 3
TYPES OF CLAIMS – COURTS OF REQUESTS – BRISTOL AND SHEFFIELD

	1830		*1835*		*1840*	
	Bristol	*Sheffield*	*Bristol*	*Sheffield*	*Bristol*	*Sheffield*
Goods sold and delivered	59%	70	65	68	62	88
Money lent, promissory notes etc.	19	6	15	23	10	5
Rent, Lodging etc.	9	7	12	8	14	3
Wages, work & materials etc.	6	11	4	1	10	3
Other	7	7	4	10	3	0%

Sources: Proceedings Books, Bristol Courts of Requests and Conscience and Sheffield Court of Requests, 1830, 1835, 1840.

Sheffield during the same period. Claims for rent exhibited the same pattern: they increased in Bristol while declining in Sheffield. These shifts may be merely circumstantial, or they may reflect changes in Sheffield's industrial and commercial structure during the 1830s.

It is instructive, as well, to try to identify who used the Bristol courts, and against whom; unfortunately no data are available from Sheffield to permit comparisons. Considerable caution must be exercised in this exercise. While plaintiffs and defendants were identified by occupation ('mason') or status ('gentleman) the interpretation of these terms, and their collapse into a few socio-economic categories, is ultimately problematic. However, in general terms we see (Table 4) that during the 1830s a majority of plaintiffs were merchants or manufacturers, while most defendants were artisans, manual workers or pursued what might anachronistically be termed 'white collar' occupations (e.g. schoolmasters, apothecaries, accountants, and solicitors).

TABLE 4

LITIGANTS BY OCCUPATION – BRISTOL COURTS OF REQUESTS AND CONSCIENCE

	1830		*1835*		*1840*	
	Pltfs.	*Dfts.*	*Pltfs.*	*Dfts.*	*Plfts.*	*Dfts.*
Artisan	12%	25	16	33	11	22
Manual Labour	8	12	7	16	4	19
'White Collar'	10	14	4	13	10	11
Merchant/Manufacturer	57	34	56	26	49	26
Misc. Middle Class	12	14	17	11	22	18%
N.A.	1	1	0	1	4	4%

Source: as in Table 2.

Yet it should not be thought that the Bristol Courts of Requests and Conscience served solely as engines for the oppression of the poor. The only group which was unambiguously poor – manual labourers – were indeed much more often likely to be defendants than plaintiffs. But they were plaintiffs only on occasion, and were never defendants in more than 20 per cent of the cases. 'Artisans' and 'white collar' workers covered a broad spectrum of occupations, some of them well-paid and relatively prestigious. They too were less likely to sue than be sued, and were themselves an important source of claims. While merchants, manufacturers, and other middle-class individuals clearly dominated the plaintiffs' side of the ledger, however, they were in turn defendants on many occasions.

Making due allowance for the imprecision of the occupational labels used, and for the ambiguity of notions of 'class', a more balanced conclusion is that the Bristol courts generally functioned to resolve the disputes of middle-class and lower-middle-class litigants. To a lesser extent they were also used to collect wages earned, and debts incurred, by members of the working class.

Small fragments of evidence from elsewhere help to place this tentative conclusion in context. For a brief period in 1842, the Rotherham Court of Requests (which then had jurisdiction up to £15 as well) recorded the occupations of parties to proceedings. Working-class parties appear about twice as often as defendants as they do as plaintiffs. Middle-class litigants (excluding 'white collar') are plaintiffs about twice as often as they are defendants.

As noted, no comparable figures are available from Sheffield. However, a significant number of cases in the Sheffield Court of Requests (as in Bristol) were multiple claims by particular plaintiffs. These accounted for between one quarter and one half of all claims in a given period. These multiple claims themselves reinforce the impression that the Sheffield court was largely used by commercial interests, and help somewhat to define the nature of those interests. For example, the anomalously high incidence of claims upon promissory notes in 1835 (Table 3) was largely attributable to a particular plaintiff who also sued a number of defendants for goods sold and delivered. This suggests that the notes may have been taken as security for unpaid accounts. In addition, a rather significant proportion of multiple claims in 1835 and 1840 (about one-third) was for either medical attention or ale and alcoholic beverages. (No linkage between the two is suggested.) If this pattern of multiple claims means anything, it may well suggest that defendants were characteristically those to whom credit would be extended. Investigation of credit practices might shed some light on the identity of defendants; intuitively one might expect that access to credit would be easier for the middle class than for workers, albeit perhaps more necessary for the latter.

Beyond these very meagre statistics, we know relatively little about the business of courts of requests. Occasionally, we hear evidence that workers used them to collect wages.[19] On the other hand, they were disparaged as 'tribunals of shopkeepers' before whom 'neither the higher nor the lower classes have much chance of obtaining justice',[20] and they were the specific target of popular protests on occasion.[21] A rather overheated critic argued that the availability of courts of requests induced shopkeepers to extend credit to the poor, which had 'a most demoralizing tendency among the working classes' and produced 'the debauchery and wretchedness of the vast population of Manchester'.[22] Other, more sympathetic, observers also acknowledge that many claims were indeed brought against debtors of 'the lower classes'.[23]

If, in fact, courts of requests were no more than instruments of debt collection, then their interest for us would be relatively limited. Judged solely on the basis of their efficiency in debt collection, it is perhaps unsurprising that by the 1830s it was widely believed that a new national system of county courts would lead to 'the more easy Recovery of small Debts and Demands'.[24] But there was another view of courts of requests, another concern which persisted during the long battle over the establishment of the county court system. That view emphasised the communal characteristics of courts of requests.

The only published account of the daily working of a court of requests comes, unfortunately, from the pen of an author whose enthusiasm for them is matched only by his unusual humanity, instinct for justice, and common sense. William Hutton, who served for many years as a commissioner of the Birmingham Court of Requests, was known as 'the English Benjamin Franklin'.[25] His Birmingham, the Birmingham of the last decades of the eighteenth century, was obviously not the same city fifty years on, although apparently somewhat akin to it in terms of civic tradition.[26] Hutton's account of his work on the court must therefore be read subject to two *caveats*: it is not only the projection of his unique personality, but it is also a reflection of the time and place to which it relates. Nonetheless, Hutton shows us how a court of requests may have functioned as a useful communal forum of dispute resolution, within a tradition of humane values, informal processes, and indigenous customs which has since largely disappeared from view.

Hutton's humanity was unabashedly paternal: 'I have considered the suitors as my children, and when any of this vast family looked up to me for peace and justice, I have distributed both with pleasure'.[27]

But it apparently did run deep. He expressed sympathy for animals, young people in difficulty with the law, and religious minorities.[28] He articulated a commitment to adjudication 'according to good conscience': 'if the commissioners cannot decide *against* law, they can decide without it'.[29]

Such a commitment would hardly be pursued within the framework of the technical rules of pleading, evidence and legal doctrine: 'The straight, the easy, the concise road to justice is blocked up, and the traveller is led through the dark, long and intricate windings of the law.'[30] Thus, Hutton did not hesitate to 'promote peace between contending parties',[31] to pursue 'the most concise mode of conducting a trial [by] examin[ing] the parties and their evidences', rather than emulate courts of law where 'he who knows it best is forbidden to speak',[32] and to take notice of well-known facts concerning local characters and customs.[33]

His concern for justice was not confined to procedure. It extended to substantive outcomes as well. We find him ingeniously ensuring that all who drew water from a communal well should contribute to the costs of its repair; dismissing a legal argument based on high authority because 'it was not perfectly in point' and would yield 'an absurdity beneath Lord Mansfield', its author; and enforcing the claims of two members of a sick benefit club against the stewards who allegedly dissolved it, defying 'a lusty lawyer of Northfield who ... drew out all the artillery of the courts above ... and threatened destruction' while pointing out the stewards' right to claim indemnification from the other club members.[34]

One cannot escape the feeling, finally, that Hutton and his fellow commissioners were men very much rooted in their community (which by formal qualification and daily occupation they obviously were). For example, customs relating to wage claims, the treatment of servants, landlord-tenant obligations, and peculiarities of specific trades,[35] were all vindicated by decisions of the Birmingham Court of Requests when almost certainly they would not have survived the scrutiny of a court of law.

By identifying this combination of characteristics – humane intentions, informality, community-consciousness – we raise the possibility that the Birmingham Court of Requests in Hutton's heyday, the 1780s, was very different from the busy court in Sheffield, or even Birmingham, fifty years later.[36] Hutton's court may well have functioned as a communal court, although he was obviously sensitive to its commercial importance.[37] The Sheffield court very likely did not. What is implied by this possible difference between the commercial and the communal models of courts?

It is tempting to characterise the struggle over the shape of local justice from 1830 to 1850 as a contest between the claims of commerce and those of community. But this would be misleading. As we shall see, changes in the courts of requests and debates over their replacement by the new county courts in 1846 were largely responses to the assertion of professional interests and ideology. The commercial model is thus significant primarily because it tells us what the court might have been expected to become but did not, the communal because it remains, even today, a goal of idealistic social and legal reformers.

4. *From Courts of Requests to County Courts: 1830–1850*

From 1828, when Lord Brougham delivered his epochal speech on legal reform, considerable attention was focussed upon local courts, including courts of requests. Even before the completion of an enquiry into common law courts (including local courts), Brougham had introduced a bill for the establishment of a national system of 'district courts'.[38] However, such comprehensive legislation was still fifteen years away.

In response to complaints about oppression, corruption, inconvenience, inefficiency and jurisdictional idiosyncracy, a series of measures was proposed and passed which altered the character of all local courts. Some local jurisdictions were suppressed;[39] others were rationalised by increasing their monetary and subject-matter jurisdiction and by extending their boundaries to coincide with those of the new municipal corporations.[40] Measures were undertaken to improve the facilities, staff and procedures of local courts.[41] And a steady barrage of criticism was maintained against egregious abuses.

In fact, few such abuses were charged against courts of requests,[42] although it is true that they were sometimes unable to cope with increasing caseloads and to meet expectations of high efficiency in debt collection. Their most significant defects were structural: commissioners were unpaid, preoccupied with their own affairs, and not always available for duty; court fees were low and insufficient to carry the costs of adequate staff or facilities. These would be characteristic problems for communal courts in rapidly expanding and changing trends. The jurisdiction of courts of requests was geographically limited. Thus, they were unable to issue process, compel attendance, or enforce judgements against defendants whose goods or persons were removed beyond their borders. These defects would obviously be more serious for courts of a commercial than those of a communal character. Courts of requests were able to arrange for the payment of debts in instalments,[43] and to establish a 'tariff' of imprisonment scaled to the size of unpaid debts,[44] meliorative measures in context, and consistent with both communal and commercial expectations. However, the abysmal state of their underfinanced debtors' prisons must have done little for communal harmony, while acting *in terrorem* to enforce commercial obligations. Finally, their limited jurisdiction forced many disputes into the inhospitable superior courts, presumably pleasing neither debtors nor creditors in the end.

But while all of these criticisms of courts of requests were expressed throughout the 1830s, on the whole they were directed towards improvement, rather than abolition, of the courts. Only the legal profession exhibited fundamental hostility to them, and even that hostility was not universal or implacable. Thus, on the eve of their abolition in 1846, courts of requests were the subject of a surprisingly benign obituary in a legal journal which had been persistently critical of their shortcomings:

> The proceedings were cheap, expeditious, domestic, generally certain, almost always final; much knowledge of local habits and trade bargains was brought to bear upon the adjudication; and remedies were placed with the reach and comprehension of persons whom proceedings more solemn, technical, and therefore more

> expensive, would have disabled of all redress. On the other hand these courts wanted intrinsic authority; their jurisdiction was limited in point of territory, restricted in amount, often doubtful in respect of matter; though numerous when considered as anomalous and exceptional tribunals, they were in fact too few.[45]

'Reform' of courts of requests, as well as of other local courts, was thus apparently required. But what 'reform'? in whose interests? and with what impact upon their character?

By the 1830s, one important change was already under way. Whereas Hutton had been able to boast that courts of requests '[created] judges in the lower class, taking the power out of the hands of professional men',[46] substantial property qualifications for commissioners had gradually been introduced.[47] From 1830, moreover, much effort was devoted by those very 'professional men' to vindicating their particular interests. This effort focussed on three issues: the suppression of other modes of dispute resolution in favour of formal adjudication; the assurance that adjudication would be conducted according to common law, rather than other normative systems; and the guarantee that adjudication would involve the participation of lawyers.

The triumph of formal adjudication can be briefly recounted. Hutton's testimony suggests that mediation and informality played an important role in at least some courts of requests, and may indeed have contributed to their effectiveness in resolving disputes amongst neighbours and those involved in ongoing employment, trade, or tenancy relationships. Brougham's original bill to create a new system of district courts envisaged that their judges would also be 'judges of arbitrament and reconcilement',[48] a scheme he pursued in vain virtually until his dying day.[49] And a number of witnesses before the Commission on Common Law Courts favoured the use of arbitration and mediation. But it was not to be.

The legal profession was intensely hostile. A judge cannot be everything at once, urged a barrister, 'judge, advocate, attorney, arbitrator, referee and pacificator, haranguing, adjudicating, arbitrating, conciliating and reconciling'.[50] The Commission was prepared to recommend only limited departures from conventional court rules, in the interests of simplicity and efficiency:

> If justice . . . is to be administered according to the ordinary rules of evidence, in a court regulated by certain rules of practice, the proceeding ceases to be remedial in its effect. If, on the other hand, all such restraints be dispensed with, the tribunal becomes arbitrary, and its decisions too vague and uncertain to be satisfactory.[51]

And when it was finally enacted in 1846, the County Courts Act merely nodded at other methods of dispute resolution by authorising judges to refer matters to arbitration in appropriate cases.[52]

It would be surprising if some elements of compromise and informality did not survive in the county courts in the end. We certainly know that in their shadow negotiated settlement was widespread,[53] and that the practice of arbitration grew apace throughout the century.[54] But in formal terms, no attempt was made to preserve those aspects of the courts of requests which contributed to their communal character.

This orientation of the local courts towards more formal adjudication, on the model of the superior courts, was but one aspect of the 'reform' project of the Courts Commission (and of the legal profession). There was a clear desire to extend the reach of the common law, the law of the superior courts, into spheres previously governed by other legal regimes.

In general terms, customary law had fallen into disfavour, in part because of the interests it served,[55] in part because it was an affront to Benthamite rationality.[56] Discretion – the 'equity and conscience' jurisdiction of courts of requests – was similarly disparaged. Said the Commissioners on Common Law Courts:

> The suspicion entertained ... by Sir William Blackstone, as to the policy of erecting Courts 'with methods of proceeding entirely in derogation of the Common Law, and whose largely discretionary powers make a petty tyranny in a set of standing Commissioners', have not been removed by later experience.[57]

To what extent courts of requests actually explored the outer limits of their discretion we do not know. No doubt many decisions did not proceed from the formal rules of law.[58] But this need not imply randomness or decision-making *tabula rasa* in each case. Hutton himself remarked on the need for predictability:

> The decisions of a Bench should ever be the same. That which is law today should be law forever. If they are founded in equity, they may be adhered to with safety.[59]

Legal critics, indeed, spoke (with derision) of 'Courts of Requests law'.[60]

Perhaps we are somewhat better able to judge whether courts of requests were, in Blackstone's phrase, 'a petty tyranny'. We know enough about the manipulative use of discretion in local criminal courts at this period[61] to be able to speculate upon the quality of their civil counterparts: by comparison at least, the courts of requests do not seem to have been particularly 'tyrannical'.[62]

Ultimately, whatever their defects, it does appear that the most important accusation made against courts of requests was that they acted 'in derogation of the Common Law'.

Professor Atiyah has documented the opposition between law and discretion, between principles and pragmatism, as it was perceived by nineteenth century lawyers.[63] This opposition is seen in the successful efforts of lawyers to suppress the discretion-based courts of requests, and to replace them with the new county courts.

The presence of lay judges was an obvious barrier to the introduction of law as the basis of decision-making in courts of requests. From 1830 onward, efforts were made to diminish their role. First, the appointment of legally-trained judges was made a *quid pro quo* for passage of statutes increasing the courts' monetary jurisdiction.[64] Second, legally trained assessors were made available to assist the lay commissioners.[65] Third, the assessors were authorised to decide cases alone in defined circumstances.[66] Finally, the former immunity from superior court review was breached in 1845, at least in matters involving £10 or more.[67] Thus, while the 'equity and conscience' jurisdiction was generally not explicitly abandoned,[68] by the time the County Courts Act was enacted in 1846, the courts of requests had been all but captured by the aggressive forces of law.

In 1846, the triumph of law was made virtually complete. The old 'equity and conscience' jurisdiction was not preserved in the new county courts, which were to render decisions which were 'precisely that which a superior court would arrive at'.[69] The county courts were made courts of record.[70] Their judges were all legally qualified (save for a few former judges of courts of requests).[71] And while there was initially no provision for appeal, when this was added in 1850,[72] the superior courts finally were able to assert the supervisory jurisdiction which would ensure conformity to 'law' by the lower courts.[73] At least by 1850, then, we may say that the law of the superior courts – 'law' in the lawyer's sense – governed almost all courts in England.[74]

In the wake of the law (and, as we have seen, sometimes in its van) came the lawyers. The lawyers were committed to the virtues of law as an ideology. To decide cases except according to common law, said one, 'is at variance with our national predilections'.[75] But for them law was as well the touchstone of economic advancement. By ensuring that disputes would be decided according to law, they also ensured that they would be decided with the participation of lawyers.

The concern of lawyers in the debate over the new court system was explicit:

> The objections to Local Courts are so many .... The greatest of all is that which is by their supporters esteemed their foremost benefit; – the absence of legal advisers; – the prosecution of their suits by the parties in person .... Will no member of the House of Commons

> fight the battle of Law and the Lawyers against the reckless assaults of laymen ...?[76]

Whether this plea had some effect, or whether other influences prevailed, cannot be specifically ascertained. The County Courts Act did bring at least partial satisfaction to lawyers. They gained a monopoly of the right to represent litigants, to the exclusion of 'low attorneys' and other unqualified practitioners, although litigants were still permitted to appear in person, and many did so.[77] However, the level of fees permitted by the County Courts Act initially was very low, and far from enhancing legal incomes, the new courts 'threaten[ed] to make almost a revolution in legal economy' by siphoning off lucrative work from the superior courts.[78] By 1850, however, the fee schedule had been satisfactorily revised,[79] and all was once again well for law and lawyers.

The economic interests of the legal profession were also manifest in concerns about the selection and payment of the new county court judges. Fears were expressed about patronage and about salaries so low that they might permit the appointment only of 'the travelling drudges of the "Cheap Justice Delivery System" '.[80] Neither fear was in the end justified, and it was conceded that 'upon the whole the standard of judicial competency attained is quite as high as could reasonably be expected'.[81]

The county courts had become part of the grand edifice of the law.

5. *Conclusion*

By 1850, local justice in England had become, ironically, neither communal nor commercial, but professional, in character.

The failure of the communal model is, we may imagine, further evidence of the dissolution of communal life under the pressure of industrialisation, urbanisation, and the enhanced mobility of persons, goods, information and ideas. Only where communal life lingered, or occasionally where it could be revived,[82] is it possible to imagine the notional descendants of William Hutton putting 'a period to many thousand quarrelsome disputes, ... mak[ing] that agreement between contending parties which they were unable to make themselves'.[83]

The 'failure' of the commercial model, however, requires a rather different explanation, for this failure may have been more apparent than real. While the county courts were, in the end, reasonably hospitable to lawyers, they did not necessarily cease to serve certain commercial interests. Debt collection does indeed seem to have been undertaken more efficiently than it had been under the previous haphazard regime of local courts.

On the other hand, when commercial interests were not well served by the regular courts, businessmen could construct their own domestic tribunals or submit their disputes to arbitration.[84] Some twenty years later, their sense of alienation from law, lawyers and judges had grown to the point where the commercial spokesmen led a virtual movement of secession, and attempted to construct a new system of commercial tribunals outside the framework of the conventional courts. Using arguments early employed in the debate over local courts, lawyers managed to beat back this new challenge to the regime of lawyers' law, and as well to infiltrate (and to an extent dominate) even private arbitration.

The greatest challenge to the law of courts and lawyers, however, came not from local communities or commercial interests – but from within the apparatus of government.[85] The well-chronicled rise of administrative jurisdictions represented no less an affront to accepted notions of formal law than did the old local courts. Like those local courts, they operated on the basis of informality, discretion, and special normative systems. Like the local courts, they were largely *terra incognita* to legal practitioners. And like them, they attracted the antipathy of bench and bar.

Here too there was doubtless a mixture of ideological and economic motives. Many of the epithets hurled at local courts were used as well to bombard the new commissions and inspectorates which appeared during the 1830s and 1840s – accusations of unconstitutionality, arbitrariness, disregard for law and legal forms. And, in the case of the administration, the economic stakes were potentially very high indeed. Not only did the new regulatory regimes seem to threaten interests closely identified with lawyers; they also seemed to threaten the law's monopoly over social control, and hence the social power of the legal profession. As matters turned out, neither of these threats materialised. The impact of much regulatory legislation was deflected by political action, and lawyers soon discovered in administrative law an important new source of power and income.

Administrative tribunals, as we know, were not absorbed into the central legal system as were the local courts. Despite attempts to assimilate them to the judicial branch of government, they still retain considerable functional, and even formal, autonomy. But we can now understand attempts to project 'the rule of law' into the administrative sphere as part of a larger effort, throughout the nineteenth century, to preserve and enhance the influence and primacy of 'law' as symbolised by the superior courts, and as given substance by lawyers.

This perspective also enables us to glimpse two related, and fundamental, themes. The first of these has to do with the nature of law, the second with how it is made.

What we have witnessed in the demise of local justice, and in parallel episodes leading to the expansion of the central court system, its norms, and its personnel, is the attribution to 'law' of a very specific meaning. By the end of the nineteenth century, law can hardly be thought of except in its formal or professional sense. We lack the vocabulary to describe the processes, norms and personnel of the old local courts or the new administrative regimes, for example, except by reference to the superior courts.

The possible significance, for historical purposes, of this assumed congruence between 'law' and decisions of the superior courts is seen in connection with studies of nineteenth-century contract law. If, until 1850, the great bulk of contract disputes was resolved outside of the superior court system, and at a conscious distance from common law, what was 'the law of contracts' then? And if, as I have suggested elsewhere,[86] commercial litigation after 1850 was often diverted into arbitration and domestic tribunals, what was 'the law of contract' thereafter?

A similar point may be made in contemporary terms. How do we regard the norms which in fact determine the outcome of administrative proceedings? Are the 'red books' used in planning enquiries, or the manuals used in deciding social benefit claims, to be considered 'law'? If not, can we understand how the legal system today actually impinges on the lives of most people? And if so, are we prepared to accord such 'legal' sources and institutions the same respect, the same presumptive legitimacy, that we offer to superior court judges and their decisions?

To broaden our definition of law, then, is to put in question both our understanding of history and tacitly accepted conventions of the present.

We have also witnessed the considerable power of legal professionals to influence the processes of legal change. Linked by a common professional ideology to the bench and to senior government officials, and by ties of mutual interest to important client groups, lawyers in the nineteenth century were able to leave their mark on the changing shape of the English judicature.[87] Their capacity to do so was not unlimited, but in matters of institutional design, especially those affecting the interests of lawyers, the legal profession was already, by mid-century, in a dominant position. This dominance remains an issue today for everyone concerned with reform of the legal system. It has special significance for those who calculate the prospects of modern attempts to revive or reestablish informal expressions of law and justice.

NOTES

1. W.S. Holdsworth, *History of English Law*, London, 1969, vol. 1, p. 188, claims that '[a]t the beginning of the nineteenth century ... practically all of the judicial work of the country was done by the judges [of the superior courts]'. A relatively rare corrective is found in A. Manchester, *A Modern Legal History of England and Wales 1750–1950*, London, 1980, c. 5.
2. See generally A.L. Cross, 'The Old English Local Courts and the Movement for their Reform', *Michigan Law Review*, 30 (1931–32) p. 369; H.W. Arthurs, *Without the Law: Administrative Justice and Legal Pluralism in Nineteenth Century England* (forthcoming).
3. It has been estimated that one-third of the writs issued at Westminster in 1830 were for sums of up to £20, one-third for between £20 and £50, and the balance for over £50; yet an action could not be tried for less than £80. T. Snagge, *The Evolution of the County Court*, London, 1940, p. 8. This estimate is borne out by the experience of a Birmingham merchant at the Warwick Assizes in 1827. He sued for £25 and won. The action lasted for five days; costs against the defendant were assessed at £60; and in addition the defendant had to pay his own lawyer's fees of £50. J. Parkes, *The State of the Court of Requests and the Public Office of Birmingham*, Birmingham, 1828, p. 5. (I am indebted to Dr A. Manchester for this reference.)
4. E.P. Thompson, *Whigs and Hunters*, New York, 1975; 'The Grid of Inheritance', in J. Goody, J. Thirsk and E.P. Thompson (eds.), *Family and Inheritance – Rural Society in Western Europe 1200–1800*, Cambridge, 1976, p. 329.
5. E.P. Thompson, 'The Moral Economy of the English Crowd in the Eighteenth Century', *Past and Present*, 50 (1971) p. 56; *The Making of the English Working Class*, Harmondsworth, 1968, pp. 64ff.
6. See e.g. J. Nisbet, 'History of the Forest of Dean in Gloucestershire', *English History Review*, XXI (1906) p. 445; C.E. Hart, *The Verderers and Speech Court of the Forest of Dean*, Gloucester, 1950; J.H.B. Brown, *The Law of Usages and Customs*, London, 1875; Anon., 'Review of "The Common Law of Kent, or the Customs of Gavelkind"', *Law Magazine and Law Review* 6 (1958–59) p. 333; W. Bainbridge, *The Law of Mines and Minerals*, London, 1841; 'Local Courts of Record', *Law Magazine and Law Review*, 18 (1864) p. 219; 'Judicial Statistics (1870)', *Accounts and Papers*, 1871, [c. 422] LXVII, pp. 17ff.
7. Courts Act, Stat. 1971, c. 23, s. 41; Administration of Justice Act, 1977, c. 38, s. 23. Some of these courts were still active, see P.N. Walker, *The Courts of Law*, Devon, 1970, c. 7.
8. Typical statutes were the London Court of Requests Act, 1800, 39 & 40 Geo. III, c. 104, Cirencester Court of Requests Act, 1792, 32 Geo. III, c. 77. See generally W.H.D. Winder, 'The Courts of Requests', *Law Quarterly Review*, 52 (1936) p. 369. References for the generic characteristics of those courts will not be given in the following textual description; unusual features and important changes will be noted. A list of all courts of requests (and other local courts), together with reference to their constituent statutes or charters, jurisdiction, and caseload, is found in the *Fourth Report of the Royal Commission on Practice and Proceedings in the Courts of Common Law*, 1831–32 (239) XXV, Appendix I, part V.
9. This was a source of some concern, see Parkes, *supra*, note 3.
10. The following seems to represent a consensus of what various parts of the population earned (per week) in the 1830s:

    Farm labourers – 10s.
    Unskilled factory workers – 18s.
    Navvies, dockworkers – 20s.
    Clerks/teachers – 20–25s.
    Skilled factory workers – 20–30s.
    Skilled artisans – 25–30s.
    Lower middle class – 60–75s.
    'Comfortable' middle class – 120s.

[Sources: J.F.C. Harrison, *The Early Victorians 1832–1851*, London, 1971, c. 2, 4; H. Perkin, *The Origins of Modern English Society 1780–1880*, London, 1969, c. 5; E.P. Thompson, *The Making of the English Working Class, supra*, note 5, c. 8, 9]

11. The point is somewhat uncertain. The Cirencester Court of Requests Act, *supra*, note 8, s. 29, for example, provided: 'No proceeding [in the court of requests] shall or may be removed into any Superior Court, but ... judgments, decrees and proceedings of the said court, shall be final and conclusive to all intents and purposes.' The London Court of Requests Act, *supra*, note 8, s. 12, provided that no decision might be removed 'into any other Court by *certiorari* or otherwise howsoever'. Indeed, despite the fact that courts of requests decided well over 200,000 cases in 1830, I was unable to find a single successful challenge to a decision of a court of requests reported during that year. However, a contemporary author, D.D. Keane, *Courts of Requests*, London, 3d. ed. 1845, pp. 114–15, asserts that prohibition could be brought for want of jurisdiction or 'some act ... contrary to the general law of the land'.
12. Winder, *supra*, note 8, p. 387.
13. G.A. A'Beckett, 'Objections to the County Courts Bill now before Parliament', *Law Magazine*, 25 (1841) p. 310, at p. 313.
14. Snagge, *supra*, note 3, gives this figure as the annual average for 1822–1827.
15. Snagge, *supra*, note 3, records that in the first five years following the establishment of the County Courts, their caseload was on average 433,000. This was slightly higher than the caseload of courts of requests had been just prior to their abolition, *supra*, note 13. Only about 100,000 writs per year on average were issued at Westminster during this period, says Snagge.
16. Courts of requests were not 'courts of record' in the technical sense, and few of their records seem to have been preserved in the Public Record Office or in local archives. The most extensive records available are apparently those of the courts in Bristol and Sheffield, which were discovered through the diligent efforts of my research assistant, Heather Leonoff, B.A., LL.B. Ms. Leonoff extracted the sample data referred to *infra*. Moreover, courts of requests did not produce written, reasoned judgments, and there is little reference to them in newspapers. The only account of their decisional methods and reasoning is found in Hutton, *Courts of Requests*, Birmingham, 1787, reprinted Edinburgh, 1840; Hutton provides notes on the facts, reasoning and result in some 92 cases.
17. These were found in the Bristol Record Office. Sample figures are taken from the months of January, April and September, 1830, 1835 and 1840. In each case, all claims given in a number of weeks were included in the sample, comprising 300, 220 and 260 claims per year, respectively. Comparative figures for Sheffield were obtained by taking all claims heard on July 1 or 2, 1830, 1835 and 1840, comprising a total of 250, 300 and 265 cases, respectively. The records of the Sheffield Court of Requests (formerly the Court Baron of the Manor of Sheffield) were located in the Sheffield Record Office. The Public Record Office, Chancery Lane, holds incomplete and rather uninformative sets of courts of requests records for Rotherham, the Isle of Wight, Windsor, Keighley, and West Bromwich.
18. Answers of T. Stock, J. Cunningham, A. Palmer, R.B. Beddome, *Fifth Report of the Royal Commission on Practice and Proceedings in the Courts of Common Law*, (1833) (247) XXII, Appendix A, at 34A, 47A, 95A, 97A.
19. *E.g.* Evidence of A. Galloway, *Report of the Select Committee on Artisans and Machinery*, Minutes of Evidence, (1824) (51) V28. The Rotherham, Sheffield and Bristol Courts of Requests records all show some claims for wages and for 'work and materials'. Isle of Wight records in the early 1800s show seamen using the Court of Requests to recover unpaid wages. (The latter information was provided by Stewart Anderson, Hertford College, Oxford.)
20. 'Events of the Quarter', *Law Magazine*, 19 (1838) p. 478, at p. 481.
21. D. Jones, *Before Rebecca – Popular Protests in Wales 1793–1825*, London, 1973, c. 6; G.A. Williams, *The Merthyr Rising*, London, 1978; Hutton, *supra*, note 16, 'Biographical Memoir of William Hutton', 1840 reprint.
22. Evidence of J. Pym, *supra*, note 18, at p. 109A.

23. Hutton, *supra*, note 16, at pp. 22, 25; Evidence of Sir John Cross, *supra*, note 18, Appendix B, at 13B.
24. The full title of the County Courts Act, 1846, was 'An Act for the more easy Recovery of Small Debts and Demands', 9 & 10 Vict., c. 95.
25. *Dictionary of National Biography*, X (1908) p. 362.
26. A. Briggs, *Victorian Cities*, Harmondsworth, 1968, c. 5.
27. *Supra*, note 16, at p. viii.
28. Cases XX, XXI, LX.
29. Case XXXVIII.
30. *Supra*, note 16, at p. 7.
31. *Supra*, note 16, at p. 61, and see cases XXXIII and XXXVII.
32. *Supra*, note 16, at 12.
33. *E.g.* cases XLV, LI, LXXXIII, XCII.
34. Cases IV, XXXVIII, VI.
35. Cases LXXV, XXIV, XXXVIII, LXXXI.
36. Parkes, *supra*, note 3, attacks the Birmingham court as 'inefficient and corrupt' and reports the formation of 'a Committee for investigating and removing the evils prevalent in the court'. A litigant who felt himself badly used by the same court published a pamphlet denouncing it in more extreme terms, R. Jenkinson (*untitled*), Birmingham, 1827. The case involved the liability of a tenant to pay rent after quitting the premises, the lease being for a year, with permission to quit upon a quarter's notice. Ironically, the facts are close to those of a case reported by Hutton, although the outcome was otherwise; Hutton, *supra*, note 16, case XXXVIII.
37. Hutton observed: 'The more a people increase their trade, the more they must venture their property; how necessary is it, then, to enact such laws as will best secure that property, and, when in danger, point out the easiest method to recover it. To multiply the courts of requests and enlarge their powers, is the likeliest way to attain this end.' *Supra*, note 16, at p. 8.
38. Snagge, *supra*, note 3, at pp. 9–10.
39. *E.g.* the judicatures of Wales and Chester were abolished by An Act for the more effectual Administration of Justice in England and Wales, 1830, 11 Geo. IV & 1 Will. IV, c. 70, s. 14.
40. Municipal Corporations Act, 1835, 5 & 6 Will. IV, c.76, s. 118.
41. Better Administration of Justice Act, 1836, 6 & 7 Will. IV, c. 105; Borough Courts Act, 1839, 2 & 3 Vict., c. 27.
42. See generally 'Answers', *Appendix A* and 'Evidence', *Appendix B*, to the *Fifth Report*, *supra*, note 18.
43. Hutton, *supra*, note 16, case XXV, confirmed by Small Debts Act, 1845, 8 & 9 Vict., c. 127, s. 1.
44. Act to Regulate Courts for the Recovery of Small Debts, 1786, 26 Geo. III, c. 38, ss. 1, 2; Bankruptcy Act, 1844, 7 & 8 Vict., c. 16, s. 57; Small Debts Act, *supra*, note 43, s. 1.
45. D.D. K[eane], 'The Small Debts Act', *Law Magazine* 36 (1846) p. 189, at p. 194. Keane was the author of the *Courts of Requests*, supra, note 11.
46. *Supra*, note 16, at p. 8.
47. 26 Geo. III, c. 38, s. 8 had established a minimum property qualification for commissioners of the ownership of real property of an annual value of £20, or of personal property of £500. Some courts had much higher qualifications. For example, in Southwark, the commissioners were 'magistrates, professional gentlemen, merchants, tradesmen of the first respectability, many of whom have retired from business, and chiefly those who have served parochial office. They must possess and swear to a qualification of £2,000 . . . .' Answers of J.G. Meymott, Appendix A, *supra*, note 18, at 227A.
48. Snagge, *supra*, note 3, at p. 10.
49. 'Extract of a Letter from Lord Brougham to the Earl of Radnor', *Law Magazine and Law Review*, 10 (1860–61) p. 176, at p. 181; see also *Law Magazine and Law Review*, 16 (1863) p. 181, at p. 182.
50. 'Letters to the Lord Chancellor (from A Barrister)', *Legal Observer*, 1 (1830–31)

p. 145, at p. 147.
51. *Fifth Report, supra*, note 18, at p. 11.
52. *Supra*, note 24, s. 77.
53. Snagge, *supra*, note 3, at p. 14.
54. H.W. Arthurs, 'Commercial Relationships and Disputes: The Persistence of Pluralism' in *Without the Law: Administrative Justice and Legal Pluralism in Nineteenth Century England* (forthcoming).
55. E.P. Thompson, *Whigs and Hunters, supra*, note 4.
56. Lord Brougham had declaimed against the persistence of customary tenures 'in a thousand manors, all different from the Common Law .... Is it right that such varieties of custom should be allowed to have force in particular districts, contrary to the general law of the land?' 'State of the Courts of Common Law', *Hansard*, 18 (1828) pp. 171–72.
57. *Fifth Report, supra*, note 18, at p. 11.
58. A colloquy with two judges of the busy Tower Hamlets court in the 1830s suggests that even there a commitment to distinctive equitable, non-legal, norms of decision did persist, see Evidence of G. Offor and J.G. Hammuck, *supra* note 18, Appendix B, at p. 43.
59. *Supra*, note 16, case XVI.
60. 'Small Debts Act: A Letter to the Editor', *Law Times*, 7 (1846) p. 379.
61. See *e.g.* D. Hay, 'Property, Authority and the Criminal Law' in D. Hay et al. (eds.), *Albion's Fatal Tree*, New York, 1975, for a discussion of the magistracy in the late eighteenth century. For an account of the obstructionist role played by magistrates in connection with regulatory and protective legislation in the period 1830 to 1870, see Arthurs, *supra*, note 54, esp. c. 4, 5.
62. Even Winder, *supra*, note 8, at p. 370, who quoted Blackstone without disapproval, was prepared to concede that courts of requests were not, in fact, tyrannical.
63. P. Atiyah, *The Rise and Fall of Freedom of Contract*, Oxford, 1979.
64. Winder, *supra*, note 8, at p. 381, refers to a number of local statutes in which these changes were made.
65. Bankruptcy Act, 1844, 7 & 8 Vict., c. 96, s. 72.
66. Small Debts Act, 1845, *supra*, note 43, ss. 9, 11.
67. Small Debts Act, 1845, *supra*, note 43, s. 21.
68. See, however, the Exeter Court of Requests Act, 1841, 4 & 5 Vict., c. 73, s. 24, which required that cases be decided 'according to the laws and statutes'.
69. Keane, *supra*, note 45, at p. 240.
70. County Courts Act, 1846, *supra*, note 24, s. 3. This provision had the effect of making the county courts amenable to prerogative writ review, subject to certain restrictions in ss. 90, 108.
71. 'The Judgeships of the Courts of Requests', *Law Times*, 5 (1845) p. 446.
72. County Courts Extension Act, 1850, 13 & 14 Vict., c. 61, ss. 14–16. This change had been avidly sought by the bar, 'County Courts', *Law Magazine* 7 (1847) p. 1, but for some time after a right to appeal was established, no appeals were in fact pursued, 'County Courts', *Law Times*, 16 (1850–51), p. 157; 'The Law and Lawyers', *Law Times*, 22 (1853–54) p. 101.
73. R. Danzig, *The Capability Problem in Contract Law: Further Readings on Well-known Cases*, Mineola, 1978, at pp. 92–3.
74. In fact, technically speaking the County Courts Act did not terminate the existence of any local court; this step was left to the decision of local authorities, County Courts Act, 1846, *supra*, note 24, ss. 5, 14. A number of local courts (not including courts of record, however) remained active throughout the nineteenth century, and some until their abolition by the Courts Act, 1971, c. 23, ss. 41–3.
75. 'Old Local Courts', *Legal Observer*, 1 (1830–31) p. 121.
76. 'Local Courts', *Law Times*, 7 (1846) p. 195. Not all those who advocated legal representation were similarly motivated. For example, the Commissioners on Common Law Courts were urged to recommend that 'the Government appoint an attorney with a salary in each Court, to assist the very poor who cannot defend themselves'. W. Beale, 'Evidence', *Fifth Report, supra*, note 18, Appendix A, at 82A.

77. County Courts Act, 1846, *supra*, note 24, s. 91; Keane, *supra*, note 45, at p. 255; Snagge, *supra*, note 3, at p. 23.
78. 'County Courts', *Law Magazine*, 7 (1847) p. 1; Keane, *supra*, note 45 at p. 255; 'The Prospects of the Bar', *Law Magazine* (n.s.), 15 (1851) p. 276.
79. County Courts Extension Act, 1850, *supra*, note 72, s. 6.
80. A. Beckett, *supra*, note 13, at p. 332.
81. 'County Courts', *supra*, note 72, at p. 3.
82. For example, an attempt was made to revive the ancient miners' court of St Briavels in Gloucestershire in 1831, which led to the enactment of a statute to establish a commission of enquiry, 1 & 2 Will. IV, c. 12; several reports ensued, see esp. *First Report of the Dean Forest Commissioners*, 1835 (283) XXXVI, *Fourth Report*, 1835 (610) XXXVI; and certain ancient rights of the 'free miners' were ultimately protected, see C.E. Hart, *The Free Miners*, Gloucester, 1853, at p. 144.
83. Hutton, *supra*, note 16, at p. 8.
84. Arthurs, *supra*, note 54.
85. Arthurs, *supra*, note 61.
86. Arthurs, *supra*, note 54.
87. See generally, D. Duman, *The English and Colonial Bars in the Nineteenth Century*, Beckenham, 1983.

Notes on Contributors

Huw Pryce is a lecturer in History at the University College of North Wales, Bangor. He is currently completing a thesis on how medieval Welsh law came to terms with the church.

Jens Röhrkasten is a research student at the Free University of Berlin completing a thesis on 'The English approvers and crime 1307–1330'.

John Post is an assistant keeper of public records. He has published numerous articles on medieval English legal and sexual history.

David Lidington, former research student of Sidney Sussex College, Cambridge, is completing a doctoral thesis on the enforcement of penal statutes at the Elizabethan Exchequer.

Victor Morgan is a lecturer in English History at the University of East Anglia. His main research interests are in the social, administrative and intellectual history of Early Modern England.

James Hart is a junior research fellow of Sidney Sussex College, Cambridge. He is completing a doctoral thesis on Judicial Review and Reform in the House of Lords, 1640–1643.

Valerie Edwards is a lecturer in the Law Faculty at Birmingham University. Her main research interest is in Early Modern English Legal History.

Michele Slatter is a lecturer in Law at the University of East Anglia. She has a particular interest in the development of equity in the local courts during the eighteenth century.

Trowbridge Ford is associate professor of Political Science, Holy Cross College, Worcester, U.S.A.. He has recently published *A. V. Dicey, the Man and his Times* and is engaged upon a biography of Henry Brougham.

Harry Arthurs is a professor of Law at Osgoode Hall Law School, York

University, Toronto and from January 1985 president of York University. His book *Without the Law: Administrative Justice and Legal Pluralism in Nineteenth Century England* is about to be published.

For Product Safety Concerns and Information please contact our EU
representative GPSR@taylorandfrancis.com
Taylor & Francis Verlag GmbH, Kaufingerstraße 24, 80331 München, Germany

www.ingramcontent.com/pod-product-compliance
Ingram Content Group UK Ltd.
Pitfield, Milton Keynes, MK11 3LW, UK
UKHW022109190926
475702UK00013B/1341
* 9 7 8 1 1 3 8 9 9 0 5 8 6 *